ON THE RELATIONSHIP OF MITZVOT BETWEEN MAN AND HIS NEIGHBOR AND MAN AND HIS MAKER

ON THE RELATIONSHIP OF MITZVOT BETWEEN MAN AND HIS NEIGHBOR AND MAN AND HIS MAKER

Daniel Sperber

URIM PUBLICATIONS
Jerusalem • New York

On the Relationship of Mitzvot Between
Man and His Neighbor and Man and His Maker
by Daniel Sperber

Printed in Israel
First Edition

ISBN: 978-965-524-145-7

Urim Publications, P.O. Box 52287, Jerusalem 9152102 Israel
Typeset by Ariel Walden

www.UrimPublications.com

Library of Congress Cataloging-in-Publication Data
Sperber, Daniel, author.
On the relationship of mitzvot between man and his neighbor and man and his maker / Daniel Sperber.
pages cm
Includes index.
ISBN 978-965-524-145-7 (hardcover : alk. paper) 1. Golden rule. 2. Brotherliness—Religious aspects—Judaism. 3. Commandments (Judaism) I. Title.
BJ1286.G64S64 2014
296.3'6—dc23

2013034282

Our parents, OSKAR and HENA OLINER, of blessed memory, and SHIMON and MARGIE SUMNER, of blessed memory, were devout and righteous Jews. They led exemplary lives of meticulous observance of ritual with generous displays of Chessed and Tzedokah, with an honest and wholesome lifestyle.

The Oliner door was always open to family and friends. The kitchen counter held HENA's famous sponge cake that was happily offered to everyone who graced their home. Sunday night dinners were a constant stream of honored guests who traveled from far and near to delight in scrumptious stuffed cabbage, brisket, and heavenly desserts. OSKAR, with his twinkling eyes and deadpan expression, could bring anyone to tears of laughter.

Shimmy and Margie were loved by all. SHIMMY had the widest smile and the biggest heart. His humor, countless jokes, and dancing feet were pure sunshine. MARGIE's list of friends was endless. Her engaging personality and uncanny ability to always push the right buttons was magnetic. Her daily phone calls are still sorely missed.

Our parents were diligent in their performance of Mitzvos to Hashem and Mitzvos to their neighbors. They would be proud to be associated with this fascinating and invaluable scholarship of Halacha and Emunah.

REVA & MARTY OLINER

Lawrence, NY

2013

When man appears before the Throne of Judgment, the first question he is asked is not: "Did you believe in God?" or "Did you pray and observe the rituals?" He is asked: "Have you dealt honorably and faithfully in all your dealings with your fellow man?"

(BT *Shabbat* 31a)

Rabban Yohanan asked his disciples to reflect on the highest good that a person should strive to attain. Rabbi Eliezer said generosity; Rabbi Joshua said friendship; Rabbi Yose said concern for one's neighbor; Rabbi Simeon said considering the consequences of one's actions; Rabbi Elazar said a kind heart. Rabban Yohanan replied, "I prefer the opinion of Rabbi Elazar because your views are embodied in his." (*Pirkei Avot* 2:13)

This was – and remains – the teaching of Beshtian Hasidism. Remember his three modes of love? *Ahavat-Hashem* – love of the Almighty; *Ahavat-Torah* – love of study; and *Ahavat-Israel* – love of Israel and mankind. At the time, this formulation of Jewish commitment was called an innovation – why? For centuries and centuries Jews were taught to love God and Torah and Israel – and many sacrificed their lives for that love. But what the Besht did was new indeed: he linked the three modes together in an unbreakable bond. Before him, they were separate and divisible. In some circles, only Torah mattered. In others, only God existed. Or only man. The Besht was the first to proclaim for all to hear: The way to heaven leads through this world; the way to divine reward leads through human commitment; the way to God leads through your fellow man.

Fervor? Yes – later. Study? Yes – later. Ecstasy? Yes – later. Not on a hungry stomach. Not with a sick child at home.

(Elie Wiesel, *Somewhere a Master: Further Hasidic Portraits and Legends*, New York: 1982, 150)

Contents

Preface

THIS BOOK, as indeed many other of my books, is the result of an evolutionary process. It began as an appendix (no. 2), in a previous book, *Netivot Pesikah* (Jerusalem: 2008, 181–192). I then translated it into English, somewhat amplifying it into an article published in *Conversations* 8 (2010), 9–31. As I became more aware of the breadth and importance of the subject, I decided to further develop the theme, and the result is the present volume.

It comes in the wake of two earlier Hebrew volumes, *Darkah shel Halachah* (Jerusalem: 2007), and *Netivot Pesikah*, mentioned above. In those two volumes I sought, among other things, to demonstrate that there are certain very basic ethical values that form what we might call a conceptual bedrock upon which our halachah is based; values, such as: the dignity of the individual (כבוד הבריות), the sanctity of life (קדושת החיים), the positive nature of mitzvot (דרכיה דרכי נועם), and the foundational notion of moral rectitude (ועשית הישר והטוב). In a sense, this volume continues this theme, examining the relationship between the two major categories of mitzvot: social ones, or perhaps we should call them interpersonal ones; and ritual ones – otherwise formulated as מצוות בין אדם לחברו and מצוות בין אדם למקום, mitzvot between man and his neighbor, and mitzvot between man and his Maker. I would seek to prove that there is a hierarchic distinction between them, in which the social mitzvot have a degree of superiority over the ritual ones. And although classical rabbinic literature does not have a clear and systematic theology, or even philosophy of halachah, there is sufficient evidence in the sources to enable us to reconstruct, or perhaps more correctly to uncover, such key principles.

My argument should in no way be interpreted as seeking to belittle or diminish in any degree the importance and sanctity of ritual mitzvot. I only wish categorically to assert that they should not come at the expense of, or to the denigration of, social mitzvot.

In a different context (*Women and Men in Communal Prayer: Halakhic Perspectives*, [New York: 2010, 35–36]), I used the metaphor of a meandering river in relation to the development of halachah. It may seen that my arguments here are also somewhat meandering. However, they all have a single direction, culminating in a clear ideological, halachic and educational conclusion, namely that we must strengthen our consciousness and awareness of the need to emphasize the paramount importance of our social and societal religious obligations.

All scriptural quotations are based on the Letteris edition, except when the context requires changes in formulation. The translation of the Mishnah is usually the Danby translation, except when the context requires change or added explanations. All rabbinic citations, from the Talmud, Midrash, etc., are my own.

*

Here I should like to express my thanks to Mrs. Esther Dranger, who faithfully typed out my manuscript, and to Mrs. Batsheva Pomerantz for her careful editing, and to Tzvi Mauer of Urim Publications for his continuing support and friendship.

I owe much to my mentors: my grandfather, Rabbi David Sperber, whom I was privileged to know and serve in his latter years, and from whom I learned so much by just observing his behavior; my late parents, my father, Rabbi Samuel Sperber, from whom I learned both Torah and Derech Eretz, and my mother whose love was without bounds, and, of course, my dear wife, Chana without whom nothing would have happened, and my wonderful children and grandchildren, who constitute the ultimate source of satisfaction and fulfillment for any parent.

May they all be blessed.

Daniel Sperber
Jerusalem, 2013

Part I

Halachic Theory

I

Two Categories of Mitzvot, and the Question as to Their Relative Importance

IT IS WELL-KNOWN that all mitzvot fall into two major categories: those between man and his Maker – בין אדם למקום, and those between man and his fellow – בין אדם לחברו. The question we wish here to discuss is which of these two categories is, as it were, more weighty. Or formulated differently: if there were to be a clash between two different mitzvot from these two categories, which one would prevail?

At first blush, one might well assume that our relationship towards our Maker is clearly of such primal importance, that in all such cases we must give mitzvot directed towards Him our first priority. Indeed this seems to have been a common presumption among some people during the Second Temple times, as we learn from the very disturbing story in BT *Yoma* 23a:

> It once happened that there were two Cohanim who had equal [rights to carry out a sacrifice], and they were running up the gangway [to the altar]. One of them got ahead of his fellow by within four cubits, and he took a knife and stabbed it into his fellow-Cohen's heart... The father of the young Cohen came and found his son convulsing. He said: May he be your atonement, for my son is still convulsing (i.e., still alive), and the knife has not been made ritually impure. To teach you that the purity of [Temple] vessels was more serious for them than bloodshed.

This very shocking story reflects a not uncommon notion as to the scale of priorities to be found in certain sectors of Jewish religious society.

But the fact that we find this episode so shocking and unacceptable indicates that we must reconsider the moral and halachic presumptions underlying the tale. And indeed, on examining this issue more closely, we shall see that the opposite is the case, namely that mitzvot between man and his fellow have a priority over those between man and his Creator.

This, I believe, is clearly indicated in a famous *sugya* at the end of *Massechet Makkot* (24a). There after teaching us, in the name of R. Simlai, that there are six-hundred and thirteen commandments (mitzvot) in the Torah, the Talmud tells us that they were progressively limited, first in the time of David to eleven, then in the time of Isaiah to six, and then in the time of the prophet Michah to three, and then Isaiah again cut the number down to two, and finally Habakuk concluded with one alone. Rashi (ad loc.) explains this whole process as follows:

> In the beginning there were righteous people who were able to take upon themselves the yoke of many mitzvot. But later generations did not have such great *tzaddikim*, and if they were required to keep all of them, no one could do so meritoriously. And so David came and limited them [to eleven], so that they would be able [at least] to keep these eleven mitzvot. And so in successive generations when there is a progressive decrease [in the standards of righteousness, so the number was decreased].

Clearly, what Rashi is explaining to us is that these great authorities, seeing the state of society in their days, prioritized the mitzvot, identifying the most important to be adhered to. This does not mean that others were not to be kept, but rather that the emphasis was placed on these.

And when the Talmud enumerates these mitzvot of highest priority, it does so basing itself on biblical verses. Thus King David's list is to be found in Psalms 15:

> 1. Lord, who shall abide in Thy tabernacle? Who shall dwell in Thy holy hill?
>
> 2. (1) He that walketh uprightly, and (2) worketh righteousness, and (3) speaketh the truth in his heart.
>
> 3. (4) He that backbiteth not with his tongue, nor (5) doeth evil to his neighbor, nor (6) taketh up reproach against his neighbor.
>
> 4. (7) In whose eyes a vile person is contemned; (8) but he honoreth them that fear the Lord. (9) He that sweareth to his own hurt, and changeth not.
>
> 5. (10) He that putteth not out his money to usury, (11) nor taketh

> reward against the innocent. He that doeth these things shall never be moved.

The Talmud then gives examples of individuals who in their behavior characterize each of these principles.

And when explicating Isaiah's six principles, they refer to Isaiah 33:15:

> 15. (1) He that walketh righteously, (2) and speaketh uprightly; (3) he that dispirseth the gain of oppressions, (4) that shaketh his hands from holding of bribes, (5) that stoppeth his ears from hearing of blood; (6) and shutteth his eyes from evil.
>
> [16. He shall dwell on high . . .]

And when we come to Michah, we are referred to Michah 6:8:

> He hath shewed thee, O man, what is good, and what doth the Lord require of thee, but (1) to do justly, (2) and to love mercy, (3) and to walk humbly with thy God.

And returning again to Isaiah, we are referred to Isaiah 56:1:

> Thus saith the Lord, (1) keep ye judgment, (2) and do justice, [for thy salvation is near to come, and My righteousness to be revealed].

And finally Habakuk came and reduced it to one single commandment, as is said in Habakuk 2:4:

> . . . but the just shall live by his faith.

It should be noted that all these mitzvot, which have been given the highest priority, and many of which are generic – walk righteously, do justice – are all of a *socio-ethical* nature. Even "walking humbly with God," means, in effect, being humble before one's fellow humans. And the final Habakuk statement that "the just shall live by his faith" is best understood in the context of that whole chapter, where the prophet rails against the evils that men do:

> 5. Yea also, because he trangresseth by wine . . .
>
> 9. Woe to him that coveteth an evil covetousness to his house . . .

> 12. Woe to him that buildeth a town with blood . . .
>
> 15. Woe unto him that giveth his neighbor to drink, that putteth thy bottle to him, and maketh him drunk also, that thou mayest look upon his nakedness . . .

and so forth. It is clearly in opposition to these social ills that he stated:

> 4. Behold, his soul which is lifted up is not upright in him: but the *just* shall live by his faith.

It is, then, preeminently evident that the Rabbis of the Talmud saw that these mitzvot, which are between man and his neighbor, are of primal importance, and, more notably they do not list mitzvot of a ritual nature, or between man and Creator among the primary priorities.

This is surely the meaning of those traditions coming from the school of the Gaon of Vilna. For his disciple, R. Hayyim of Volozin – we are told by his son – said that "man was created not for himself, but in order to benefit others in every way he can" (introduction to *Nefesh ha-Hayyim*). And R. Hayyim himself, said in the name of the Gra, that "the primary labor of a person must be in matters between man and his neighbor in all their detail." (*Kol ha-Katuv le-Hayyim*, chapter *Tikkun ha-Middot*, sect. 6)

And the Gra, in *Etz ha-Hayyim* ad fin., says that "the most important part of a person's labor must be [the avoidance] of transgressions between man and his fellow in all their details."

And in this he was following on what was already stated much earlier by Rabbenu Yonah (*Shaarei Teshuvah* 3:13):

> There are among the positive commandments those which the general multitude do not pay proper attention to them, such as . . . charitable deeds, (גמילות חסדים), which is a positive commandment; for a person must make every effort to do good for his people and toil to benefit his fellow, whether he be poor or rich. And these [mitzvot] are among the most serious and the most important which are required of a person, as it is said, "He hath showed thee, O man, what is good; and what doth the Lord require of thee, but to do justly, and to love mercy, and to walk humbly with thy God?" (Michah 6:8)[1]

---

1. See R. Asi ha-Levi Even Yuli, *Shulhan Aruch ha-Middot*, vol. 2, *Halachah u-Musar* (Jerusalem: 2009, 331).

And in a more halachic style this is formulated by R. Meir ben Raphael Plotzky, in his classic *Klei Hemdah* to Deuteronomy 25:26 (section 5, subsection 4, Pietrokow: 1902, *Ki Tetze*, 228):

> Concerning the issue of one who is engaged in one mitzvah [and therefore is] exempt from another (עוסק במצוה פטור מן המצוה) – if he is engaged in a mitzvah between man and his Maker he is not exempt from a mitzvah between man and his fellow. For this rule, that a person engaged in one mitzvah is exempt from another, is because while he is engaged in one mitzvah he has no obligation to carry out another one. But this is only the case with regard a mitzvah between man and his Maker. But we have not heard that this would exempt him from a mitzvah between man and his fellow, for the ultimate end that would serve his fellow cannot be pushed aside because one is engaged in a mitzvah directed towards one's Maker.

Interestingly enough, but perhaps not surprisingly, his son, R. Elazar Yehudah Plotzky, follows in his father's footsteps in a totally different halachic context. The discussion there, in his *Hemdat Yisrael* (Pietrokow: 1903, 88) refers to the question whether the vow (*shevuah*) of a non-Jew is binding upon him (even though it is not obviously one of the seven Noahite laws). This was a well-known subject of controversy among early rabbinic authorities. R. Yehudah Rosanes, in his supercommentary (*Mishnah la-Melech*) to Rambam, *Hilchot Melachim* 10:7, and others are of the opinion that a gentile is bound to carry out his vow, otherwise he will be transgressing the laws forbidding him to bless (i.e., curse) the Lord, one of the Noahite laws. The *Hemdat Yisrael* makes a distinction between vows between man and his neighbor, which obligate a gentile, explaining that their purpose is to strengthen social covenants and property laws, which are included in the category of *dinim*, laws, to which the Noahites are committed. However, vows which are God-directed or of a ritual nature, do not obligate the gentile. (See further, *Meorot ha-Daf ha-Yomi*, no. 626, to BT *Menahot* 74–80, Iyyar 5771, 2, for additional references.)

Going back to the *Klei Hemdah* we see then, that when there is a clash between these two categories, it is the "social" mitzvah that overrides the "ritual" one.

Clearly, one must also take into account the relative status of the two mitzvot. Thus if one is of biblical authority and the other of rabbinic authority, this principle would not apply. It is only when they both belong to the same category that the social one can override the ritual one.

This is surely how we are to understand the statement of R. Shimon bar Yohai in JT *Peah* 1:1:

> R. Shimon bar Yohai said, "Honoring one's father and mother is of such great importance that the Holy One blessed be He preferred it over his own honor. It is said, "Honor thy father and thy mother" (Exodus 20:12), and it is said, "I honor the Lord with thy substance." (Proverbs 3:9). With what do you honor Him? With that with which He graced you. You separate gleanings, the corner of the field, the various tithes . . . , you make a *sukkah*, [take] a *lulav*, a *shofar*, *tefillin* and *tzitzit*, and feed the poor and the hungry and give drink to the thirsty. [All this] if you have [the wherewithal] you are obligated to do. But if you do not have the means, you are not obligated to any one of them. But when it comes to honoring one's father and mother, whether you have the means or no, you [are obligated] to honor your parent, even if you have to go begging at the doors.

(Compare BT *Kiddushin* 32a, and *Torah Temimah* to Exodus 20:12, 354, note 11; and cf. Baer Ratner, *Ahavat Tziyyon vi-Yerushalayim*, to *Peah* ad loc., Vilna: 1917, 9–10, for variant readings and roughly parallel citations in a variety of early sources.) Here, then, is a clear statement that one's duty towards one's parents overrides many mitzvot of a ritual nature, i.e., those which are God-directed.

2

On the Superiority of "Social" Mitzvot

WE FIND THIS PRINCIPLE also in the *Sdei Hemed* of R. Hayyim Hezkiahu Medini (vol. 5, 233b, Klal 45) in the name of the *Shem Aryeh*, by R. Aryeh Leibush Bolhauer [Vilna: 1873–1874], in the additional response at the end of the book sect. 3. (See also, most recently, the discussion of R. Asi ha-Levi Even Yuli, in his *Shulhan Aruch ha-Middot*, vol. 2, *Halachah u-Musar* [Jerusalem: 2009, 245].) For there he solves a certain question raised by the Tosafot to *Shevuot* 44b in the following manner:

In BT *Rosh ha-Shanah* 28a we learn that someone who takes upon himself by a vow not to receive any sort of benefit or enjoyment from a spring, is permitted to bathe in that spring for a ritual ablution (for mitzvot are not for personal benefit – מצוות לאו להנות נתנו).[1] The Tosafot ad loc. ask as follows: Surely in doing so, he will benefit according to the view of Rav Yosef in that he is a paid guardian (שומר שכר)?

Let us explain this in greater detail. Rav Yosef is of the opinion that if someone finds a lost object and keeps it till the owner comes to claim it, his legal status is that of a paid guardian (שומר שכר); the reason being, that while he is engaged in looking after the object, making sure it is in no way damaged, etc., he will be exempt from giving a poor man who comes to

1. Cf. BT *Eruvin* 31a; BT *Hullin* 89a; Rabbenu Nissim to BT *Nedarim* 15b: for carrying out a mitzvah is not considered having personal benefit. On this concept see Max Kadushin, *Worship and Ethics: A Study in Rabbinic Judaism* (New York: 1963, 213, 298).

his door a small gift of charity. This is called פרוטה ברב יוסף – Rav Yosef's penny.[2] And in that he does not have to give out a penny, it is as if he has

2. See BT *Baba Kama* 56b; (BT *Baba Metzia* 29a, 82a; BT *Shevuot* 44b); BT *Nedarim* 33b. BT *Baba Kama* actually talks of giving a *rifta*, a piece of bread, while BT *Nedarim* speaks of the *peruta de-Rav Yosef*. BT *Nedarim* also states that this is a somewhat forced legal construction. However, from the story of R. Haninah ben Dosa in BT *Taanit* 25a, we have an example of the extent to which a righteous person would engage himself in safeguarding the value of the find. We may also note that this story is not found in the majority of manuscripts of *Taanit*, and is also somewhat misplaced. See *The Treatise Taanit of the Babylonian Talmud*, ed. H. Malter (New York: 1930, 112, note to line 10). On how to look after a found object, see M. *Baba Metzia* 2:8.

And since we have mentioned the text in BT *Taanit* 25a, I cannot refrain from a further analysis of this very well-known story. As mentioned above, it is not found in most manuscripts, nor in early testimonies, such as *Ein Yaakov*, *Menorat ha-Maor*, etc., and was declared both by scholars (*Dikdukei Soferim* ad loc., and Malter), as well as classical commentaries, *Maharsha*, to be a late addition. It appears at the end of a series – *a catena* – of tales describing the piety and poverty of R. Haninah ben Dosa and his wife. They both lived in penury, and were miracle workers, but for others rather than themselves. One of the stories tells how he had goats, which the neighbors claimed were doing them damage. He replied that if this was the case, then bears would devour them by night. But, if the claim was untrue, they would bear the bears on their horns by nightfall. And so it was, that by nightfall the bears appeared borne on the horns of the goats. There then follows another tale about how he helped a neighbor who had planned building his house, but mistakenly had ordered roof beams that were too short. R. Haninah ben Dosa miraculously lengthened the beams so that they protruded a cubit on either side, and Pelimo asserts that he saw this building.

The Talmud then asks: How come R. Haninah ben Dosa had goats? Surely he was extremely poor, and, furthermore, one was not permitted to have goats in Palestine (אין מגדלין בהמה דקה בארץ ישראל) (BT *Baba Kama* 79b). The reply, in the name of Rav Pinhas, is as follows:

> It once happened that someone passed by the entrance to R. Haninah's house, and left there some chickens, [two, according to a manuscript that Malter found]. His wife found them, and brought them in. R. Haninah told her not to eat the eggs, and they hatched, and soon there were many chickens, which troubled the couple. So they sold them and with the proceeds bought goats. Some time later the original owner of the chickens was passing by with a friend, and remarked to him that it was here that he had left his chickens. R. Haninah heard him, called him in and asked

> him if those chickens had any sign to identify them as his. He replied, yes, and gave the signs, and R. Haninah gave him the goats. And these are the goats, says the Talmud, which bore the bears on their horns. [This latter statement is in Aramaic, whereas the story, unlike the other ones in the series, is in Hebrew.]

We have already noted that R. Haninah ben Dosa was extremely poor. Indeed, the Talmud, *Taanit* 24b, relates in the name of Rav Yehudah in the name of Rav (Babylonian *amora*, mid-3rd cent. C.E.) that each day a voice (*bat kol*) comes forth from heaven declaring: "The whole world is nourished by the merit of Haninah my son, and for Haninah my son it suffices that he has a *kav* of carobs from Sabbath eve to Sabbath eve." Yet despite his poverty he took upon himself to look after the find, until its owner be identified.

According to BT *Baba Metzia* 28b, and thence to Rambam, *Hilchot Gezeilah ve-Aveidah* 13:15, and *Shulhan Aruch Hoshen Mishpat* 267:26, chickens found should be publicly announced for several months (perhaps twelve), the eggs sold, and the proceeds used to cover the expenses involved in feeding them, etc. If, in the end, the income is greater than the outlay, the "profit" is shared equally by the finder and owner. Sales are carried out in the presence of a Beit Din. However, none of these procedures were carried out by R. Haninah. He did not sell the eggs to cover his expenses, but fed the chickens at his own expense, despite his extreme penury. Only when the number of chickens became too troublesome did he sell them – it is not mentioned whether this was before a Beit Din, or not – and bought goats with the proceeds. He then continued to feed and look after the goats, which obviously required more food and were worth much more than (two) chickens, until the owner was identified. He then gave him the goats, not requesting any payment for his work and monetary outlay, and not requesting an equal share in the increased value of the "find." All in all, the message of the tale is that he went far beyond the letter of the law in the mitzvah of returning a lost object (השבת אבידה). This, of course, is an extreme example of לפנים משורת הדין, in the case of a mitzvah between a person and his neighbor.

Incidentally, this tale does not answer the Talmud's question on how R. Haninah had goats, when they were not permitted in Eretz Yisrael. The later commentaries make various suggestions in this regard, but they are all somewhat forced. Indeed, this is one of the arguments that the *Maharsha* brings to prove that this is a late addition.

This tale was very popular, and appeared in numerous folkloristic collections, such as *Sefer ha-Maasiyyot*, etc., and is frequently related in kindergartens.

The degree to which righteous scholars were meticulous in observing this mitzvah is exemplified by what we told of R. Yisrael Salanter. (See further on him below.) For it is related that once on the eve of Yom Kippur people saw him running after a cat, trying to persuade it to enter his house. People were astonished earned it. Hence, he is a paid guardian.[3] According to this view, if, while the gentleman is having his *ritual* ablution, a poor man would come begging for a donation, he would be exempt, since he is already engaged in a *mitzvah*, and thus he would have monetary benefit from not giving the "penny." How then, ask the Tosafot, can he be permitted to bathe in the spring when he has vowed to have no sort of benefit from it? The answer that the *Pnei Aryeh* offers is that such exemption from charitable giving is only the case when the mitzvah he is engaged in is towards his fellow man, looking after the lost object. But if he is engaged in a ritual mitzvah, towards his Maker, he is in no way exempt from the mitzvah of giving charity, which is a mitzvah directed to his fellow man. This then is fully in line with what we saw to be the principle in the *Klei Hemdah*.

And while this may appear to be a rather radical view formulated by later authorities, actually it is already to be found in the Rosh (Rabbenu Asher), in his commentary to *Peah* 1:2. For there he wrote (ed. Samuel Edwin, Marlborough, Australia, no date):

> For the Holy One blessed be He is more desirous of mitzvot that are done to the satisfaction of human being, than these which are between man and his Maker.

---

at his behavior most especially at this most hallowed hour at the beginning of the most holy day that he should concern himself with a cat! It finally turned out that he had in his house books that he had borrowed from others, and was worried lest during Yom Kippur, when everyone was out of the house at the synagogue for most of the day, mice might come and damage the books, (D. Katz, *Tenuat ha-Musar*, vol. 1 [Tel Aviv: 1952, 353]; A. Tobolsky, *Hizaharu be-Mamon Haverchem* [Bnei Brak: 1981, 240]). Katz (ibid., 250) writes that Reb Yisrael did not distinguish between the two categories of mitzvot, and indeed preferred those between man and his neighbor. (On the halachic aspects of this tale, see Y.Y. Neuwirth, *Shemirat Shabbat Kehilchatah*, 2nd ed. [Jerusalem: 1988], 346:35, or most likely, this was before the onset of the fast.)

3. See *Torah Temimah* to Gen. 45:22, 312, n. 7, who argues that the fact that the brothers of Josef did not pay up the fine of 300 shekels, and that Josef decided to forgo his right to this fine, was as though he had given them this sum. According to this, the fact that you have not given the penny to a poor man, is as though the poor man gave you that penny, even though he was unaware of the fact, and consequently you are a "paid guardian."

And on this Rabbi Elhanan Wasserman wrote in his *Kovetz Maamarim* (ed. R. Eliezer Simchah Wasserman, his son, Jerusalem: 1963, 42–43):

> For "among two hundred is to be found a hundred," [a common rabbinic idiom], meaning that in all mitzvot between man and his fellow there is also a component between man and God. Why then should they be lessened by being between man and his fellow? And it is for this reason that the Rosh saw mitzvot between man and his fellow as being more weighty, for they contain both elements.

A somewhat different formulation of this basic principle may be found in a statement of R. Yisrael Salanter, founder of the Musar movement, based upon the verse in II Samuel 24:14, "[And David said unto God, I am in a great strait:] let us fall now into the hand of the Lord; [for his mercies are great:] and let me not fall into the hand of man" – Better a failure between man and God, than one between man and man (Dov Katz, *Tenuat ha-Musar*, vol. 1, Tel Aviv: 1952, 304, note 7). And another of his aphorisms is: Even at the hour when one stands in fear and trembling before the awesomeness of judgment, one is not free from an obligation to take care not to tread on one's neighbor's foot (305, note 12). (See below, section 23 on R. Yisrael Salanter.)

Much the same message is to be found in a totally different literary context, a "*derush*," that is a moralistic sermon. I cite in extenso a passage from Yerahmiel Shulman's *Peninei ha-Hochmah*, Jerusalem: 1964, 80, (as brought in A. Tobolsky's *Hizaharu be-Chevod Haverchem*, Bnei Brak: 1981, 79). Its starting point is with the Mishnah in *Sukkah* 2:1:

> If a man slept under a bed in a *sukkah* he has not fulfilled his obligation. R. Yehudah said: It was our custom to sleep under the bed in the presence of the Elders, and they said nothing to us. R. Shimon said: "Tabi, the slave of Rabban Gamliel, once slept under the bed, and Rabban Gamliel said to the Elders, 'See Tabi, my slave, that he is a learned scholar, and knows slaves are exempt from [the law of] the *sukkah*; and so he sleeps under the bed.'"

Rabban Gamliel explains that slaves, just as women, are exempt from all time-related mitzvot; consequently, Tabi was exempt from the mitzvah of *sukkah* and therefore slept under the bed.

R. Yohanan Sofer, the Rabbi of Erloi, then asked rhetorically:

> Why was Rabban Gamliel so impressed with Tabi, and his behavior? Do you need to be a learned scholar to know that a slave is exempt from the mitzvah of *sukkah*? Who is not aware of the fact that slaves, like women, are exempt from time-related mitzvot? And surely Tabi, Rabban Gamliel's slave, would be cognizant of such a well-known legal principle! However, he answers, in the Yerushalmi (*Sukkah* 2:1), we read that Tabi acted in this manner in order to leave more room for the other scholars in the *sukkah*, since the space was limited. From here we learn clearly that there were before Tabi two alternatives: to sleep in the *sukkah* and carry out the mitzvah of *sukkah*, which is a very precious one, and concerning which the Rabbis said that it was equal in measure to all the Torah (*Piyyut* to the second day of Sukkot); and even if women and slaves were exempt, nonetheless they can take upon themselves to carry out such mitzvot and receive merit therefrom, as is well-known [in accordance with the view of Rabbenu Tam]. The alternative was: to be scrupulous in mitzvot between man and his neighbor, and leave more room for the comfort of the Rabbis, so that they feel not cramped in the limited space of Rabban Gamliel's *sukkah*. And Tabi decided to prefer the mitzvah between man and his neighbor, and to forgo the mitzvah of *sukkah*, which is one between man and his Maker. It was this decision that so impressed Rabban Gamliel, so much so, that he proudly declared: "See Tabi, my slave, what a *Talmid Hacham* he is!" For he is wise and discerning enough to understand this moral imperative, and to be scrupulously careful in matters concerning his neighbors.

The Yerushalmi then continues to enquire: If this was the case, that Tabi wished to make room for the Rabbis, why did he have to sleep under the bed? He would not be carrying out the mitzvah of *sukkah*. Surely, he could as well have slept outside the *sukkah*? The answer given there is that: Tabi, the slave of Rabban Gamliel, wished to listen in to the Torah discussions of the Rabbis; i.e., he was not willing to forego the pleasures of learning Torah from the Rabbis.

The *derush* ends by extolling Tabi's behavior, that he would crawl under a bed in order to have the privilege of learning Torah, but at the same time would take extreme care not to cause any sort of discomfort to others.

The overall message that we may derive from this exposition, is that even the desire to carry out a mitzvah and gain much merit therefrom, coupled with the desire to learn Torah, was here overridden by the thought of causing a measure of discomfort to others, because the social, or perhaps we may call them moral mitzvot, override the ritual (or perhaps the religious) ones.[4]

We may find this line of reasoning in yet another somewhat related halachic context. There is a well-known question that troubled the Rabbis throughout the generations, namely, why is it that so many people in so many different communities do not sleep in their *sukkot* at night. Surely

---

4. Of course, this kind of exposition does not purport to expound the Mishnah in accordance with its simple straightforward meaning – *peshat* – but to uncover some deeper ethical principle contained therein. As such, it reflects the personal moral *Weltanschauung* of the exponent-preacher more perhaps than what the Mishnah actually teaches.

We may, perhaps, add an additional example of this kind of halachic thinking. The *Shulhan Aruch Orah Hayyim* 242:1, at the very beginning of the laws of Shabbat, rules that even the poorest of people should make great efforts to honor the Shabbat with (three) suitable meals. The *Beur Halachah* ad loc. (s.v. לכבד) remarks as follows:

> And if he has but little money, and his employee comes to claim the wages of the work he completed for him that day . . . , it would appear that he has to give the worker his money, in order to fulfill that which is written, "At his day thou shalt give him his hire, neither shall the sun go down upon it; [for he is poor, and seteth his heart upon it; lest he cry against thee unto the Lord, and it shall be sin unto thee]" (Deut. 24:15), even though by doing this nothing will remain for him with which to honor the Shabbat; and he should persuade him to wait till after the Shabbat, for the obligation to pay a worker on time is a biblical obligation, whereas this (honoring Shabbat) is only מדברי קבלה, i.e., rabbinic. And even according to those authorities who view [the obligation to honor the Shabbat] also as being of biblical authority... (the mitzvah of payment on time) is a positive and a negative commandment, and a positive commandment (of honoring the Shabbat) cannot override a positive and a negative one (BT *Yevamot* 21), and therefore this does not come under the category of "he claimed from him and he does not have what to give," in which case he does not transgress the commandment of delaying payment.

We see how the Hafetz Hayyim, (the author of the *Beur Halachah*) carries out what appears to be a complex internal dialogue with himself to justify the payment to the laborer on time even at the expense of honoring the Shabbat. This is, perhaps, characteristic of his ethical-halachic posture, in which interpersonal mitzvot have overriding importance. And though he does not overtly use this as part of his argumentation, I believe it reflects his overall halachic thinking.

one is obligated to spend all of one's time in the *sukkah* during the seven days of the festival, in so far as is possible, and even a short nap is mandated in the *sukkah* (lest it becomes a long sleep), according to the *Shulhan Aruch Orah Hayyim* 639:2 (based on BT *Sukkah* 26a and JT *Sukkah* 2:5 ad fin.).

Putting aside any socio-historical explanation (already offered by the Rema, R. Moshe Isserles, in *Orah Hayyim* 639:2), such as that in northern European communities Sukkot falls during a wintry period, which can be both very cold and rainy, and therefore sleeping in a *sukkah* would be most uncomfortable and even stressful, and, as is well-known, a *mitz'taer* (מצטער) – he that feels uncomfortable (cold, etc.) – is exempt from sitting in the *sukkah* (BT *Sukkah* 26a, in the name of Rava, *Shulhan Aruch Orah Hayyim* 640:4; and see my *Minhagei Yisrael*, vol. 3, Jerusalem: 1994, 75–77). R. David b. Shmuel ha-Levi (1586–1667, Poland), in his *Turei Zahav* (usually called *Taz*) to *Orah Hayyim* 639:9, gives quite an alternative explanation, expanding on one already offered by the Rema himself (ad loc.). He writes that the reason is that a husband is obligated to please his wife during the festival periods, and since women are not obligated to dwell in the *sukkah* – because dwelling in a *sukkah* is a time-related mitzvah – if he does not wish to separate himself from his wife, this is considered a mitzvah, and this is the case even when she is a menstruant (*niddah*), for it is pleasing for her to be in the same room as her husband (cf. BT *Eruvin* 63b). And this constitutes the mitzvah, because of the principle of *teshvu ke-ein taduru* (תשבו כעין תדורו), one's dwelling in the *sukkah* should be of the same nature as when one normally dwells in one's home (BT *Sukkah* 28b, and cf. 26a, and cf. Tosafot 28b, s.v. *teshvu*). This reasoning appears in a variety of Rishonim and Aharonim, as arrayed by R. Ovadiah Yosef in his *Hazon Ovadiah: Sukkot*, Jerusalem: 2005, 195–196. There he adds that according to BT *Pesachim* 72b, a person is obligated to please his wife at all times (אפילו שלא בעונתה), and even if he is involved in carrying out the mitzvah of dwelling in the *sukkah*, he is not exempt from satisfying his wife's desires, for

> as stated by the *Shem Aryeh*, (additional response at the end of the book, section 3), they did not say "One who is involved in one mitzvah is exempt from another," except when they are both of the same category, such as when both are mitzvot between Man and God; but one who is involved in a mitzvah between Man and God, it is not reasonable to suggest that he be exempt from one that is between Man and his neighbor.

And elsewhere in that same volume (166, 168–169), R. Ovadiah Yosef discusses the rule that travelers (הולכי דרכים) are exempt from dwelling in the *sukkah* by day (BT *Sukkah* 26a), arguing that the rabbis only permitted them from functioning outside the *sukkah*, if they were engaged in trading in order to bring sustenance to their families in straightened circumstances, for such activity is considered a mitzvah (see Rema, *Orah Hayyim* 248 ad fin., and *Magen Avraham* 531:7). Similarly, in 163, 164 he argues that those who travel during Sukkot to raise funds for public (Torah) institutions, are considered *shluchei mitzvah* (שלוחי מצוה), mitzvah emissaries, who are exempt from dwelling in the *sukkah*. And, here too, their mitzvah is of a social nature. Thus, once again, we find the social human-oriented mitzvah superseding that which is God-directed.

The law of *mitz'taer* just mentioned above, is in itself, clear evidence of the sensitivity of the halachah to human needs and sensibilities. And though a homiletic basis may be brought for this ruling, this does not obscure or conceal the basic value of necessitating mitzvot to be pleasant (*darchei noam*, דרכי נועם) to those *humans* who wish to fulfill them, even at the expense of God-related commandments. In many ways, this parallels the discussion in BT *Sukkah* 30b, which deals with the rejection of certain identifications for the "*anaf etz avot*" and the "*kappot temarim*" (Leviticus 23:40), on the basis that they are thorny and would scratch or wound a hand holding them. And the Torah would not demand of us to carry out a mitzvah that would harm us. For "her ways are the ways of pleasantness [and all her routes are peaceful]" (Proverbs 3:17). Thus, a biblical injunction is defined on the basis of a non-Pentateuchal verse! This again underscores the centrality of the human disposition in the structure of one halachah. (See more details on this in my *Darkah shel Halachah* [Jerusalem: 2007], 51 et seq.; and *Netivot Pesikah*, Jerusalem: 2008, 130 et seq.)

I believe this notion is also to be found in the Ramban. On the verse in Leviticus 23:22, "And when ye reap the harvest of your land, thou shalt not make clean riddance of the corners of thy field when thou reapest, neither shalt thou gather any gleanings of thy harvest; thou shalt leave them unto the poor and to the stranger: I am the Lord your God," he writes as follows:

> Rashi wrote, [though not in our Rashi]: The Scripture repeated itself to make a person transgress two prohibitions . . . .

Rashi seeks to answer the question why this verse appears after the section dealing with the bringing of the *omer*. Moreover, these commandments of *peah*, etc., have already appeared in Leviticus 19:9–10, in a very similar formulation. However, Ramban, rejecting Rashi's explanation, suggests:

> And, in my view, the correct interpretation is that the harvesting mentioned refers to what is brought at the beginning of the section (verse 10), namely that when you come into the land and reap the harvest, and bring a sheaf of the first fruits of the harvest (*bikkurim*), you should not reap the corner of your field for the *omer*, nor glean the gleanings, meaning that the mitzvah [of the *omer*] does not supersede those prohibitions.

The Ramban here is teaching us that the mitzvah of bringing the *omer* before the altar of God cannot push aside those mitzvot directed to helping the poor.[5]

Indeed, this is surely the explanation for the statement found in Tosefta *Berachot* 1:2, ed. Lieberman, 2:

> Said R. Yehudah: Once I was walking after R. Akiva and R. Elazar ben Azaria, and it was time to say the *Shema*, and I thought they had given up on saying it. But [then I realized] that they had been involved in communal affairs (צרכי ציבור).

And in the parallel text in Yerushalmi *Berachot* 1:2: "and they were involved in mitzvot. I read the *Shema* . . . , and then they began, and the sun was already above the hills."

And in Tosefta *Berachot* 2:6, ed. Lieberman, 7:

> Said R. Elazar be-R. Tzadok: When Rabban Gamliel and his court at Yavneh were involved in communal affairs (צרכי ציבור), he would not interrupt [for prayer], so as not to confuse his thoughts (להסיח מלבו).[6]

And in Yerushalmi *Berachot* 5:1, we read in the name of R. Yirmiah: "He who is involved in communal affairs, it is as though he is involved in learning Torah (בדברי תורה)." And this statement was understood by the

5. R. Hayyim ibn Atar, in his *Orah Hayyim* ad loc., follows this interpretation.
6. Cf. BT *Berachot* 11a.

Rishonim to mean that he does not have to interrupt for prayer.[7] (See *Shulhan Aruch Orah Hayyim* 93:4.)

From all the above sources, it seems clear that involvement in communal affairs – צרכי ציבור או רבים[8] – a social commitment, takes precedence over various forms of prayer, a ritual obligation.

We find further confirmation of this basic proposition, namely that "social mitzvot" take a certain precedence over "ritual" ones, in a very interesting passage in R. Yosef Engel's *Otvin de-Oraita*, Lvov: 1896, *Klal* 13. The point of departure is a difference of opinion between the *Derishah* and the *Taz* as to whether one who was unable to pray one of the mandatory prayers because of some compelling reason (אנוס – *anus*) is obligated to make it up in the following prayer, or is exempt therefrom (see *Taz*, *Orah Hayyim* 108:1). The source of their disagreement lies in the question as to whether one who does not carry out a mitzvah because he was unable to do so (*anus*) is actually totally exempt of that time, and consequently is not obligated to make it up, or he is obligated, but unable to fulfill that obligation, therefore he must make it up. R. Yosef Engel settled this conflict of opinions, arguing that in the case of a mitzvah between man and his Maker, God, as it were, would have no complaint or find any fault in one who could not fulfill his commandment; hence, in such a case he is completely exempt, and need not make it up. For God only requires of a person that which he can carry out. But when dealing with a mitzvah relating to one's fellow human, such as paying up a debt, or building a protective fence (*maakeh*) on the roof, etc., who would suggest that one who was unable to do so at a given time is exempt in the future! Clearly he has to find another opportunity to fulfill his social obligations. In this way he explains some passages in the Talmud (BT *Hagigah* 2a, BT *Yevamot* 2a, Tosafot to *Baba Batra* 13a, etc.), but that part of his argumentation is beyond the scope of our discussion. (I am grateful to Rabbi David Bagno for bringing this passage to my attention.) For further implications of this whole question, see the detailed and complex related discussion in

7. See L. Ginzberg, *Perushim ve-Hiddushim la-Yerushalmi*, vol. 1 (New York: 1941, 131–133); vol. 4, ed. David Halivni (New York: 1961, 64–71). See further *Beur Halachah* to *Orah Hayyim* 38:5, and the various commentators to the *Shulhan Aruch* for detailed discussion of these rulings.

8. On the difference between *tzorchei tzibbur* and *tzorchei rabbim*, see Moshe Zvi Polin, *Sefer ha-Mitzpeh al ha-Rambam*, vol. 2, (on *Hilchot Keriyat Shema*) (Jerusalem: 2007, 93–100).

R. Ovadiah Yosef's *Hazon Ovadiah – Yamim Noraim*, Jerusalem: 2005, 370–372.

Finally, I believe there is a remarkable corroboration of this basic principle in an explicit biblical ruling. The Bible in Leviticus 14:33–36 tells of a house that was afflicted with some kind of leprosy. In verse 36 we are told:

> Then the priest shall command that they empty the house, before the priest goes into it to see the plague, that all that is in the house be not made unclean: and afterward the priest shall go in to see the house.

Only after all the contents of the house have been removed the priest enters, examines it and determines whether or not it is indeed plagued, and whether the afflicted stones have to be removed and "cast into an unclean place without the city" (verse 40). For this kind of plague causes the house and all that would have been in it to be impure.

The Mishnah in *Negaim* 12:5 (and parallel sources) adds R. Meir's comments:

> R. Meir said: And which of his goods would it render unclean? If thou wouldest say. "His articles of wood, or of cloth or of metal," these he may immerse and they become clean. For what has the Law taken thought? For his earthenware vessels [which cannot be made clean by immersion, but must be broken], even his cruse and his ewer [cf. M. *Kelim* 3:2]. If the Law there takes thought for that property of a man that is of least worth, how much more for property that he prizes most....

From here Rashi to *Menachot* 86b (Ms.) learns the principle that the Torah was concerned for the assets of Israel. (See our extensive discussion of this issue in *Darkah shel Torah*, Jerusalem: 2007, 93–99, 140.)

This biblical directive, that the owners of the plagued house should remove all their belongings before the priest comes to examine it, is truly remarkable. Prior to the priest's visit there is already a suspicion of impurity. The impurity, if it be there, is of biblical status, and it is a well-known axiom that "doubtful impurity in a private domain is impure" (ספק טומאה ברשות היחיד ספקו טמא, see e.g., Tosafot *Avodah Zarah* 37b; *Sdei Hemed*, by R. H.H. Medini, vol. 3, 126, etc.).

Likewise, for all prohibitions of biblical authority, when in doubt rule stringently (ספקא דאורייתא לחומרא). So the earthenware vessels removed from the *possibly* afflicted house ought, according to standard halachic understanding, be impure. Nonetheless, the Torah rules that they remain pure as long as the priest has not examined the house and its contents. So much so, that a priest could eat his *terumah* in those vessels! Surely the Torah is here teaching us that the concern of the economic welfare of the unfortunate owner of the house outweighs even the ritual rules of impurity. (See below section 15, near note 6).

And not merely economic welfare must be considered. For in BT *Moed Katan* 7b–8a we learn (based on the verse in Leviticus 13:14), that the priest does not necessarily rush off to examine the house when suspicions of plague are raised. For a bridegroom "there is a delay of seven days (the "seven days of banqueting"), for both his house and his garments; and so too during the foot-festivals [there is a delay] of seven days. Here, then, other kinds of sensitivities come into play, be they the emotional state of the bridegroom (and presumably his bride), and not negatively to affect the joyous festive activities.

(It is true that there is an opinion that ספקא דאורייתא לחומרא is of rabbinic authority – מדרבנן. However, the dominant view is that ספקא דאורייתא לחומרא מדאורייתא. See the copious material cited in *Sdei Hemed*, vol. 5, pp. 184 and 216.) It is also clear that the laws of *negaim* – leprous afflictions – have their own unique characteristics. Thus, the priest plays a very dominant part in the whole proceedings. See e.g., Rambam, *Hilchot Tumat Tzaraat*, chapters 9 and 14. (Likewise, see *Torah Temimah* of R. Baruch Halevi Epstein, to Leviticus 13:22, 230–231, note 104.) However, the ethical lessons emerging from this complex of rulings is surely meaningful to all – even in contemporary times.

Furthermore, in the light of what we have seen thus far we can also more fully understand how during the foot-festivals the pilgrims in Jerusalem all had the status of *haverim*, i.e., they were not suspect of bearing impurity, and everyone could eat and share with everyone else. (See JT *Hagigah* 3:1, 79d; M. *Hagigah* 3:6; BT *Hagigah* 26a; Rambam *Hilchot Metamei Mishkav u-Moshav* 11:9; and cf. *Shut R. Betzalel Ashkenazi* [Lemberg: 1909], section 1, a responsum from c. 1574.) Apparently the value of social unity during these festive occasions temporarily superseded the ritualistic laws of impurity. (And see below section 15.)

3

Two Categories of Sinners

IN THE LIGHT of the above we can perhaps better understand the well-known rabbinic statement that while sins against God are expiated on Yom ha-Kippurim, those against fellow humans are not expiated on Yom ha-Kippurim until the sinner appeases him that was sinned against, (BT *Yoma* 85b, and cf. *Numbers Rabbah* 11:7).[1]

---

1. In *Yoma* 85b, we find the following statement:

> Sins between man and his Maker Yom ha-Kippurim atones; sins between man and his fellow Yom ha-Kippurim does not atone until he appeases his fellow. This is what R. Eleazar ben Azariah taught: "that ye be clean from all your sins before the Lord" (Lev. 16:30) – sins between man and his Maker Yom ha-Kippurim atones; sins between man and his fellow Yom ha-Kippurim does not atone until he appeases his fellow. Said R. Akiva: Blessed are you, Israel, before whom do you purify yourself and who purifies you? Your father in Heaven.

And in *Numbers Rabbah* ibid. we read:

> R. Akiva said: One text says "and that will clear [the guilty]" (ונקה), and another text says "that will by no means clear [the guilty] (לא ינקה), (Exod. 34:7; Num. 14:18)! But [the meaning is that] something between you and your Maker "will clear," and something between you and your fellow "will by no means clear . . ."

We must, however, not overlook the view of Rabbi [Yehudah ha-Nasi], who in BT *Yoma* ibid. (and in parallels in BT *Shevuot* 13a and BT *Keritot* 7a) states in a *baraita* that

> All sins in the Torah, whether he repented or not, Yom ha-Kippurim atones for them, with the exception of homiletically demeaning the Torah (מגלה פנים בתורה) . . . , and violating the covenant (i.e., circumcision), which, if he repented Yom ha-Kippurim will atone, and if not, Yom ha-Kippurim will not.

There is a discussion among the later authorities as to whether when he said "all sins" he meant also to include those between man and his neighbor, or he only was referring to those between man and his Creator. Some argue that since he specifically excludes some sins, all others must be included in his primary statement, i.e., also those between man and his neighbor. Others reject this argument for a variety of reasons. This issue is discussed by R. Yaakov Hayyim Sofer, in his *Shuvi ha-Shulamit*, vol. 5 (Jerusalem: 2008, sect. 7, 31–33), who shows that R. Moshe ben Shem Tov ibn Haviv (15th cent.) in his *Tosefet Yom ha-Kippurim* to BT *Yoma* ibid., (which I have not actually seen), explicitly states that Rabbi also would agree that Yom ha-Kippurim does *not* atone for sins between man and his neighbor, and this too was the opinion of the author of the *Minhat Hinuch*, R. Yosef Babad (Vilna: 1923, Mitzvah 364, sect. 32, 27b), who adds that this is also true of death, which would not atone for such sins without a person's repentence. So too notes R. Yosef Engel, in his *Gilyonei ha-Shas* to *Yoma* ibid. (Vienna: 1929, 85b). However, R. Sofer ends his discussion by suggesting that this may not be the opinion of the Tosafot (to BT *Shevuot* ibid.). See also his remarks in the following sect. 8, 33–34. In summary, however, the more dominant consensus is that Rabbi too agrees that sins between man and his neighbor require repentance in order that Yom ha-Kippurim atone them.

I found yet another halachic differentiation between these two categories, expounded in *Meorot ha-Daf ha-Yomi*, no. 420 (2007) to *Yevamot*, 38–44. It is dealing with a passage in BT *Yevamot* 39b. I quote it in full:

> The order of *halitzah* (the ritual for end of a levirate relationship) includes "calling out" (קריאה). The sister-in-law cites the verse in Deut. 25:7, "My husband's brother refuseth to raise up unto his brother a name in Israel, he will not perform the duty of my husband's brother." And the brother-in-law replies to her, saying, "I like not to take her" (25:8).
>
> Concerning these declarations the *Shulhan Aruch* rules (*Even ha-Ezer* 169, *Seder Halitzah* 6) that the brother-in-law must understand what his sister-in-law said, and what he declares in return. The Gaon of Vilna, explaining this requirement (ibid., sect. 39), states that the source is in the Gemara in *Yevamot* which deals with the formulation of the "*get halitzah*" (the bill of divorce for the levirates). This is a document which is written for the sister-in-law who has fulfilled the mitzvah of *halitzah*, and serves as evidence that having done so she is permitted to remarry. The Gemara

(*Yevamot* ibid.) explains that this document is written, among other reasons, because the court said to the brother-in-law, "Should you wish to marry her, you may do so, and if not, present your foot."

Why then is it necessary to mention in the *halitzah* document that the court explained the nature of the process? Surely it would suffice to declare that the *halitzah* process took place, she removed his shoe, etc., and thus the mitzvah was carried out? We see then, that he has to understand what he says, and proclaiming the biblical verses without understanding their meaning is to no avail.

Rabbi Kanievsky, in his *Nahal Eitan*, expounds the laws of the "decapitated calf" (עגלה ערופה). In the course of his disquisition, he debates whether the elders have to understand what they are saying, when proclaiming, "Our hands have not shed this blood, neither have our eyes seen it" (Deut. 21:7). For, on the one hand, the ruling is that when saying *Shema* and prayers, benedictions and the Grace after Meals, even if one does not understand their meaning, one has fulfilled the obligation (with the exception of the first verse of the *Shema*, and the first blessing of the *Amidah*, see *Shaar ha-Tziyyun* 193:3). On the other hand, those participating in the *halitzah* ceremony must understand the meaning of their proclamations.

In his opinion, the distinction between these two categories is clear and simple. One must distinguish between what a man says merely for himself, as when he speaks to his Creator, as opposed to when he speaks to others. When the Torah commanded to declare verses, it is sufficient that there be an act of speech. Not so when the Torah required that one speaks to someone else. The act of speaking in itself is not enough. It has to pass on to others who understand it and receive the information given. And clearly that cannot be the case, when the speaker himself does not understand what he is saying.

Saying *Shema* blessings, prayers, *Kiddush*, *Havdalah*, Grace after Meals – all these are said to God alone. Therefore, ex post facto, also he who does not understand the meaning of the words has fulfilled his obligation, as long as he is aware that he is not merely mumbling, but making a benediction or a prayer to God. But the statements in the *halitzah* ceremony are not merely verses, but statements to the levirate and the court, and without understanding, these statements are totally in vain. This distinction has its implications for many kinds of proclamations where there is no clear indication as to whether the understanding of them is essential or not. The proclamation in the case of the *eglah arufah* is directed to God alone, argues Rabbi Kanievsky, and hence, need not be understood on the part of the declarers. So too *Vidui Maaser* (declaration concerning separation of tithes). However, the declarations in the chapter dealing with the *sotah*

> (adulteress), where the Cohen reads certain verses to her, and makes her take an oath, they must be understood by the woman, for they are declarations from person to person.

From the above analysis, we see that there is a clear difference between statements between man and his neighbor and statements between man and his Creator. And, of course, we are speaking of statements and declarations in the context of mitzvot. For a similar distinction between two types of declarative mitzvot, see R. Yitzchak Nissenboim, *Kinyanei Kedem*, second edition, ed. Y. Shapiro (Jerusalem: 1978, 187–192).

It has also been noted that there are no *berachot* on social mitzvot, and no debate on whether they require *kavannah* (intent). See, e.g., Aharon Levine, *Avnei Hefetz* (Munich: 1948, 31), and, most recently, the discussion of R. Shlomo Mordechai Einhorn, in his *Maaseh Hoshev* (New York: 2011, 134–140), citing, inter alia, the *Klei Hemdah* to *Parshat Va-Yehi*.

Even though this is the generally accepted principle, there are apparently exceptions to it, as I learned from a fascinating yet unpublished article by Prof. David Henschke. He points out that the mid-13th century R. Eliyahu of Londrish (London) writes that in his opinion *all* mitzvot require a blessing. "And on occasions I say 'who has commanded us on his mitzvot to rise before the aged,' or 'to honor the Sage,' and all such positive commandments." (See his commentary to *Berachot*, ed. Y.L. Sacks [Jerusalem: 1956], 32, cited in a slightly different fashion in *Sefer Haredim*, by R. Eliezer Azikri, to JT *Berachot* 6:1, etc.). Hundreds of years later R. Aaron of Worms, the Rabbi of Metz and member of Napoleon's Sanhedrin, stated that one should make blessings over unusual mitzvot, such as returning lost articles, or making a fence for the roof. (*Meorei Or*, called *Beer Sheva* [Metz: 1819], 4b.) So too, R. Yitzhak Isaac Safrin of Komarno, in 19th cent. Galicia, also stated (*Shulhan ha-Tahor* [Jerusalem: 1965], 70, section 214/1, etc.):

> Over all mitzvot one must make a [full] blessing *be-shem u-malchut*: over honoring one's parents, paying wages on time, charity and good deeds. For there is a general principle "over all mitzvot one makes a blessing" . . . and all who make more such blessings which are mandated will be blessed by the Lord a hundred holy blessings; so one should make blessings over every mitzvah, great or small. (But see below, sect. 21, n. 4.)

And there are additional such references in his book (sect. 188, etc.), and Henschke has found further examples of this practice. However, these are definitely minority opinions and do not represent the standard practice.

(Incidentally, concerning the passage in JT *Berachot* 6:1 on which the *Haredim* cited R. Eliyah of Londrish, see my comments in *Minhagei Yisrael*, vol. 2 [Jerusalem: 1991], 137–138 in n. 23.)

My grandfather, Rabbi David Sperber, of blessed memory, in his commentary to Tractate *Avot* 3 (*Michtam le-David*, Brooklyn, NY: 1997, 64) linked this concept to the statement of Rabbi Haninah ben Dosa (*Avot* 3:11):

> He in whom the spirit of mankind finds pleasure, in him the spirit of God finds pleasure; but he in whom the spirit of mankind finds no pleasure, in him the spirit of God finds no pleasure.

And perhaps this is how we should understand another statement by the same R. Haninah ben Dosa (3:12):

> He used to say: He whose deeds (מעשיו) exceed his wisdom (חכמתו), his wisdom endures; but he whose wisdom exceeds his deeds, his wisdom does not endure.

I would suggest that deeds refer to social mitzvot, while wisdom – *hochmah* refers to Torah. R. Haninah ben Dosa is teaching us that in order that one's learning endure and be meaningful, it cannot be divorced from practical interpersonal mitzvot.[2]

And, indeed, this is one of the interpretations of R. Yitzhak Abohab, in his commentary to *Avot*, *Magen Elohim*, ed. Y.S. Spiegel, Petah Tikva: 2007, 168, who writes:

> The explanation: He whose deeds exceed his wisdom – meaning: when a person's moral behavior and the honesty of his relationship with others, such as in business transactions come first, (שקדמו לו חכמת המדות ומשאו ומתנו באמונה) his wisdom will endure. But if a person studies (קורא ושונה),[3] but is not honest in his business transactions, . . . then his wisdom (i.e., his study [of Torah]) will not endure.

On the need for *kavannah* in the performance of mitzvot in general, see the brief survey in R. Isaac Cohen's *Acts of the Mind in Jewish Ritual Law* (Jerusalem: 2008, 58–61).

2. See below, sect. 4 dealing with the status of Torah study, namely that "learning Torah is a utilitarian endeavor" with functional objectives.

3. This terminology in rabbinic literature always refers to study of Torah – Oral and Written.

And this is in fact an elaboration of R. Yonah Girondi's more laconic explanation of R. Haninah ben Dosa's aphorism.[4]

And in this context we should recall the famous difference of opinion among the later authorities, some of whom hold that if the sinner does not appease his fellow, then those sins against God will also not be expiated by Yom ha-Kippurim, (cf. above, note 1).[5]

---

4. R. Baruch ha-Levi Epstein, in his commentary to *Avot*, entitled *Baruch she-Amar* (Tel Aviv: n.d., 113–114), connects this passage with what we read in BT *Yoma* 86a:

> We have learned in a *baraita*: "And thou shalt love the Lord thy God" (Deut. 6:5) – that the Name of Heaven be made beloved by you. A person who studies Torah (קורא ושונה) and serves the Rabbis, and his business transactions with people are honest and his conversations with people are calm and peaceful, what do people say of him? Blessed be his teacher who taught him Torah. Woe to unto those people who have not learned Torah. This person who learned Torah, see how pleasant are his ways, how correct is his behavior. Concerning him the verse says, "And He said unto me, Thou art My servant, O Israel, in whom I will be glorified" (Isa. 49:3). But he who studies Torah and serves the Rabbis, but his business transactions are not honest, and his conversations with people are not calm and peaceful, what do people say of him? Woe to unto him, who learned Torah. Woe unto his father who taught him Torah; woe to his teacher who taught him Torah. See how corrupt are his ways, how ugly is his behavior. Concerning him the verse says, "when they said to them, these are the people of the Lord, and are gone forth and of his land" (Ezek. 36:20).

R. Epstein summarizes saying that from here we may learn that one whose actions and moral behavior are good and admirable, his wisdom – the wisdom of the Torah – will endure in the world, because the multitude will learn from his example... Not so, the learned scholar whose actions and behavior are reprehensible; he is the cause of people being driven away from the Torah and its message.

All of the above comes to teach us, what is really quite obvious, that even intensive Torah learning and knowledge, when it is not accompanied by decent behavior, is not only purposeless, but even pernicious, and may lead to the desecration of the Name of God (*hillul ha-Shem*).

5. There is a well-known controversy among the later authorities whether according to R. Eleazar ben Azariah sins between man and his fellow where there was no appeasement also warrant the atonement of sins between man and his Maker. This is the view of R. Yishayah Pinto in his commentary to R. Isaac Alfasi (the *Rif*) apud the *Ein Yaakov*, and so too R. Hayyim Palache (in *Birkat*

It is perhaps pertinent here to recall what R. Dov Katz wrote (in his *Tenuat ha-Mussar* vol. 4, Tel Aviv: 1957, 119–120) concerning the Hafetz Hayyim, namely that he made repeated efforts to change the order of recitation of *Tefillah Zakah* on the eve of Yom ha-Kippurim.[6] He urged that the congregation read the later part first, the *vidui* – confession of sins

---

Moadim le-Hayyim), and Yaavetz, (in a responsum *Shetei ha-Lehem*, sect. 31). On the other hand, the Hida, in *Birkei Yosef* to sect. 606, subsect. 1, is of the opposite opinion. See R. Yosef Engel's note to *Yoma* ibid., *Peri Hadash*, sect. 606:1, R. Yosef Shaul Nathanson, *Shoel u-Meshiv Reviata*, vol. 3 (Lemberg: 1877, sect. 64); Responsa *Yehaveh Daat*, by R. Ovadiah Yosef, vol. 5, sect. 44, and *Hazon Ovadiah: Yamim Noraim* (Jerusalem: 2005, 220–222).

Here we may add that the view that atonement for sins between man and God require prior appeasement between man and his neighbor seems to be borne out by the passage in BT *Yoma* 87a that Rav went to appease a butcher on the *eve* of Yom Kippur. And, indeed, this is the standard custom that one begs forgiveness from one another *before* Yom Kippur. However, interestingly enough, R. Moshe ben Yehudah Machir (Ein Zeitun, Tzefat 17th cent.) in his *Seder ha-Yom* (Jerusalem: 1978, 218), writes:

> *After* Yom ha-Kippurim it is the custom to appease one another and ask forgiveness for any mistake or sin against one another. And the reason is because Yom ha-Kippurim only atones for sins between man and God.

The editor ad loc. notes that he has not found a parallel to this practice of appeasement *after* Yom Kippur. However, R. Aharon (Stolinsky) of Karlin, in his *Beit Aharon* (Pietrokov: 1914), (*Shabbat Shuvah*) refers to the Maharal of Prague as having said that first one appeases God and afterwards, after Yom Kippur, one's neighbor. R. Yisrael Dendrovitch, in an article in *Moriah* (31:7–8, 2011, 173), states that he has not found this in the writings of the Maharal, but points to the *Seder ha-Yom*. Perhaps R. Aharon of Karlin mistakenly confused the two authorities. This view of the *Seder ha-Yom* is cited by R. Avraham Yitzhak Friedman, in his *Likutei Mahariah*, vol. 3 (Brooklyn, NY: 1965, 96a), who, however, adds that "in all the decisors (*poskim*) it is stated to do so *before* Yom Kippur. And this undoubtedly is the overall consensus," (see Dendrovitch, ibid., 174).

However, what is of interest for us in this context is that apparently according to this view the atonement for sins between man and God are *not dependent* upon man's appeasement of his neighbor, for only thus can we understand the otherwise inexplicable practice of appeasement of friends *after* Yom Kippur.

6. On *Tefillah Zakah*, see what I wrote in *Minhagei Yisrael*, vol. 4 (Jerusalem: 1995, 274), and in my *On Changes in Jewish Liturgy* (Jerusalem, New York: 2010), 55–56.

between man and his neighbor – before that of the ones between man and God, which constitutes the first part of *Tefillah Zakah*. His reasoning was that this prayer is quite lengthy, and people often do not manage to recite the whole of it and end in the middle in order to hear the *Kol Nidrei* prayer, "especially as many members of the congregation bang on the tables when they see the sun setting, demanding that one begin *Kol Nidrei*." In this way they miss out the most important part of the prayer, the *vidui* of sins between man and his neighbor. (See also R. Aryeh Leib ha-Cohen, the Hafetz Hayyim's son, in his *Michtevei ha-Rav Hafetz Hayyim, Ztl*, second edition, New York: 1953, part 2, *Derachav Nimukav ve-Sihotav*, 16–17, and especially 21–22.)

And if I be permitted some degree of homiletic license, I would cautiously suggest the following:

It is well-known that Yom Kippur is the Day of Atonement and consequently of judgment. It is the day when the divine decision is made as to whether we are granted an additional year of life, or not, whether we be rich or poor, etc. But the rabbis gave us yet another further chance to repent, thus delaying the final judgment till Hoshana Rabbah, at the end of the festival of Sukkot. Indeed, the Rambam to Numbers 14:9, calls it ליל החתום – *Leil ha-Hatum* (or *ha-Hitum*), the "Night of Final Reckoning." And in some *mahzorim*, they would recite on this day *U-ne-Taneh Tokef*, with the following phrase: בראש השנה יזכרון, ביום צום כיפור יכתבון ובהושענא רבה יחתמון: On Rosh ha-Shanah they will be remembered, on the fast of Yom Kippur they will be written, and on Hoshana Rabbah their fate will be sealed. (See on this in further detail in my *Minhagei Yisrael*, vol. 6, Jerusalem: 1998, 174–175, note 5.) Why, then, did the rabbis add this additional day of judgment?

Perhaps we may suggest, in accordance with those views that without pacifying one's enemies, one is not forgiven also of those sins against one's Creator, and possibly on Yom Kippur we have not been able to make peace with those against whom we sinned, therefore, another opportunity was given.

On Yom Kippur, we declared at the beginning of the *Kol Nidrei* service, that we allow all the "sinners" to join us in prayers. Those "sinners" are those we regard as sinners, because they did not act in a way we thought correct and proper. (The commentaries explain that they acted against rabbinic enactments.) In welcoming them into our midst – our synagogues – we are in a way seeking to pacify them, to declare our acceptance of them, and thus rectify our untoward acts against them. On the verse in Leviticus 23:42, "all that are Israelites born shall dwell in booths" the rabbis declared, "It is fitting that all Israel dwell in one *sukkah*," (BT *Sukkah* 27b). Here, again, is an expression of welcome to all Israelites, be they whatever they be. Just as on Yom Kippur we welcomed them into our synagogues to join with us in prayer, so on Sukkot we welcome them to join with us in rejoicing in our *sukkot*. Indeed, this is the all-too-well-known symbolism of the "Four Species," one of which has neither fragrance nor taste, i.e., representing those who have neither Torah nor righteous deeds. Nonetheless, all Four Species are bound together, to express the unity of Israel, throughout its whole spectrum. (See BT *Menahot* 27a; *Leviticus Rabbah* 30:12, ed. M. Margaliot [Jerusalem: 1958, 709–710]; *Tur Orah Hayyim* 619, 651; BT *Keritot* 6b.) Here again we have a strengthening of the notion of acceptance of those who differ from us. And this being, in a sense, a form of pacification of those against whom we have perhaps acted improperly, Sukkot enables us to complete the atonement for sins against our neighbors, thus enabling us to attain a *complete* atonement, both for those sins as well as those against our Creator. Hence, Hoshana Rabbah, the end of Sukkot (the end of our dwelling in *sukkot*) is, indeed, the most suitable day to constitute the *Yom ha-Hitum*, the Day of *Final* Judgment.

We see then that an untoward relationship towards our fellow neighbors, prevents, as it were, a positive relationship towards God.

It is interesting to note that the principle that Yom ha-Kippurim atones sins between man and his Creator, but not necessarily between man and his neighbor, unless he has succeeded in pacifying him, was known to medieval Muslim scholars. Thus Al-Maqdisi, tenth century, in his description of Judaism writes:

> They claim that on this day [*Id Rāsh Hashanā*], God forgives them all their sins and offences, except three: adultery with a married woman [*gilui arayot*], *injustice of a man towards his brother* [my emphasis, D. S.], and the denial of God's divinity.

(See Camilla Adang, *Muslim Writers on Judaism and the Hebrew Bible, from Ibn Rabban to Ibn Hazm* [Leiden, New York, Köln: 1996, 260, with relevant bibliography, on 48–50, 84–87.])

And here I cannot restrain myself from recalling the wonderful story that R. Yehudah Leib Maimon records in his *Toldot ha-Gra* (Jerusalem: 1970, 7), concerning the rabbi of Frankfurt, R. Avraham-Abush, a contemporary of the Gaon of Vilna:

> They relate that once the *shochtim* (slaughterers) of Frankfurt came before him with a query concerning [the kashrut of] a lung, a matter

on which the Rema and the rest of the Polish authorities ruled most stringently. The incident took place on the eve of a festival, and the matter was one which potentially involved a very considerable monetary loss for the impoverished slaughterer. The members of the Beit Din wished to rule stringently and declare the meat not kosher (in accordance with the view of the Rema), but R. Avraham-Abush began to search for ways of finding it kosher. The judges of the Beit Din insisted on their position that it is impossible to rule leniently against the view of the Rema and his colleagues, but R. Avraham-Abush argued with them, discussing the halachic issues involved, and finally ruled that the meat was kosher. The members of the Beit Din were astonished, asking him: How could one possibly rule leniently declaring it kosher against the ruling of the Rema and the great authorities of Poland who held the same opinion?!

R. Avraham-Abush replied to them as follows: I prefer at the end of my days when I come [before the Heavenly Court] to argue my case with the Rema and his colleagues, rather than with this poor slaughterer. The slaughterer is a simple man, and it will be very difficult for me to argue my case with him before the Heavenly Court, if he brings me to court claiming that I declared his animal *tareif*, and that in doing so I caused him great monetary loss (הפסד מרובה),[7]

---

7. On this halachic concept, see what I wrote in *Darkah shel Halachah* (Jerusalem: 2007, 117–118, 140–141, 175–177); *Minhagei Yisrael*, vol. 3 (Jerusalem: 1994, 53–54); idem vol. 8 (Jerusalem: 2007, 263); *Encyclopedia Talmudit*, vol. 10 (Jerusalem: 1961, 32–41).

Bension Cohen of New York (in an internet communication from Sept. 15, 2010) would wish that there be here an amplified explanation of R. Avraham-Abush's ruling so that it be more clearly understood. He would interpret it as follows:

> ... both the slaughterer and the Rabbi were caring for the poor, they were concerned about *Mitzvot she-Bein Adam le-Havero* as well as the *Mitzvot Bein Adam la-Makom*. The lung is one of the least desirable organs for a butcher, generally sold to the poor. The strict rendition of *treifa*, the slaughterer argued, would make all the poor who rely on this meat not to have the ability to celebrate the holiday with a little meat, making the poor unnecessary anguish, before *Yom Tov*. Therefore, ... the Rabbi who recognized the potential anguish of the poor not having cheap meat for *Yom Tov* as well as the greater monetary loss required of them to purchase clearer portions of the meat, rendered a lenient *psak* predicated on the *shitah* ... presented in this ... (chapter). There is a double consideration of *Kevod*

> and that I damaged his business on the eve of the festival. But I am sure that when I lay out my arguments before the Rema and his colleagues, we will reach an agreement....

The logic in R. Avraham Abush's position is clarified in a similar tale told by Yaakov Rimon and Yosef Zundel Wasserman in the book, *Shmuel be-Doro: R. Shmuel Salant z"l, Rabbah shel Yerushalayim 1841–1909, Hayyav u-Poalav*, Tel Aviv: 1961, 122–126:

> Once upon a time some learned rabbis were arguing with him (R. Shmuel Salanter) on a case where he had ruled "kosher," and needless to say he refuted their counter-arguments. One of them turned to him and said to him: "You have refuted our arguments, but what will happen when you come before the Heavenly Court and have to

---

> *ha-Kelal* and the recognition of the *Tzaar*. The explanation presented... while very lofty presents an argument made by a true Gadol.

My thanks to Mr. Cohen for this insightful amplification, which is certainly much clearer and more forceful than a mere reference to the concept of *hefsed merubeh*, which might lead one to the erroneously simplistic conclusion that when it comes to money the Rabbis are ready to be lenient, (as Cohen writes, warning us against such an understanding). This is, indeed, partially true, but requires a detailed understanding of the concept of *hefsed merubeh*, for which reason I gave some basic references.

Here we may add that there is a general misconception that it is easier to rule stringently – *le-humra*, thus avoiding the dangers of permitting the forbidden. However, the Rosh, in his response, *Klal Bet*, sect. 17 ad fin., writes, "and he who rules forbidding something (והאוסר) must bring clear and strong evidence, for the Torah was concerned for the property of Israel (כי התורה חסה על ממונם של ישראל).

Further details may be found in R. Yitzhak Yosef's *Ein Yitzhak*, vol. 3 (Jerusalem: 2009, 298–306, 596).

A different approach to a similar situation is told of R. Yosef Dov Soloveitchik. It was his way to be extremely stringent in cases of kashrut for himself. But when it came to others, he feared mistakenly to declare something not kosher, thus causing damage and as it were stealing other people's property. On one occasion, he felt he had no alternative but to declare some meat non-kosher, "even though according to the *Shach* it is kosher, I may not cause you monetary loss and be considered a thief according to the view of the *Shach*." There and then, on the spot he took from his purse the value of the animal and gave it to the butcher, (A. Tobolsky, *Hizaharu be-Mamon Haverchem* [Bnei Brak: 1981], 249).

> argue with the Beit Yosef and the Rema?" they asked. He replied as follows: "Surely you will agree with me that it will be better for me to argue my case with them, since I believe that I understood in depth their opinion, rather than having a claim against me on the part of the ox [i.e., on the part of the owner of the ox] that I incorrectly declared *tareif*..."[8]

Both these tales have a common denominator: namely that if the rabbi ruled incorrectly, declaring *tareif* meat kosher, he has sinned against God, and Yom ha-Kippur will atone for this sin. But should he have ruled kosher meat as *tareif*, he will have caused damage, hurt and monetary loss to the slaughterer, and this is a sin against his fellow-man for which Yom ha-Kippur does not automatically atone; and hence he preferred to err on the side of leniency rather than risk erring on the side of stringency.[9]

We find much the same idea reflected in the Netziv (R. Naftali Zvi Yehudah Berlin), in his *Haamek Davar* to Genesis 20:7, "[Now therefore restore the man his wife; for he is a prophet], and he shall pray for thee, and thou shalt live":

> According to what we have explained ... that the sin was that [Avimelech] caused grief to our forefather Abraham, surely he only needed to appease him, and there was no need for prayer. However, from here we may learn that one who sins against his neighbor also sins against God, and it is not sufficient to appease one's neighbor alone. One must also beg forgiveness from God. And for this reason he needed Abraham's prayer, in order to be completely expiated.

---

8. Cf. below, sect. 27.

9. See my discussion in *Darkah Shel Torah*, 140–141. Here we may add the following story brought by Meir Tamari in his *Al Chet: Sins in the Marketplace* (Northvale, N.J. and London: 1996, 24):

> A *shochet*, "ritual slaughterer," once came to the Chafetz Chaim for advice, saying, "The laws of *shechitah* are so many and difficult I am afraid that I may sin and cause others to sin through an infringement of them. I think I will go into business." The Chafetz Chaim's reply was simple and direct: "If your major concern is the safety of your soul, you should remain a *shochet*. The laws of the marketplace and of money are far more numerous and onerous, while God, your partner, is an ever-present witness and judge to any deviations."

4

Ha-Osek be-Mitzvah Patur min ha-Mitzvah: The Case of Prayer and Torah Study

We find in *Sefer ha-Rokeah*, section 369 ad fin., that a person who is sitting in the synagogue, wrapped in his *talit* and with his *tefillin* on his head and is reciting liturgical songs, must, nonetheless, rise up before his teacher, since he can carry out both actions and he will receive fine rewards in both worlds. Now there are early authorities who hold that the principle that one who is engaged in one mitzvah is exempt from another is also the case when both could be carried out. (See *Shulhan Aruch Orah Hayyim* 38:8, and in the *Beur Halachah*, ibid., and also R. Yaakov Hayyim Sofer, *Brit Yaakov* [Jerusalem: 1985], section 2, 36; R. Ovadiah Yosef, *Hazon Ovadiah: Sukkot* [Jerusalem: 2005, 167].) The author of the Rokeah, R. Elazar of Germaiza, was a disciple of R. Yehudah (b. R. Shmuel) he-Hasid, the author of *Sefer Hasidim*. And it is the view of R. Yehudah he-Hasid that even if one can carry out both mitzvot, one is exempt from doing so, if one is engaged in a prior mitzvah; and this, indeed, is the view of R. Elazar Rokeah himself (Rokeah, *Hilchot Sukkah*, section 299; see Sofer). Why then should one who is engaged in praising the Lord in the synagogue, have to rise up before his teacher? Surely he is already engaged in a mitzvah, and therefore exempt from others! The answer, I suggest, is because ritual synagogue worship is directed towards God, but respect for one's teacher is a mitzvah between man and his fellow, and he is therefore not exempt from it. So too the Hida, R. Hayyim Yosef David Azulai, rules, that even in the hour of prayer one rises before a Torah scholar, (*Birkei Yosef Orah Hayyim*, section 244:1; and see Sofer, note 8 on page 37; and see most recently the discussion of R. Yitzchak Eliyahu Stessman, *Kimah ve-Hidur* [Jerusalem: 2011, 88–91], with additional references).

Indeed, the severity of not rising before one's teacher is expressed by R. Eleazar in very extreme terms in BT *Kiddushin* 33b:

> Any scholar who does not rise before his teacher is called a wicked person (רשע), and will not live long and will forget his learning.

(See also R. Yaakov Hezkiyahu Fisch, in his *Ve-Haarachta Yamim*, ed. Y.M. Sofer, [Jerusalem: 2010, 71–72].)

To this we may add what we are told of the Arizal, by his disciple R. Hayyim Vital, that he was very particular in paying his workers exactly on time and without delay. And if he did not have the money with which to pay these wages, he would delay his afternoon prayer (*minhah*) until close to sunset in order to search out a loan with which to make the payment. Only afterwards would he hurriedly *daven minhah*. He would explain himself by saying: "How can I pray to the Lord, may He be blessed . . . , when such an important mitzvah is incumbent upon me, and I have not carried it out?" (See R. Hayyim Vital, *Shemonah Shearim: Shaar ha-Mitzvot* [Jerusalem: 1872], *Parshat Tetzeh*; Avraham Tobolsky, *Hizaharu be-Memon Haverchem*, vol. 2, [Bnei Brak: 1981, 211–212].)

In a somewhat different vein, but with much the same principle as its basis, we read in *Niflaot Beit Levi*, by A. Kleiman (Pietrokov: 1911, 32, [Yiddish]), cited in Louis I. Newman and Samuel Spitz, *The Hasidic Anthology: Tales and Teachings of the Hasidim* (New York: 1944, 178:2, 480) as follows:

> A teamster (=wagon driver) sought the Berditchover's (Reb Levi Yitchak of Berditchov's) advice as to whether he should give up his occupation because it interfered with regular attendance at the synagogue.
>
> "Do you carry poor travellers free of charge?" asked the Rabbi. "Yes," answered the teamster. "Then you serve the Lord in your occupation just as faithfully as you would be frequenting the synagogue."

(However, see A.Y. Pfoifer, *Ishei Yisrael* [Jerusalem: 1998, 104, section 11, and notes ad loc].)

And indeed, the Rambam in *Hilchot Talmud Torah* 3:4, followed by the *Shulhan Aruch*, *Yoreh Deah* 246:8, rules:

> If there came before him [the choice of performing] a mitzvah and (i.e., or continuing) learning Torah, if that mitzvah could be carried

> out by another, he should not interrupt his learning; but if not, he should carry out that mitzvah and then return to his study. And when it comes to giving charity, one should always give charity first.[1]

This indeed is the conclusion to be drawn from the *sugya* in Yerushalmi *Pesahim* 3:7 (and parallel to JT *Hagigah* 1:7). There we read that R. Abahu, who lived in Caesarea, sent his son R. Haninah to study in Tiberias, in the Yeshiva of R. Yohanan.

> They came and informed him that [his son] was engaged in charitable activities (i.e., in the burial of dead). He sent him a message, saying to him: "Are there no graves in Caesarea that I sent you to Tiberias?" (i.e., for such activities you could have stayed at home).

The Talmud continues that it was already decided at Beit Nitzeh in Lod that "study is greater for it leads to deeds," (see below). However, the rabbis of Caesarea qualified this by saying:

> This is the case when there is someone else to carry out the deeds. But if there is not anyone else to carry them out, the deed comes before [the study], (i.e., has precedence).

We then are told a tale:

> R. Hiyya, R. Yosi [and] R. Ami were late coming to R. Eleazar [for their lesson with him]. He asked them, "Where were you?" They replied, "We were involved in charitable activity" (meaning in the burial of someone). "Was there no one else [who could do this?]" he asked of them. They replied, "He was a neighbor [according to the *Pnei Moshe*, or a proselyte – according to the *Korban ha-Edah*," i.e., and there was no one else to deal with his burial.]

Incidentally, we may add here that the interpretation of the *Pnei Moshe* is supported by a passage in *Sefer Haredim*, (by R. Eleazar Azikri, [Safed: 1533–1600]), *Mitzvot Aseh . . . ha-Teluyot be-Lev* 22, which states that:

---

1. See *Le-Hair Hilchot Tzedakah be-Or Yekarot* (Jerusalem: 2010, 6–7). And see below sect. 16 on the overriding importance of charity, and Appendix.

> A person is obligated to act charitably towards his neighbors and his relations more than to other people, as is clearly stated in the Bavli and the Yerushalmi.

(See S. Lieberman, *HaYerushalmi Kiphshuto* [Jerusalem: 1934, 426] and his other comments.)

And the parallel text in JT *Hagigah* 1:7., begins with an additional passage, namely:

> R. Yehudah, when he would see a dead person (i.e., a burial) or a bride (i.e., a marriage procession), [and people] praising them (i.e., honoring them in the processions), he would turn to his students (נותן עיניו בתלמידים), and say: "The [dealing with] the dead precedes the study of Torah (תלמוד)."

And a somewhat similar notion, but expressed in a Hassidic vein, may be found in a story related in Yehezkel Shraga Fraenkel's *Rabbenu ha-Kaddosh mi-Shinyeve* (Ramat Gan: 1992, 256–257). He relates that once the Rabbi of Warsaw came to visit the *Divrei Hayyim*, R. Hayyim of Sanz. The Sanzer Rebbe asked him, "Do you learn?" "Yes," the Warsaw Rabbi replied. The Rebbe repeated, "Do you always learn?" The reply was, "When someone who is embittered and needs help comes to me, I close my *gemara* and deal with him, to help and encourage him." "This is what I wanted to hear," said the Sanzer, "whether you have the good sense to close your *gemara* when someone needs your help,[2] both in word and in deed, and in any case to encourage him and bolster his spirit."[3]

Here we must make something of a digression, which is not really a digression, as this touches upon a very important point. For the Mishnah in *Peah* 1:1 states that: "the study of Torah is equal to all of them," i.e., even to those mitzvot listed in the Mishnah which are social ones, such as hon-

---

2. See, for example, the practice of the Brisker Rav, Reb Hayyim Soloveitchik, as described in Aharon Sorasky, *Marbitzei Torah u-Musar bi-Yeshivot Nusah Lita mi-Tekufat Volozin ve-ad Yameinu*, vol. 1 (Jerusalem: 1976, 110).

3. Cf. BT *Shabbat* 127a: Said R. Yohanan: Great is the hosting of guests as are those rising up early to the House of Study [of Torah], as we have learned: to make room for guests [to avoid] hindrance in the House of Study. But Rav Dimi of Nehardea said: It is greater than rising up early to the House of Study. For we learned: "for guests," and only afterwards "to avoid hindrance in the House of Study." And see below sects. 11 and 12 on hosting guests.

oring one's parents, doing charitable deeds, bringing peace between rival individuals, etc. The question we ask ourselves is: is the study of Torah (תלמוד תורה) a ritual or a social mitzvah? Into which category does it fall? For if the former, according to our suggestion how can it be superior to those other social mitzvot?

To clarify this issue we must go back to a very ancient discussion that took place in the attic at Beit Nitzeh in Lod, between R. Tarfon and the Elders. For this question was put before them: which is greater, or more important תלמוד או מעשה, learning or deeds? R. Tarfon answered: Deeds are greater. While R. Akiva said study is greater. And they all replied: Study is greater for it leads to deeds (BT *Kiddushin* 40b).[4] That is to say the importance of study is in that it constitutes the key to the proper execution of the mitzvot. This is also the meaning of R. Shimon the son of Rabban Gamliel's statement in *Avot* 1:17: Not the expounding of the law (*midrash*) is the chief thing, but the doing [of it] (*maaseh*). And this is amplified by Rabbenu Bachya in his commentary ad loc.: that the aim of man's labor in Torah is not that he should just learn a lot, but that [his learning] should lead to deeds, as we have learned from the verse [in Deuteronomy 5:1], 'and ye may learn them [i.e., the statutes and judgments], and keep and do them.' And this is further amplified in *Shulhan Aruch ha-Rav*, by R. Shneur Zalman Mi-Ladi, in his *Hilchot Talmud Torah* 4:2, by telling us that "it is impossible to fulfill all the mitzvot in all their details without intensive study and knowledge of them. And for this reason it is equal to all of them," i.e., not intrinsically, but as a means to their proper application.[5]

This issue has been analyzed recently by R. Yitzchak Shapiro, in his article in *Hakirah* 9, (2010), 221–243, entitled "To know the Forbidden

---

4. On this text see Benedict Thomas Viviano, *Study as Worship: Aboth and the New Testament* (Leiden: 1978, 105–109). Directly related to this is the text in JT *Pesahim* 3:7, and JT *Hagigah* 1:7, cited above, from which the Rabbis learned that if others can carry out these charitable activities, a person should not interrupt his Torah studies. And this seems to be the dominant view among the *poskim*. See further BT *Moed Katan* 9a; *Shulhan Aruch Yoreh Deah* 246:18; Meiri to BT *Shabbat* 9a and *Moed Katan* ibid.; Rabbenu Yeruham 22a in the name of the Ravad, etc.

See R. Asi ha-Levi Even Yuli, *Shulhan Aruch ha-Middot*, vol. 2, *Halachah u-Musar* (Jerusalem: 2009, 243–244).

5. See R. Mordechai Shmuel Ashkenazi's magnificent commentary to *Hilchot Talmud Torah Mi-Shulhan Aruch Admor ha-Zaken*, vol. 5 [=ha-Rav] (Kefar Habad: 2000, 86).

and the Permitted: An Analysis of Rambam's View of the Purpose and Goals of Talmud Study." He shows that the Rambam's view, as expressed in his letter to his disciple R. Yosef,[6] is that "learning Torah is a utilitarian endeavor, with extracting halachic conclusions its functional objective" (227).[7] He goes on to show that "the simplicity and obviousness [of this position] might go unnoticed if not for its staggering ramification and total incompatibility with contemporary realities in *derech halimud*" (227–228). For as he earlier showed (223–224): "the Aharonim do identify an aspect of Torah study, unrelated to fulfillment of the other mitzvot, based on the verse והגית בו יומם ולילה – 'but thou shalt meditate therein day and night' (Joshua 1:8, cf. BT *Menachot* 99b). This mitzvah of '*limud ha-Torah*' is distinct from the mitzvah of '*yediat ha-Torah*,' and can be fulfilled regardless of the subject matter that is learned, whereas the mitzvah of *yediat ha-Torah* requires a curriculum that is limited to 'halachah' (or at least the sharpening of one's mental acuity, which is necessary for accurate application of halachah). However, one may fulfill both facets of the mitzvah simultaneously only by learning halachic subject matter."[8]

---

6. Ed. Y. Shilat, *Iggrot ha-Rambam*, vol. 1 (Jerusalem: 1987, 254–259); and see editor's note on 257–258 to line 4).

7. At the simplest level, there is, in the Rambam's view, an obligation upon one who has learned Torah, also to teach it to others. See *Hilchot Talmud Torah* 1:2, and so too in the listing of the positive commandments at the beginning of his *Mishneh Torah*, no. 11. (This list is also that of the Rambam, as attested by the author of the *Magid Mishneh* in his introduction to *Hilchot Eruvin*, and the *Kesef Mishneh* in *Hilchot Hannukah* 3:6; Responsa *Noda bi-Yehudah Kama, Orah Hayyim*, sect. 29; *Petah ha-Dvir*, vol. 2, sect. 194, subsect. A. See R. Yaakov Hayyim Sofer, *Drupteki de-Oraita*, vol. 1 [Jerusalem: 1987, 45]. And see further his remarks, 68–69, on the need to teach others.) Of related interest is the article of Sarah Pessin, "Maimonides and the Sacred Art of Teaching," apud *Adaptations and Innovations: Studies in the Interaction between Jewish and Islamic Thought and Literature from the Early Middle Ages to the Late Twentieth Century, Dedicated to Professor Joel Kraemer*, ed. Y. Tzvi Langermann (Paris & Louvin: 2007, 285–298). See also, most recently, the remarks of R. Aharon Lichtenstein, in H. Sabato and A. Lichtenstein, *Mevakshei Panecha* (Tel Aviv: 2011, 212–215).

8. See the material R. Yitzchak Shapiro brings from the letters of R. Yisrael Salanter (no. 27), in this regard. See also *Kuntres Aharon shel Shulhan Aruch ha-Rav, Talmud Torah* 3:1, ed. Y.A. Lev (Ashdod: 1989, 39 et seq.).

And see R. Aharon Lichtenstein's very comprehensive study entitled "Does Involvement in Torah Study Exempt One from Mitzvot?", which appeared in *Alei Etzion* 16 (5769 [2009]), 71–107, which examines this issue in depth, dealing

This is the view of the Meiri, as formulated in his commentary to BT *Berachot* 7b:

---

with questions of delaying procreation, *Megillah* reading, prayer, all mitzvot, etc., and seeks to explain Rambam's position that "*ha-osek be-mitzvah patur min ha-mitzvah*" theoretically applies to Torah study too, when "it is studied with the purpose of performing" (91); and cf. ibid., 105, for his suggestive interpretation of the view of the *Maharach Or Zarua*. His study of this very complex issue is extremely rich and requires intense study.

See also Moshe Zvi Polin, *Sefer ha-Mitzpeh al ha-Rambam*, vol. 1, (on *Hilchot Talmud Torah*) (Jerusalem: 2005, 11–26), that studying (*lilmod*) and teaching (*lelamed*) are two interconnected mitzvot. See Ramban *Hilchot Talmud Torah* 1:1; *Hilchot Hagigah* 3:1: that anyone who is obligated to study is obligated to teach, and cf. ibid., 1:4. I think this is the meaning of the statement in *Seder Eliyahu Rabba*, ed. Friedman, p. 63 = *Tanna Debe Eliyahu*, transl. W.G. Braude & I.J. Kapstein (JPS, 1981, 183) that "one who toils in Torah is like a lamp which provides light for the eyes of many." And in this connection, it is also worth reading Benjamin Blech's article "Personal Growth or Communal Responsibility: A Question of Priorities," *The Torah U-Madda Journal* 2 (1990), 134–142. However, to give a slightly different point of view, see *Hatam Sofer* to *Nedarim* 81a; R. Hayyim Volozin's *Nefesh ha-Hayyim, Shaar Dalet*, sect. 3; *Ruah Hayyim* to *Avot* 6:1, and the introduction to *Eglei Tal*.

A very extreme expression of this view is to be found in R. David Baharan's "*Hanhagot u-Piskei Halachah*," in *Otzrot Yerushalayim*, vol. 13 (Jerusalem: [2010?]), 40, where he insists one must learn halachah every day, and it is not sufficient to learn merely Gemara. He goes on to say that one must learn *Shulhan Aruch Orah Hayyim* or *Hayyei Adam*, and he who does not do so will surely have no part in the World to Come. (See also ibid., 41–42.)

See further R.S.Z. Auerbach, *Halichot Shlomo . . . al Moadei ha-Shanah*, ed. Y. Terner and A. Auerbach (Jerusalem: 2007), 537–539, who also is of the opinion that there are two aspects to Torah study: the one being to study in order to learn how to act properly, and the other as an independent positive commandment which is not just in order to know how to act, but the actual practice of learning as an end in its own right. He expands on this position bringing biblical and rabbinic sources to bear out this point of view. However, here too he agrees that ultimately this is in order "to purify his body through the light of Torah, in order to cleave to God . . . who orders the world (אשר הליכות עולם לו), and without which the world cannot subsist (ובלא קיומם – אין מקום קיום לעולם)" so that in the final reckoning this non-action-orientated study is nonetheless direct to תיקון עולם, the betterment of *our* world, (see ibid., 536).

> The knowledge of how the Torah actually expresses itself indeed requires serving or observing Torah scholars. While intellectual learning is the cause of wisdom, observing the Sages is the cause of knowing how the Torah manifests itself. This is both true for monetary matters as well as that which is prohibited and permitted.

Hence, we may well understand the statement of Rav in BT *Megillah* 3b, that *Talmud Torah* is greater than the sacrifice of the daily offerings (*temidin*).

Here we may also call attention to R. Meir Triebitz's insightful analysis (in his introduction to R. Daniel Eidensohn's *Daas Torah: A Jewish Sourcebook* [Jerusalem: 2005, 31–35]). He begins by noting that God commands us twice to study Torah: once in Deuteronomy 11:19, and again in Deuteronomy 4:9–11. He analyzes the differences between these two formulations in all their details – e.g., one in the plural and the other in the singular; one talks of teaching, the other telling; one focuses on parents to children, while the other lists three generations. He concludes that "the two verses which obligate us to learn the Torah actually refer to two types of study. One refers to the study of the legal part of Torah, and the other to the study of Torah's theology. Each form of study is deemed a separate scholarly enterprise." He characterizes these two forms of study as "legal" (i.e., halachic) study, and "faith" study, which he states "deals primarily with Aggadic parts of the Torah." But for our purposes it is important to emphasize that both verses, that is to say both classes of study, require the student also to be a teacher, and to pass on his learning to future generations. Hence, Torah study has a social aspect too.

This is a very broad subject that requires a study in its own right, and we cannot enlarge on it here. But what emerges very clearly is that the mitzvah of Torah study is in a very special category, for without it one would not know how to carry out ritual or social mitzvot correctly. Nonetheless, the *Or Zarua* and the Rav Baal ha-Tanya agree that one interrupts learning Torah to fulfill other mitzvot, if both cannot be carried out at the same time, and one is not exempt because one is already involved in a prior mitzvah.[9]

---

9. See *Kuntres Aharon* ibid., in the editor's *Midrashei ha-Kuntres*, 36; and also *Kuntres Aharon, Talmud Torah* 4:3, that one interrupts learning for persuading others to give charity, where others are less persuasive, or helping in burying the dead, etc. See R. Mordechai Shmuel Ashkenazi, ibid., 87 et seq.

This is clear from the *baraita* in BT *Ketubot* 17a (BT *Megillah* 3b, 29a) that we interrupt our study of Torah (מבטלין תלמוד תורה) not merely for a *met mitzvah* and to accompany the dead (הוצאת המת), but also for wedding ceremonies (הכנסת כלה) – all supreme social mitzvot.[10] And in this way, we

---

See further R. Ovadiah Yosef, *Hazon Ovadiah: Sukkot* (Jerusalem: 2005, 168), on the special status of *Talmud Torah*, because it is mandated at all times (מצוה תמידית), and, hence, cannot exempt from other mitzvot, as this would free us from all other mitzvot (citing the *Birkei Yosef* of the Hida 38:7).

This subject has most recently been examined in considerable detail, with a wealth of sources, by R. Asi ha-Levi Even Yuli, in his *Shulhan Aruch ha-Middot*, vol. 2, *Halachah ve-Musar* (Jerusalem: 2009, 243–247). He shows that there are two opposing views. For the *Yosef Omez*, by R. Yosef Juspa Kahn Neurelingen (c. 1639), (Frankfurt am Main: 1908, [reprint, Jerusalem: 1965] 316), writes that the Rabbis said: Anyone who is involved in Torah learning and not in *gemilut hasadim*, acts of charity, is as one who has no God. And therefore he wrote that a Torah scholar should make sure that every day he should carry out one act of charity. And the *Seder ha-Yom* (by R. Moshe ibn Machir [Venice: 1599], and numerous editions) wrote that one must not interrupt the learning of Torah for any mitzvah which can be carried out by another, with the exception of acts of charity. And therefore the enthusiastic should take this to heart and pursue acts of charity as one pursues life itself. (And see the continuation of this passage.) Even Yuli further refers us to Responsa *Aderet Tiferet* (by R. Avraham Dori, vol. 4, sect. 44), who following on the words of the *Seder ha-Yom* seeks to find additional support for this view in the Rambam, citing the *gemarot* in BT *Megillah* 3b, 29a; BT *Ketubot* 17a as further proof, in that one interrupts Torah learning to accompany the dead to his final resting place. (See below on this subject.) He then refers us to the *Sdei Hemed* to which we referred earlier on. However, this runs counter to the prevailing majority view found in a multitude of rabbinic sources, to which he referred on 243–244, and therefore very convincingly he rejects and refutes this argument on 246–247. See there in detail. However, the above just underscores what we have tried to point out, namely the complex ambiguity of the status of Torah study.

10. See Rema, *Even ha-Ezer* 65:1; *Ba"h* ibid., that even the leading Torah authority, *Gedol ha-Dor*, does so. And even public learning is so interrupted, (*Pnei Yehoshua* to BT *Ketubot* ibid., on the basis of *Tosafot Megillah* ibid.). However, see D. Friedman, *Piskei Halachot*, vol. 3 (Warsaw: 1901, 35), argues that nowadays, that we are not intimately acquainted with the laws and our studies *are* directed to their correct understanding, therefore, we do not interrupt Torah learning for wedding ceremonies. See, in detail, on all the rules related to this subject, B. Adler, *Ha-Nisuim ke-Hilchatam*, 2nd ed., vol. 2 (Jerusalem: 1985, 394–395).

may better understand the passage in *Avot de-R. Natan*, chapter 41, (ed. Schechter, Vienna: 1887, 133):

> It once happened that R. Tarfon was sitting and teaching his disciples, and a bride went past him. He ordered that she be brought into his house, and told his mother and his wife that they should bathe her, anoint her, and decorate her with jewelry, and dance before her until she goes to her husband's house.

Apparently, he interrupted his teaching in order to carry out the mitzvah of *hachnasat kallah*.[11]

And indeed we read in the letters of the Hafetz Hayyim (*Michtevei ha-Hafetz Hayyim he-Hadash*, vol. 2, Bnei Brak: 1986) II, 86:

> You occasionally see a Jew who [in a praiseworthy way] learns Torah [as much as possible] and values his time [not wasting a minute]. But if he does not set aside part of the day to do deeds of kindness, what a lack of intelligence!

And interestingly enough, this also becomes evidence from the commentary of R. David ha-Nagid, the Rambam's grandson, to *Avot* 1:15. There Shammai is cited as saying: "Make thy [study of the] Torah a fixed habit (קבע); .... And receive all men as its cheerful countenance." And this is explained by the Nagid to mean that even when you are engaged in your fixed period of Torah study, you should not desist from receiving people cheerfully, thinking that in doing so you are "wasting" Torah-study time.[12]

Clearly *hachnasat kallah* is related to the mitzvah of procreation, which is one of the paramount duties of a man, in Jewish halachic thought. See my *Netivot Pesikah* (Jerusalem: 2008, 162–163, n. 251). (And cf. below, sect. 30.)

Here we may add that a communal positive mitzvah always takes precedence and outweighs a private individual's positive mitzvah. A teacher sitting *shiva* is forbidden to learn and teach Torah. However, he is permitted to do so if the community needs him (*Shulhan Aruch Yoreh Deah* 384:1). See Tzvi Marx, *Halakha and Handicap* (Jerusalem: 1992–1993, 228).

11. See Schechter's note in his edition of *Avot de-R. Natan*, n. 24, and p. 131, n. 10.

12. *Midrash R. David ha-Nagid* to *Avot*, ed. BenTziyyon Kipnis (Jerusalem: 1944). The Arabic original appeared in *Na Amon* 1901. However, there are some doubts as to the attribution of authorship. See *Milhamot Ha-Shem* by R.

So apparently he regarded proper interpersonal relationship of such importance as even to override one's involvement in Torah learning. And this presumably goes under the category of *kevod ha-beriyot*, respect for the individual. (Cf. below, sections 15 and 19.)

We are reminded of the statement of Reb Yisrael of Rizhyn (died 1850), who expounded the verse in Psalms 115:16, "the heavens are the heavens of the Lord; but the earth hath He given to the children of men."

> There are two kinds of *tzaddikim*. Those of the one sort learn and pray the livelong day and hold themselves far from lowly matters in order to attain holiness. While the others do not think of themselves, but only of delivering the holy sparks which are buried in all things back to God, and they make all lowly things their concern. The former, who are always preparing for Heaven, the verse calls "the heavens," and they have set themselves apart for the Lord. But the others are the earth given to the children of men.
>
> (Martin Buber, *Tales of the Hasidim: The Later Masters*, New York: 1948, 53–54)

Here, he is contrasting the Lithuanian *mitnagdim*'s way, (in a double-edged complementary fashion), with that of the Hasidim, while we well know with which way he personally sided.

At the same time we should recollect how Yehudah ha-Levi in his *Kuzari*, begins his definition of the religious man according to Jewish tradition with the negative statement that "in Jewish opinion, the religious man is *not* to be defined as one who cuts himself off from the world" (Book III, sect. I, ed. Hirschfeld, Leipzig: 1882, 140–141). Perhaps he was combating predominant contemporary Sufi views on extreme asceticism. (See Franz Rosenthal, "A Judaeo-Arabic Work under Sufic Influence," *HUCA* XV 1940, 440, and cf. page 465 for an extreme view of this form of asceticism, and note 104.)

Avraham ben ha-Rambam, ed. M. Margaliot (Jerusalem: 1953, 38, n. 8); A. Katz, *JQR* 48 (1957), 140–160; *Midrash R. David ha-Nagid* to Genesis, ed. A. Katz (Jerusalem: 1964, 16–18). On R. David ha-Nagid himself, see A. Strauss (Ashtor), *Toldot ha-Yehudim be-Mitzrayim ve-Suriah tahat Shilton ha-Mamelukim*, vol. 1 (Jerusalem: 1944, 117–128).

5

The Different Kinds of "*Ish*" according to the Divrei Hayyim

THE DIVREI HAYYIM, R. Hayyim Halberstam (Munkatz: 1906), further explained the notion of the two types of personality: the one whose piety is directed not only towards God, but also towards his fellow man, as opposed to one whose piety is exclusively God-directed, and hence is not really pious, by reference to the verse in Genesis 32:25:

> ". . . And then he [Jacob] wrestled a man (*ish*) with him until the breaking of the day." Whereas, in the case of Josef the verse states (37:15), "And a certain man (*ish*) found him wandering in the field," and the man asked him, saying: "What seekest thou?" On this latter verse Rashi explains that the "man" was the angel Gabriel. However, on the former verse Rashi tells us that the "man" was the "spirit of Esau" (*saro shel Esav*), i.e., the Satan. In both cases the same word *ish* – "man" is used. How then did Rashi know that in the one case the "man" was Satan, and in the other the angel Gabriel? To which the Sanzer replied: In the case of Josef, the *ish* asks him "What seekest thou?" He showed interest in Josef and sought to help him and point him in the right direction. He was surely an angel. But in Jacob's case, the man who had been struggling with him for a whole night until daybreak, when Jacob asks him for a blessing, his only answer is, "Let me go, for the day breaketh" (32:27), and Rashi explains: My time has come to sing [the praises of the Lord].
>
> The Sanzer continued:
>
> When someone comes to you requiring help, and asks for a blessing, and you suddenly have no time but have to hurry off to ascend

to spiritual heights and to sing the praises of God, then you must be *saro shel Esav*, possessed of the Satan.[1]

1. I have found this same tradition attributed to R. Aryeh Levin, by his son R. David Levin. See Simha Raz, *Tzaddik Yesod Olam: Masechet Hayyav shel R. Aryeh Levin* (Jerusalem: 1996, 146–147), where this homily is used to justify not delaying rushing off to a hospital, to visit the sick, even at the expense of a regular Torah lesson (*shiur kavua*). Presumably, he learned it from the Sanzer.

6

The Difference between a *Tzaddik* and a *Hacham* according to the Djikover Rebbe

MUCH THE SAME IDEA, namely that the true *tzaddik* must be involved not only in spiritual matters, but also material, is expressed in the somewhat more complex homilitical exposition of the Hasidic master, Reb Yehoshua Horwitz of Djikov (1848–1913). His "Toira" runs thus:

> "These are the generations of Noah: Noah was a just man and perfect in his generations, and Noah walked with God" (Genesis 6:9). The *Baal ha-Turim* (Rabbenu Yaakov ben Rabbenu Asher, author of the *Tur*) commented that "and Noah walked with God" – את האלקים התהלך נח – the final letters of these words when spelled in reverse become חכם, *het*, *kaf*, *mem*, *hacham*, a wise man, but in the verse he is called "a just man" – *tzaddik*. This is to be understood on the basis of what we have learned from the Sages that if a man has sickness in his house he should go to the wise man in his town. We must understand why they recommended going to the *hacham* of the town and not the *tzaddik* of the town.
>
> The answer lies with differentiation between the nature of the *hacham* and the *tzaddik*. For the *tzaddik* sits alone, always involved in his closeness (*devekut*) to God, and is not aware of his human surroundings and their needs, and consequently cannot influence them in their material requirements, because he regards as a descent (*yeridah*) even to pray to God for materialistic necessities. But the *hacham*, though he too serves God and walks in His just paths, nonetheless pays attention to all the needs of this world, to help with children, life (i.e., health) and sustenance בנים חיים ומזוני. And this is what was meant by the statement of R. Shimon in *Avot* 2:9: Who is

> wise – *hacham*? He who sees forthcoming [events] (הנולד),[1] namely, that he sees that out of material things may also grow spiritual things . . . , and consequently the *hacham* will pay attention also to material matters, praying for them that they be successful. And it is for this reason the Sages recommended going to the *hacham* [rather than the *tzaddik*]. And this is what the *Baal ha-Turim* wished to hint to us that in a true *tzaddik* there must be both aspects, both the involvement in spirituality as well as in material needs. For if he be a spiritual *tzaddik* alone, he will not benefit his fellow humans. But Noah had both these aspects: he was a *tzaddik*, but also a *hacham*.[2]

It would then appear that this is a very basic principle in halachic and ethical thought, that mitzvot between man and his fellow have some kind of greater virtue than those directed merely towards one's Maker. And, of course, we should always remember the classic statement of the Ramban to *Parshat Kedoshim* (Leviticus 19:2), concerning the *naval bi-reshut ha-Torah*, "the vile scoundrel acting (as it were) within the parameters of the Torah," whose social behavior is disgraceful though it does not appear to contravene any explicit biblical prohibition. But this is a very extreme example of circumventing explicit biblical commandments.

---

1. There is no such statement in *Avot* 2:9. It is a conflation of Ben Zoma's statement in *Avot* 4:1 and R. Shimon's, ibid., 2:9.

2. Cited by Menashe Schiff, in his *Tzaddikei Olam*, 2nd ed. (Ashdod: 2010, 190–191), from R. Horowitz's *Ateret Yeshua, al ha-Torah* (Cracow: 1919, *Parshat Noah*). And see also ibid., 819, citing R. Asher Yeshaya of Ropschitz (*Tiferet Banim Avotam, Ropschitz*, 53b), who, basing himself on this same verse, counseled a certain young Rabbi that, although there are *tzaddikim* who sit peacefully while involved in mystical exercises and smoking their pipes, "but you should not stray from the path of the righteous in teaching and influencing the community." These texts clearly reflect Hasidic thinking on the duties of the "Rebbe." See also R. Hayyim Mordechai Bronrot, *Setirat Zekenim*, vol. 1, part 2 (Jerusalem: 1948, 62–63), on these two types of *tzaddikim*.

I am reminded of the *Darâwis*, as described by T. Canaan, in his article "Mohammedan Saints and Sanctuaries in Palestine," *JPOS* 7 (1927), 78: "He is so absorbed by his supposed inner life that he ignores all else . . ." (The term *Darâwis* is commonly explained as derived from the Persian, and as meaning "seeking doors," i.e., mendicant; Canaan ibid., 77, n. 2.)

7

Murder and Theft versus Idolatry, Incest and Homosexuality

WE FIND THE following principle reflected in a passage in Rambam, *Hilchot Rotzeah* 4:9. There he writes as follows:[1]

> Even though there are more serious sins than murder, they do not destroy the order of society (אין בהן השחתת ישובו של עולם) like murder. Even idolatry, and it goes without saying that incest and the desecration of the Sabbath, are not as [serious] as murder. For these sins are of the [category of sins] between man and the Holy One blessed be He, while murder is of [the category of] sins between man and his fellow man.

And again in *Hilchot Geneivah* 7:12, he writes:

> The punishments for sins of [false] measures (עונשין של מדות) are more severe than those of incest. For this one is between him and his Maker and this one is between him and his fellow man.

He is basing himself on BT *Baba Batra* 88b, where we read in the name of R. Levi: "The punishment for sins of measures are more severe than those of incest." And there follows a homiletic discussion on how this is derived from biblical verses.

And when the Rambam talks of "sins of measures" he is referring to

---

1. This is also quoted in the *Semag* [*Sefer Mitzvot-Gadol*], negative commandment no. 163.

different forms of cheating such as stealing through the use of inaccurate weights and measures. (See the whole chapter 4, *Hilchot Geneivah.*)[2] Indeed, there is a tradition in the name of the late R. Aharon Soloveitchik that when he was asked concerning the gravity of the sin of homosexuality, he replied, "It is terrible. It is almost as great a sin as cheating in business."[3]

But perhaps most surprising is what we read in BT *Sanhedrin* 108a:

> Said R. Yohanan: Come and see how great is the power of [the sin of] *hamas* – violence. For surely, the generation of the flood transgressed all [transgressions], but they were not condemned until they turned to theft, as it is written, "for the earth is filled with *hamas*; and behold, I will destroy them with the earth" (Genesis 6:13); and it is written, "Violence (*hamas*) is risen up into the rod of wickedness; none of them shall remain, nor of their multitude, nor of any of theirs: neither shall there be any waiting for them" (Ezekiel 7:11).

Hamas in this homily is equated with theft, which brought about their condemnation and destruction more than all other transgressions! And cf. *Genesis Rabbah* 31:1, ed. Theodor-Albeck 278: ... for they were steeped in theft. (Cf. ibid., 31:5, 279, on the difference between theft – *gezel* – and *hamas*, a violent form of robbery.)[4]

So too, the same R. Levi (BT *Baba Batra*, 88b) states that "theft from an individual is more serious than theft from that which has been dedicated

2. This whole notion in the Rambam was discussed in detail by R. Hayyim Rappaport, in a note in *Or Yisrael* 15/3 (59), 2010, 243–244. See also R. Yosef Kafih's commentary on the Rambam ibid., 255–256. See also the Netziv's explanation in his *Haamek Davar* to Deut. 25:13–16. See also the material cited in A. Tobolsky, *Hizaharu be-Mamon Haverchem* (Bnei Brak: 1981, 273–274, 282–283, 304, 305).

3. See further Meir Tamari, *Kesef Kasher: Sugyot Musar be-Mishar* (Jerusalem: 2005, 49–50); and also in his *Al Chet: Sins in the Marketplace* (Northvale, N.J. and London: 1996, 9), (where he also refers us to *Hoshen Mishpat* 331:1, and *Meirat Einayim* ad loc.), and also ibid., 27; Edward Zipperstein, *Business Ethics in Jewish Law* (New York: 1983, 49–53), etc.

4. Cf. M.M. Kasher, *Torah Shelemah* ad loc., vol. 2 (Jerusalem: 1935), 398, n. 151, for parallels. The author of the *Torah Temimah* ad loc. offers a rationale why theft or robbery can be seen as more serious a sin than forbidden sexual relationships (Gen., p. 83, n. 17).

to God (מגזל גבוה)." Here again we see the relative weight of these two categories of mitzvot, and conversely, *aveirot* – sins.

Moreover, we shall see below (section 16 ad fin.) that even the most serious sin of idolatry can at times be outweighed by charitable hospitality. (And see also below, section 13.)

8

The Kol Bo's Great Question on Impurity, and Josef's Coffin

We may add yet another possible aspect. The *Kol Bo*, *Hilchot Evel ve-Tumat ha-Guf*, ed. David Avraham, vol. 7, Jerusalem: 2002, 71, raises what he calls "a very weighty question" – תימא גדול, namely that "there are two mitzvot which contradict one another," (or as the *Orhot Hayyim* emended: "seem to contradict one another," note 314), namely: the seriousness of coming into contact with corpse-related uncleanness, and the very important mitzvah of burying an untended corpse – a *met mitzvah*.[1] He goes to considerable depths to solve this apparent contradiction (71–75,

---

1. On the status of *met mitzvah*, see what I wrote in my commentary to *Derech Eretz Zuta, Chapters Five to Eight*, Ramat Gan: 1990, 179–182. (And see above, sect. 4, n. 9.) See further the interesting text in *Numbers Rabbah* 8:4, on how King David collected the bones of Saul and Yonatan, etc.

Here I shall cite certain sections from *Derech Eretz Zuta* 8:10, p. 138:

> But he who transgresses the words of the Sages is deserving of death. And he who maligns [will] be maligned. Said R. Akiva: This was the beginning of my serving before the Sages. Once, when I was going on the wayside, I found an [untended] corpse, and I attended it [by carrying it] some four miles until I brought it to a graveyard, and buried it. And when I came and related the matter to R. Eliezer and R. Joshua, they said to me: For every single step you took you are guilty as though you shed innocent blood. I said to them: My teachers, how so? [And] if, when I intended [to act] worthily [I sinned and am as] guilty, how much more so when I did not intend [to act] worthily. From that moment I have not moved away from serving scholars. He used to say: Who has not served scholars is deserving of death.

This text is found in JT *Nazir* 7:1, 56a, and *Semahot* 4:19, ed. Higger (New York: 1931, 125). (See *The Tractate "Mourning,"* ed. and transl. D. Zlotnick [New Haven and London: 1966, 45.]) It is frequently found in the Rishonim and Aharonim, such as Tosafot to *Megillah* 29a, catchword מבטלין, in the name of *Massechet Derech Eretz*, idem to *Ketubot* 17a, catchword מבטלין תלמוד תורה להוצאת המת, in the name of *Hilchot Derech Eretz*; Responsa of R. Moshe Mainz (Maharam Minz), no. 17, sect. 2, ed. Salonica (1804, 14c), in the name of *H.* (הלכות=ה') *Derech Eretz*; *Rashbatz* (R. Simeon b. Tzemah ibn Duran, in his *Magen Avot*, cited in *Avot de-R. Nathan*, ed. Schechter [Vienna: 1887, 176], missing in printed ed.), cited in the name of *Md.* (מדת=מד') *Derech Eretz*; Ramban (Nahmanides), *Torat ha-Adam*, ed. Chavel (Jerusalem: 1962, 13), from JT *Nazir*; *Sefer ha-Eshkol*, ed. Auerbach (Halberstadt: 1868, 2, p. 175); anon. (absent in Albeck ed.). Several authorities cite it from *Semahot*, such as: *Beit Yosef* to Tur *Yoreh De'ah* 364, catchword הרמב"ם, in the name of *Evel Rabbati*, chap. 4 (=*Semahot*); Isaac Aramah, *Akedat Yitzhak*, Lech Lecha, chap. 17, from *Massechet Semachot*; *Or Zarua* by R. Isaac of Vienna, 2, 85c, sect. 479, in the name of *Massechet Semahot* (while ibid., 1, 110d, in the response section, no. 5, cites it with the prefix *tanya*). See further, M. Gaster, *Sefer ha-Ma'asiyyot*, (*The Exempla of the Rabbis*) (London-Leipzig: 1924, no. 97, p. 68); *Ma'alot ha-Middot*, Eshkol ed., 47 (anon.); *Zichron Torah* by R. Moshe [bar Yosef] Figo (Constantinople: 1553–1554, Prague: 1623), sect. זכות. See also references in Higger, *Massechtot Ze'irot* (New York: 1928, 142).

There are a good many variations between the versions, which are noted in my edition of *Derech Eretz Zuta*.

Met mitzvah, literally translated is a mitzvah corpse. See Lieberman, *Tosefta ki-fshutah* 3, p. 325, n. 31, who suggests that the phrase *met mitzvah* is derived from *met milhemet mitzvah*, the body of a man slain in a war in which he was obligated to fight; that is to say, the corpse of a man slain during a battle against an invading army. During the battle it would be dangerous to transfer the corpse to a proper burial ground, and therefore he was interred on the spot. Furthermore, at times the enemy denied the dead real burial as a matter of policy, as was the case with "the corpses of Betar," which remained exposed until a successor of the Emperor Hadrian permitted them to be buried (BT *Berachot* 48b; *Lamentations Rabbah* 2:4, etc.) (See further Zlotnick ibid., 21–22; D. Halivni, *Mekorot u-Masorot, Mo'ed – to Eruvin* [Jerusalem 1982, 41, n. 1]; M. [A.] Bloch, *Sha'arei Torat ha-Takkkanot* 1 [Vienna: 1879, 63–64, n. 18].)

Among the ten ordinances enacted by the biblical Joshua, according to BT *Bava Kama* 81ab, one reads: an [untended] corpse acquires its immediate area for burial. (So too in BT *Eruvin* 17a; BT *Sotah* 45b; BT *Sanhedrin* 47b. See further JT *Nazir* 7:1, 56b; ibid., 9:3, 57d; JT *Sotah* 9:4, 23c; JT *Bava Batra* 5:1, 15a.) And in T. *Eruvin* 2 (3):6, ed. Zuckermandel, 140, ed. Lieberman, 93–94, we read: An encampment going out to battle . . . [on] the place that they are slain, there they and the editor's notes ad loc.). However, we would suggest that the laws of impurity are basically ritual laws, and hence God-related laws, whereas the burial of an untended body is a person-related law, since the dead were thought to be sensitive to their state, and certainly live people would wish to be properly buried, as well as relatives of the deceased, as this is a *hesed* and *nahat* for them as well.[2] Hence, the mitzvah of burying a *met mitzvah* has priority over the laws warning us against becoming impure by contact with the dead. And we have seen above that it even has priority over study of Torah (see above, note 1).

We may also call our attention to what is related in Numbers 9:6–7:

> And there were certain men, who were defiled by the dead body of a man, that they could not keep the Passover on that day; and they came before Moses and before Aaron on that day: And these men said unto him: "We were defiled by the dead body of a man: wherefore are we kept back, that we may not offer our offering of the Lord in his appointed season among the children of Israel?"

On this the Talmud in BT *Sukkah* 25ab asks:

> Who were these people who were dealing with a *met mitzvah*, a dead person that no one else was dealing with?

---

are buried. See further, *Semahot* 4:16–17, ed. Higger (New York: 1931, 123–124) (and his references to line 66, and Zlotnick, 21–22, 116–117). There 4:16, we read:

> If a priest finds a *met mitzvah*, he must attend to its needs and burial. When is a corpse a *met mitzvah*? Wherever he did call out and the townspeople did not hear his cry . . . Rabbi says: It is always a *met mitzvah*, until enough pallbearers and those to inter it are there... (translation: Zlotnick).

According to biblical law a priest may not come into contact with a dead body, since this would make him polluted, impure. It is interesting to note that the Romans also took considerable pains to keep the priestly class away from death pollution. See the material assembled by Hugh Lindsay, in his chapter "Death Pollution and Funerals in Rome," apud *Death and Disease in the Ancient City*, ed. Valerie M. Hope and Eireann Marshall (London and New York: 2000, 156).

2. I have discussed this issue at considerable length in my forthcoming volume: *The Jewish Life Cycle: Custom, Lore and Iconography: Jewish Customs from the Cradle to the Grave*, vol. 2.

The Talmud in BT *Sukkah* 25b discusses the question, who were these "certain men" who were unclean, and gives several suggestions. The first is that of R. Yitzhak, who identifies them as the bearers of Josef's coffin. Apparently he was of the opinion that the mitzvah of bearing a dead man's coffin overrode the biblical commandment of eating the paschal lamb,[3] and bearing a dead man's coffin, as being involved in dealing with the dead, is a mitzvah between man and his neighbor, whereas eating the paschal lamb is a ritual obligation. And so too, according to the last opinion given in that Talmudic passage, that they were dealing with an abandoned corpse, a *met mitzvah*, with whom no one else was concerned. Here again, the Sages were convinced that this mitzvah overrode that of the eating of the paschal lamb.

Rashi, ad loc., comments that this was not necessarily a *met mitzvah* (who has a special status), for even if it were their own dead . . . they would have been obligated to deal with them. See the *Torah Temimah* (109–110, note 4), from whose discussion it emerges that even when a relatively minor mitzvah of a social nature comes before one, and carrying it out would obviate the carrying out of a more serious one of biblical status, one nonetheless carries out the minor one. We would add that seeing to the burial of a dead person is seen as a mitzvah between man and his neighbor, and is called by the Rabbis *hesed shel emet*, true benevolence, in that it is one for which one receives no recompense. But within a person's lifetime one knows that someone will always see to one's last rites and burial. Hence, doing so is a person-directed mitzvah, whereas, the sacrifice of the paschal lamb is a God-directed mitzvah; hence, the former overrode the latter.[4]

---

3. See *Sdei Hemed*, ibid.

4. Similarly a person who is involved in collecting bones for secondary burial (ליקוט עצמות) is exempt from prayer, etc. See BT *Berachot* 18a; *Semachot* 13:1, ed. Higger, 200–201, *Shulhan Aruch Yoreh Deah* 403:9. (As to whether the reading there should be "looking after the corpse" or "the bones," see *Beit Hillel*, ad loc., and this is dependent on the readings in the Talmud and *Semachot*, etc.) In such a situation one may not take upon oneself to pray, etc. – לא יחמיר – because this would dishonor the bones – מפני כבוד עצמות. Here we may also note that, though biblical law strictly forbids a Cohen to become impure, and to come into contact with a dead body, it does take into account his basic emotional relationship to his close relatives, permitting contact with them when they die. And so we find in Lev. 21:1–3:

> And the Lord said unto Moses, speak unto the priests the sons of Aaron, and say unto them: There shall none be defiled for the dead among his

Indeed, it is from this biblical episode the Sages derived the ruling of the Mishnah in *Sukkah* (2:4) that "they that are sent forth on a pious duty are exempt from the [law of] *sukkah*." Rashi defines there "men of given duty" as those who among other activities are going to welcome their mentor or to collect funds in order to bring about the release of hostages.[5]

> people. But for his kin, that is near unto him, that is for his mother, and for his father, and for his son, and for his daughter, and for his brother. And for his sister a virgin, that is nigh unto him, which hath no husband; for her may he be defiled.

The prohibition against defilement is ritual law. But this is apparently overridden by humane needs. The Talmud, in BT *Zevahim* 100a, goes so far as to say that even if the Cohen does not wish to become impure in such case, the court forces him to do so. The ritual law should not be adhered too, even when the Cohen so desires, in the face of the Torah's clear recognition of human needs. See on these laws, in a clear and succinct manner, R. Baruch Yashar (Schlichter), *Torat ha-Cohen ve-ha-Levi be-Yamenu* (Jerusalem: 1967, 90–99). Similarly, this applies to an *onen* who is exempt from mitzvot.

This was already pointed out by Max Kadushin, in his *Worship and Ethics: A Study in Rabbinic Judaism* (New York: 1963, 215, 216). His conclusion is formulated somewhat differently from mine, but gives much the same message: "All these instances are, of course, prime examples of the association between the concept of mitzvot and the ethical concepts."

5. And see Tosafot ad loc., and *Shulhan Aruch Orah Hayyim* 640:7, and cf. ibid., 38:8 and supercommentaries.

9

Biblical Precedents: Erasing God's Name

Perhaps we can already find this principle, namely that מצוות בין אדם לחברו supersede מצוות בין אדם למקום, indicated in the Bible itself. The Rabbis expressed this in *Derech Eretz Zuta* chapter (=*Perek ha-Shalom*) 11:9 as follows:

> Said R. Yishmael: Great is peace. For we find that the Holy One blessed be He conceded that His Name, that is written in holiness, be erased in the water, in order to bring peace between a man and his wife.

He is, of course, referring to the case of the woman suspected of adultery, and to the biblical ruling (Numbers 5:11–31) that special curses, containing God's name, be placed in the water which would erase them and then she would drink the potion (verse 22) – and this despite the very serious transgression of erasing the name of God, as derived from the verses in Deuteronomy 12:3–4, " . . . and destroy the names of them [idols] out of that place. Ye shall not do so unto the Lord your God." (See BT *Makkot* 22a; Rambam, *Yesodei ha-Torah* 6:1.)[1]

---

1. See my detailed discussion on all the parallels in my edition of *Derech Eretz Zuta* (Jerusalem: 1994, 217–218).

Indeed, in that chapter there is a whole series of statements permitting, or justifying, deviation from the absolute truth in order to bring peace between people (sects. 5, 6, 7, that the Torah deviated from the truth for this reason, and so too the prophets, etc.). And this is summarized in a statement of Rabbi [Yehudah the Prince], (ibid., sect. 5 ad fin.):

> All sorts of lies are forbidden, but it is permitted to speak falsely in order to foster peace between man and his neighbors.

And R. Natan's opinion, in BT *Yevamot* 65b, is that this is not only permitted, but is a mitzvah. See my discussion, ibid. And all this, despite the explicit statement in Exod. 23:7: "Keep ye far from a false matter."

10

The Folly of Doing What Is Not Required: Being *Machmir* with Different Types of Mitzvot

WE MAY MOVE yet one stage further, quoting a passage from the Hida, in his book *Yair Ozen* (Lemberg: 1865, fol. 109a):

> That which is written in the Yerushalmi *Berachot*, chapter 2 ad fin., and *Shabbat* 1:1, that he who is exempt from something and does it is considered an ignorant person, while in many other cases our decisors said that he who takes upon himself additional stringency, may he be blessed.[1] (See *Shulhan Aruch Orah Hayyim* section 639:2, and

---

1. See JT *Berachot* 2:9: He who takes upon himself additional stringency, may he be blessed. Said R. Zeira: "So long as [in doing so] he does not degrade others." On which the *Pnei Moshe* ad loc. commented: For himself he can take upon himself stringencies (*humrot*). But if this is in the presence of others, he should not do so, because in doing so he is, as it were, degrading others who do not wish to act beyond the letter of the law. See on this passage the material cited by Y. Tamar, in his *Alei Tamar* ad loc., vol. 1 (Givatayim: 1979, 93). (But see Responsa of *Radbaz*, part 4, sect. 1368; *Maharatz Hayut* to BT *Niddah* 34a.) These sources stress the severe limitation on *humra* (stringency) which may well lead somehow to harming others.

And see *Michtevei ha-Rav Hafetz Hayyim*, by his son R. Aryeh Leib ha-Cohen, 2nd ed. (New York: 1953, part 2, 30, sect. 63, subsect. 8):

> On Pesach he would not eat *sheruyah* and not *kneidlach* (matzah cooked with water or other liquids), only potatoes. Once it happened when I was as yet a young boy that a distinguished guest came and stayed with us. . . . on the last day of Pesach, and they honored him with *chremslach*, and

compare with subsection 7, ibid.)[2] One may explain [this difference]

---

he too ate of them in the guest's honor (i.e., even though this was not in accordance with his normal custom).

See *Shulhan Aruch Orah Hayyim* 515:1, and *Magen Avraham*, ibid., on the special status of guests (see below), what may one do to honor them. But here we may add: and not to shame them.

However, this was not so difficult and painful a compromise, since the whole *humra* of *sheruyah*, or, as it is called in Yiddish *gebrochts*, is weak, and the Gaon of Vilna and the Hatam Sofer both permitted it. See, in detail, on this issue in my *Minhagei Yisrael*, vol. 2, (Jerusalem: 1991, 144–146). Indeed, there was a custom, that even those who kept this *humra*, would eat *gebrochts* on the last day of Pesach in the diaspora, but they may have had a complete extra set of dishes for that day. That, indeed was the practice in my maternal grandfather's house.

2. In subsect. 2 we read that one who takes upon himself not even to drink water outside the *sukkah* is praiseworthy (הרי זה משובח), even though "it is permitted to drink water … outside the *sukkah*" (ibid.). However, the *Birkei Yosef* of the Hida wrote (cited in *Shaarei Teshuvah* ad loc.) in the name of the *Tzedah la-Derech* (by R. Menahem b. Zerah) that this is a *humra yeteira*, an unnecessary stringency, and so too the *Maharil*. In subsect. 7 we read that if it rains to the degree that the soup will be spoiled, one does not sit in the *sukkah*, and he who does so does not fulfill the mitzvah of dwelling in the *sukkah* and receives no reward therefore and is considered a *hedyot* – fool. And on this the *Beur Halachah* remarks in the name of *Bechorei Yaakov* (by R. Yaakov Ettlinger, Altona 1736) that this is only if sitting in the *sukkah* in the rain is distressing (שמצטער), because such rain indicates that the Divine does not want him to act thus and it is as though he wishes to force his will over his Master. See further *Shaarei Teshuvah*, sect. 13, citing the *Shevut Yaakov* of R. Yaakov Reischer, vol. 3, sect. 45, concerning an event that took place in Metz in 1723, where rains came down during the night soaking the *sukkot*, and there were three who wished to delay their meal till after midnight, even though there was still a heavy rain. They wished to wear broad-brimmed hats with which to protect themselves, and the *Shevut Yaakov* strongly objected, chastising them, saying that they should not be cleverer than the Sages of the Talmud and the decisors of the past and present. (See also *Mishnah Berurah* to *Orah Hayyim*, ibid., sect. 67, and *Shaar ha-Tziyyun*, ibid.) The *Shaarei Teshuvah* continues to refer us to the *Magen Avraham* 645, who rails against "the ascetics who wish to sit in the *sukkah* even when heavy drops of rain come down, declaring that what they do is certainly not good," and citing the Yerushalmi we referred to above. See the lengthy continuation of his discussion. See also *Kaf ha-Hayyim*, of R. Yaakov Hayyim Sofer, *Orah Hayyim* 639 nn. 37, 77, 92, referring to the Ramban and the *Ritba* to *Kiddushin*

31, that one is only called a *hedyot* when carrying out an act which has not been commanded to be a mitzvah. But if he "adds," as it were, to an existing mitzvah, he is not considered a *hedyot*. And in this way it is explained why women can take upon themselves to carry out time-linked mitzvot (מצוות עשה שהזמן גרמן), to which they are not really obligated. He further refers us to the Hida, in *Ein Zocher, peh*, sect. 13 (which is the same as what we quoted from his *Yair Ozen*).

The apparent contradiction between these two principles has been the cause of considerable discussion both among early authorities and latter-day ones. Here we shall give a somewhat random sample of references which may indicate to some extent the complexity of the issue. And clearly, the Hida's solution is not the only one.

On the actual passage in Yerushalmi *Berachot*, see Baer Ratner, *Ahavat Tziyyon vi-Yerushalayim, Berachot* (Vienna: 1901, 63), for variant readings, to which may be added, *Arugat ha-Bosem*, by R. Avraham be-R. Azriel, ed. E.E. Urbach, vol. 2 (Jerusalem: 1947, 70).

See *Raviah*, vol. 2, ed. A. Aptowitzer, second edition (Jerusalem: 1964, sect. 597, 340); cf. vol. 1 (Jerusalem: 1964, sect. 56, 33 [on women keeping time-linked mitzvot]); Responsa of *Rivash*, (R. Yitzhak ben Sheshet, 1326–1408), sect. 43, ed. David Metzger (Jerusalem: 1993, vol. 1, introduction, 114–119), discussing the view of the Ravad, in his notes to *Gittin*, (*Rif* 19a) and Ramban (18a), that if the Children of Israel took upon themselves to give tithes after the destruction of the First Temple (JT *Sheviit* ad fin.), why is that not called *hedyotut* – idiocy. See the various suggested solutions to this question. And on the passage in JT *Berachot*, see L. Ginzberg, *Perushim ve-Hiddushim ba-Yerushalmi*, vol. 1 (New York: 1941, 419–420). See further H.M. Bronrot, *Setirat Zekenim*, vol. 1, part 1 (Jerusalem: 1948, 59–60). This, as mentioned above, is merely a random sampling of the numerous discussions on this complex subject.

And while we are discussing laws related to the mitzvah of *sukkah*, we may make the following halachic observation, which links up, in some measure, with our general theme.

First we must establish a basic fact that in a "stolen *sukkah*" one cannot fulfill the mitzvah of dwelling in a *sukkah*, see *Shulhan Aruch Orah Hayyim* 637:3, (and the definition there of a "stolen *sukkah*" – *sukkah gezulah*). The *Mishnah Berurah* (n. 18) ad loc. explains that this is because the biblical verse states: "The feast of Tabernacles you should observe for *yourself* for seven days" (Deut. 16:13) – literally: "The feast of Tabernacles make for *yourself*" תעשה לך – "excluding a stolen one which is not yours – לך" (*Mishnah Berurah*). This applies not only to the *schach*, but to the walls too (*Pri Megadim, Bechorei Yaakov, Beur Halachah*, ibid.).

However, the *Shulhan Aruch* (ibid.) modifies the former statement as follows:

> If he stole wood and made from it a *sukkah*, even though he did not fix them with anything (i.e., like nails), [if he sat in it] he fulfilled [the mitzvah], for

> by stating that "he is considered ignorant" only with regard mitzvot directed towards his Maker. But mitzvot directed towards his fellow humans there is never an exemption from them, for we have been directed in a generic fashion to go beyond the letter of the law (לפנים משורת הדין) as we learned in BT *Baba Metzia* 30b . . . , etc.[3]

(See below, section 20 on "the righteous man who is not good.")

> the Sages instituted that the [original] owner of the wood can only claim the value of the wood, (i.e., but not the wood itself).

This is based on the Mishnah in *Gittin* 5:5, where we learn from the testimony of R. Yohanan ben Gudgadah that if one stole a beam and built it into one's house, the original owner can only claim its monetary value, "because of the enactment for the benefit of the penitents" (מפני תקנת השבים). Rashi (BT *Gittin* 55a) explains that if he would be required to take apart his house in order to return the beam, he would not do so. And following on this Mishnah, Ravina in BT *Sukkah* 31a states that the same is true of a stolen beam in a *sukkah*.

The *Mishnah Berurah* (ad loc.) states clearly that:

> Even though from the point of view of biblical law (*mi-deoraita*) it is disqualified (פסולה), . . . nonetheless, the Sages already instituted in order that people be penitent (i.e., and repay the value of the theft) that he only pay the value of the wood, . . . and he may make a benediction on [sitting in] it.

We see, then, that the Sages' desire that the theft be reimbursed was so powerful that it overcame the biblical requirements that the actual stolen object be returned (Lev. 5:23, BT *Baba Kama* 67a, 94b, 112a). The "enactment for the penitents" – *Takanat ha-Shavim* – even legitimized a biblically disqualified *sukkah* even when the stolen beam had not been firmly fixed into the *sukkah* (and presumably could be removed from it without taking apart the whole structure?). The interpersonal mitzvah of returning the theft in its rabbinic form of monetary reimbursement overcame the biblical mitzvah of a ritual nature. The result, of course, is also to ease the thief's ability to carry out the ritual mitzvah of dwelling in a sukkah, but this is, as it were, a byproduct of the rabbinic enactment, though certainly not an undesired one.

And see further the penetrating philosophical discussion of this issue in Yohanan Silman's study entitled "*Mitzvot ve-Averot ba-Halachah: Tziyut u-Meri O Tikun ve-Kilkul*," *Dinei Yisrael* 16 (1992), 183–201.

3. The continuation of the Hida's statement is somewhat cryptic and requires elaboration. He writes as follows:

. . . for we have been directed in a generic fashion to go beyond the letter of the law, as we learned from Rav Yosef, and as is said there in BT *Baba Metzia* 30 where R. Yishmael be-R. Yossi asks: [surely he is] an elder person and it is not in accordance with his dignity? And the reply is: He acted beyond the letter of the law, as we learned from Rav Yosef, etc., see there carefully.

The Hida's intention is to refer us to BT *Baba Metzia* 30b, which reads as follows:

> R. Yishmael be-R. Yossi was strolling along the wayside when he came upon a man weighed down under the burden of faggots (see Rashi). He stopped to take a rest and put down the burden, and said to him: "Help me." "And how much are they worth?" [asked R. Yishmael be-R. Yossi]. "Half a *zuz*," he replied. He gave him half a *zuz* and renounced his ownership over them. The man then reclaimed them. Again he gave him half a *zuz*, and renounced his ownership over them, and saw that the man was about to reclaim them. He said to him: "I have renounced my claims over them to the whole world excluding you."

The Talmud then asks:

> But surely R. Yishmael be-R. Yossi was an elderly person, and this was not commensurate with his dignity [and hence he was not obligated to help the man].

The reply given by the Talmud, based on Exod. 18:20, is:

> R. Yishmael be-R. Yossi acted beyond the letter of the law. For Rav Yosef taught: "and thou shalt show them" (Exod. 18:20) – this is *beit hayyechem*; "the way" – charitable deeds; "where in they must walk" – this refers to visiting the sick; "in it" – this refers to burial; "and the work" – this is the law; "that they must do" – this means *going beyond the letter of the law.*

And see further what the Hida wrote in his *Birkei Yosef, Yoreh Deah* 333; idem, *Mahzik Berachah, Yoreh Deah* 61:16; idem, *Petah Enayyim*, vol. 2, 16ab; R. Hayyim Cohen, *Lev Shomeah* (Livorno: 1885, *Maarechet Kaf*, sect. 33); R. Avraham Palache, *Avraham Ezkor* (Izmir: 1899, sect. 46); R. Hayyim Pontrimoli, *Petah ha-Dvir* (Izmir: 1755–1773, 31:4); *Sdei Hemed, Klelalim Maarechet Lamed, Kelal* 29, vol. 4, 53a. See also my *Netivot Pesikah* (Jerusalem: 2008, 159, n. 246), that there are many opinions that the court can force the litigants to act beyond the letter of the law, basing themselves on the statement of R. Yohanan in BT *Baba Metzia* 30a, as explained by the anonymous editor of the Talmud, that the Second Temple was only destroyed because the courts ruled in accordance with the strict letter of the law, and not beyond it. From this, the *Sdei Hemed* (referred to above) concludes that this obligation must be of biblical authority, or else how could such a terrible punishment be brought upon them. See also *Mordechai* to *Baba Metzia*, chap. 2, sect. 257; Rema, *Hoshen Mishpat* 12:2; second opinion;

idem, Responsa no. 32, ed. A. Ziv, 188, and editor's note (and see below in this note ad fin.); *Bah, Hoshen Mishpat*, sect. 12, that one coerces to act beyond the letter of the law. See below on BT *Baba Metzia* 83a.

See further the responsum of the *Bah* no.12, that the court can force Shimon to waive his legal rights and refrain from opening a liquor store, which would damage Reuven's store. And see also Teshuvot *Tzemah Tzedek, Hoshen Mishpat* 418:11. See also, S. Belkin, *In His Image: The Jewish Philosophy of Man as Expressed in Rabbinic Tradition* (London, New York, Toronto: 1960, 216–217), on "the duty of the individual to conduct his life, *where his fellow man is concerned* [my emphasis, D.S.], in accordance with the higher moral law."

In this connection we may recall the very illuminating tale told of the great Hasidic master, Reb Meshulam Zusha of Anipoli. It is related that once he brought a piece of cloth to his wife to give to a Jewish tailor to make her a dress. When the tailor concluded his work, he brought it to Reb Zusha's wife, at the same time sighing. She asked him: "Why are you sighing so?" He told her of his distress. For he had just arranged the engagement of his daughter, and the fiancé, when he saw that he was engaged in sewing a new dress for a woman, assumed that it was intended for his bride. And when he heard this was not the case, he was angry and upset. R. Zusha's wife was filled with pity, so she took the dress and gave it to the tailor as a present.

When she told her husband the story, he immediately asked her: "And did you pay the tailor for his work?" She was astonished, replying: "I gave him the dress as a present; why then should I pay him?" Reb Zusha replied: "The tailor is a poor man, and he worked hard all the week to sew this dress for you, and not for his daughter. Eagerly he awaited his payment so as to be able to bring sustenance to his family. And now what will they eat? If it fell to you to give a present to the daughter, can you therefore excuse yourself from payment; surely this is extortion from an employee." Forthwith, his wife did as her husband wished, and paid the tailor his wage. (See A. Tobolsky, *Hizaharu be-Mamon Haverchem* [Bnei Brak: 1981, 219], and his reference to R. Shaul Nathanson's Responsa *Shoel u-Meshiv Tinyana*, vol. 3, sect. 42, for the halachic issues involved in a similar such case, and compare Tobolsky, 259–260, the story told of R. Yehoshua Leib Diskin, and cf. BT *Baba Metzia* 83a, cited below.)

See on this subject what I wrote in *Darkah shel Halachah* (Jerusalem: 2007, 99–101); S. Shilo, "On One Aspect of Law and Morals in Jewish Law: *Lifnim Mishurat Hadin*," *Israel Law Review* 13:3, 359–390; S. Berman, "*Lifnim Mishurat Hadin*," *Journal of Jewish Studies* 29 (1975), 86–124; idem 28 (1977), 181–193; A. Kirschenbaum, *Equity in Jewish Law: Beyond Equity: Halakhic Aspirationism in Jewish Civil Law* (Hoboken, NJ: 1991, 109–136, 212–222) (critique of Berman's view); A. Lichtenstein, "*Musar ve-Halachah be-Masoret Yisrael: Ha-Im ha-Masoret Makirah be-Etikah she-Einah Teluyah be-Halachah?*," *Deot* 46 (1977),

In this way the Hida sought to resolve a question against the Rambam (*Hilchot Gezelah ve-Avedah* 11:17), who wrote that: "He who goes on the straight and virtuous path and acts beyond the letter of the law, will return a lost object wherever it be, even if this is not in accordance with his dignity." According to the Hida, even though this person is not obligated to return the lost object, because it is beneath his dignity to do so, he should nonetheless do so, and is not to be considered an ignorant one, since this is a mitzvah directed to his fellow man.

He further expands on this principle in his homily to *Shabbat ha-Gadol*, in *Devarim Ahadim*, Jerusalem: 1986, homily 22, p. 424 (in the Livorno ed., 1788, 119a). This comes as part of his discussion on the obligation to

---

5–20; Eugene Korn, "Legal Floors and Moral Ceilings: A Jewish Understanding of Law and Ethics," *The Edah Journal* 2/2 (2002), 4–10.

In *Darkah shel Halachah* (100, n. 145), I brought the position of R. Ben-Tziyyon Meir Hai Uziel, in his *Michmenei Uziel*, vol. 3 (Jerusalem: 2005, 221), who, when discussing the passage in BT *Ketubot* 27b about Rav Hisda's firm legal stance, remarks that, "One needs great care and deep understanding to find clear principles and boundries, in order to distinguish between what appear to be opposing principles: 'One does not act mercifully in judgment' (אין מרחמין בדין), and 'beyond the letter of the Law' (לפנים משורת הדין)."

I also pointed out that while the Rema in *Hoshen Mishpat* 12:2 rules that: "A court cannot force [a person] to act beyond the letter of the law, even if it should seem to be the right thing to do (*Beit Yosef* in the name of the Ri and the Rosh); but some are of a differing view (*Mordechai, Baba Metzia* chap. 2)." And even though generally speaking the Rema prefers the first opinion, he cites (*Hochmat Shlomo*), it would appear from his responsum no. 32, that he, nonetheless, recommends forcing one to act beyond the letter of the law. (See Kirschenbaum, 125, n. 82.) For this is what he writes there (*Shut ha-Rema*, ed. A. Ziv [Jerusalem: 1971, 188]):

> Nonetheless, if the damage to Reuven, in opening the windows of the synagogue, to his house or his courtyard is not great, he should not have positioned himself according to the strict measure of the law, but beyond it and to give honor to his God and to beautify our House of God. And he who does not give importance to the honor of his Creator (see Mishnah *Hagigah* 2:1: that it would have been better had he not been born), etc., and one coerces an entrance beyond the letter of the law, as did write the *Mordechai*, chapter *Eilu Metziyot* (sect. 257), and even though there are those who differ on this issue.

act beyond the letter of the law. He then cites the famous passage in BT *Baba Metzia* 83a. There we read that:

> Raba bar bar Hana had some porters who broke his wine barrels. He seized hold of their garments. They came to Rav and complained. Rav told him to return the garments. He said: "Is this the law?" Rav replied, "Yes, [citing the verse], 'that thou mayest walk in the way of good men'" (Proverbs 2:20). He returned the garments to them. They said to him, "We are poor, and we worked very hard the whole day, and we are hungry and we have nothing." [Rav] said to him, "Go, give them their wages." He asked, "Is this [truly] the law?" "Yes," [he replied], "'and keep the paths of the righteous'" (2:20).

The Hida suggests that Raba bar bar Hana, as it were, knew the principle that if one is not obligated to do something, and nonetheless does it, one is considered a *hedyot* – an idiot; he therefore queried Rav's ruling. And the answer was: only when we are speaking of ritual mitzvot, but not when we are speaking of social mitzvot. There, one goes beyond the strict letter of the law, in order "to walk in the way of good men, and keep the paths of the righteous."

This explains what we find in *Shulhan Aruch Orah Hayyim* 63:2, that "one who wishes to act in a more stringent fashion, and stand for the reading of the *Shema* when he had been sitting, is called an *avaryan* – sinner." See *Magen Avraham* ad loc. section 3, for his explanations, and see *Tur Orah Hayyim* section 61, in the name of the Midrash, that "the Holy One blessed be He said that he did not trouble Israel to read [*the Shema*] standing . . ." etc. (See also *Turei Zahav* (*Taz*) to *Orah Hayyim* 61:1, and R. Shlomo Luria's *Yam shel Shlomo* to *Baba Kama*, chapter 3, section 41, cited in the *Magen Avraham* above.) Of course, here we must also remember that standing during the recitation of *Shema* is obligatory according to the view of Beit Shammai (M. *Berachot* 1:3; BT *Berachot* 11a), and cf. ibid., 13b, on the view of R. Yohanan. (See further *Pri Megadim* ad loc. *Mishbetzot Zahav* 2, and *Eshel Avraham* 2 on *avaryan*, etc; and also the remarks of R. Yedidiah Schwarts in *Moriah* 38 [11/12, 371–372], 2012, 275.) The *Magen Avraham* saw this behavior as *yuhara* – arrogance. In the light of the Hida's explanation that we brought above, this ruling is more fully understandable.

There is, I believe, further corroboration of the Hida's solution in a somewhat complex question of an apparent contradiction in the area of ritual sacrifices. But this requires some preliminary information.

There is a certain class of sin offerings the nature of which is dependent upon the economic status of the person obligated to bring the sacrifice, (see Leviticus 5:6–13). The rich man brings for his "trespass offering" "a lamb or a kid of the goats" (verse 6). And one who cannot afford this brings "two turtle-doves or two young pigeons" (verse 7). And if this is too much for him, he brings for his offering "the tenth part of an ephah of fine flour for a sin offering" (verse 11). This, in rabbinic parlance is called a "*korban oleh ve-yored*," actually "an offering which goes up and down," in other words a gradiated offering. And if a rich man were to bring a poor man's offering, he would not have fulfilled his obligations (BT *Keritot* 28a, BT *Yoma* 41b). But a leprous person who was poor who brought the rich man's offering has fulfilled his obligation (ibid.). R. Shimon of Sans (a Tosafist) even writes that for this "he should be blessed" (to M. *Negaim* 14:12).

However, in *Sefer ha-Hinuch* to *Mitzvah* 123, basing himself on BT *Yoma* 41a, we read concerning the sin of entering the Temple in a state of impurity *(tumat mikdash ve-kodshav)*, which also mandates a "graduated" offering, that:

> He does not fulfill his obligation with a meal offering of a fowl unless he is poor. But if a poor man brought a lamb or a goat, he has *not* fulfilled his obligation – i.e., the offering is invalid. And the reason is that the Lord blessed be He had mercy upon him and freed him [from the expensive offering], and it is not proper that he force himself to bring more than what he can afford . . .

At first glance it would appear that these two rulings contradict one another. For in the former case, he is *blessed* for bringing more than he was actually obligated to bring, and in the latter, his offering is actually invalid! There has been considerable discussion to explain the view of the *Hinuch*. (See references in *Meorot ha-Daf ha-Yomi* 673, to BT *Keritot* 27, *Meilah* 6, 23, Nisan 5772, 2.) However, I would suggest as a simple explanation that the solution depends on the nature of the sin. Entering in the Temple area in a state of impurity is a sin against one's Creator. In such a case, one acts in accordance with the exact ruling, and if one goes beyond it, one is a "*hedyot*," and hence one's offering is invalid. However, the offering brought by the person who has been cured from his leprosy, according to rabbinic tradition is because he spoke calumny against his neighbors (*motzi-shem ra*, a word-play on *metzora*), and, hence, his sin was one against his fellowman. This they learned from Miriam's punishment of becoming leprous in Numbers 12:10; see e.g., *Sifra Metzora* 5:5, 8; Rambam, *Hilchot Tumat Tzaraat* 16:10. (And see *Leviticus Rabbah* 17:3, ed. Margaliot, 374–377, where out of the ten sins which are punished by leprosy, eight of them are sins against one's fellow being. And so also *Deutronomy Rabbah* 6:8–10.) Hence, the atonement – i.e., the *tikkun* – can well be over and above the formally required offering (*machmir*), so that the poor man who offers a rich man's sacrifice is not to be considered a "*hedyot*," and his offering is not only valid, but he is therefore to be blessed.

According to the above explanation, we have additional support for the Hida's contention, from a completely different area of halachah.[4]

---

4. We mentioned in passing (above, n. 3) the concept that certain activities are not commensurate with a senior person's dignity, relieving him of certain obligations (זקן ואינו לפי כבודו). The principle finds its roots in the verse in Deut. 22:1: "Thou shalt not see thy brother's ox or his sheep go astray, and hide thyself from them; thou shalt in any case bring them again unto thy brother." And ibid., v. 3: "In like manner shalt thou do with his ass; and so shalt thou do with his raiment; and with all lost things of thy brother's which he hath lost, and thou hast found, shalt thou do likewise: Thou mayest not hide thyself." (And cf. v. 4.)

And on this, the Talmud remarks (BT *Baba Metzia* 30a):

> "And hide thyself from them." Our rabbis taught: At times you hide from them, at times you don't. In what case [do you hide]? [In the case] of a priest in a graveyard (who may not make himself impure), or an elderly person (זקן – perhaps a scholar) when it is not commensurate with his dignity . . .

This concept should perhaps be related to the concept of human dignity discussed below, sect. 15.

Here I should like to give an additional example of the use of this concept. The *Tur* (*Orah Hayyim* 395), followed by the *Shulhan Aruch* (ibid., 366:13), related that there is a mitzvah of rabbinic status to arrange an *eruv hatzerot* (cojoining buildings to form a common court to permit transferring objects from one house to another on Shabbat). The Talmud (in BT *Eruvin* 68a) cites Rabba bar Rav Hanan as asking Abbaye, "How come in the alleyway of your two great authorities (Abbaye and Rabbah), you do not have an *eruv hatzerot*?" Abbaye replied that it was not commensurate with Rabbah's dignity to go from household to household to make the necessary arrangements.

II

Hospitality towards Guests and to the *Shechinah*

AND THIS, INDEED, is the simple and deep understanding of the statement found in BT *Shabbat* 127a:

> R. Yehudah in the name of Rav said: Greater is the hosting of guests than the hosting of the *Shechinah*,[1] as it is said (Genesis 18:3), "And he [Abraham] said: My Lord,[2] if now I have found favor in Thy sight,

---

1. There are some truly remarkable statements that must give us pause. Thus in BT *Sanhedrin* 103b we are told that the idolater Michah, whose idolatrous incense would intertwine with that of the holy place of Shiloh, was not counted among those who have no place in the World to Come, because his fare was prepared for all passersby. And furthermore, in Judg. 17:1, we read "and his name was Michiahu." Now it is a well-known principle that evil persons have their name before the word "his name was," such as נבל שמו – "Naval was his name," גלית שמו – "Goliath was his name," etc.; whereas, with righteous people "and his name" comes before the actual name. Thus ושמו מרדכי – "and his name was Mordechai," ושמו מנוח – "and his name was Manoah," etc. How come, then, that Michiahu, the idolator, appears in the biblical text as though he was a righteous person? The answer given is: Because he received guests, therefore his name is written after the manner of the righteous (*Numbers Rabbah* 10:14). See my *Greek in Talmudic Palestine* (Bar-Ilan: 2012), 169–170, n. 1.

2. The Hebrew word here is *Adonai*, with a *kamatz* under the *nun*. Rashi and Rambam explain that he was talking to the leader of the three angels, requesting him not to leave, but calling all of them "my lords." This interpretation is based on the fact that *adonai* is a plural form; but the continuation of the verse, "if now I have found favor in *thy* sight, pass not away, I pray *thee*, from *thy* servant," is in

the singular. (These interpretations base themselves on *Genesis Rabbah* 48:9; BT *Yoma* 37a.) Onkelos and Pseudo-Yonatan, on the other hand, translate this word as referring to God. There are practical halachic implications to this aggadic controversy. For if the word means merely "my master," it is a "secular name" (*shem hol*), and certain special demands upon a scribe writing it are not required. Whereas, if the meaning is "God," it is a "*shem kodesh*," a sacred name, to which those special requirements apply. See BT *Shevuot* 35b, where we read: "Haninah ben Ahi R. Yehoshua and R. Elazar ben Azariah in the name of R. Elazar ha-Modai said: "This too is holy." According to which view is the statement of R. Yehudah who said, "Greater is the hosting of guests than the hosting of the *shechinah*?" It is in accordance with [the view of] that couple. Cf. *Soferim* 4:10, ed. Higger, 143, *Massechet Sefer Torah*, chap. 4 (and references cited in Higger's note to lines 29–42 ibid.). We shall see below that this homiletic controversy has additional practical halachic implications.

Since this is a very critical text we should discuss it in some further detail. *Adonai* (*Adonoi*) with a *kamatz* throughout *Tenach* refers to God. When referring to a group of people, the plural form of "My Lords" is *Adonai* with a *patah*, as in Gen. 19:2, when Lot addresses those same angels, saying, "Behold now, my Lords (*Adonai*), turn in, I pray you, into your servant's house . . ." It therefore is to be expected that the commentators understand our text with "*Adonoi*" – with a *kamatz* – as referring to God, as indeed did the *Targumim* mentioned above. So too is the opinion of R. Eleazar ha-Modai in BT *Shevuot* 35b, BT *Shabbat* ibid., etc. So too emerges very clearly also from *Seder Eliyahu Rabbah* (12) 13, ad init., ed. M. Ish Shalom (Vienna: 1901 [second ed. Jerusalem: 1960], p. 54); English translation *Tanna Debe Eliyyahu*. Transl. W.G. Braude and I.J. Kapstein (Philadelphia: 1981), 186, where we read:

> Such was Abraham's desire to please those who share in divine wisdom that he asked God, who had come to visit him after his circumcision, to wait [while he dined with the angels], saying, *My Lord, if now I have found favor in Thy sight, please wait a while for Thy servant* (Gen. 18:3). Hence it is said: In order to try and be hospitable to disciples of the wise who have come to dine with him, a man may ask permission to put off [even his Sovereign]. It took courage indeed on Abraham's part to say to God: *My Lord . . . wait a while for Thy servant.*

On the other hand, in *Massechet Derech Eretz* 4, (=*Pirkei Ben Azzai* 2:2, ed. M. Higger. *Masechtot Derech Eretz* [Brooklyn, NY: 1935, 175–176]) we read as follows:

> When Abraham our forefather saw the angels, the *Shechinah* came and stood above him. He said *to them* "My Lords, wait for me while I dismiss the Divine (אפטר מן השמים), who is greater than you . . ."

Clearly, the author understood *Adonai* as referring to the angels. Indeed, this follows the alternative view in *Shevuot* and *Soferim* ibid., that this is a "secular name." And this is the first opinion cited by Rashi ad loc., "the most important of them [i.e., the angels]"; and so too in Ramban, who, nonetheless, notes the use of the *kamatz*, explaining that an angel may be thus addressed because of its elements of divinity. Likewise Sforno.

The question we must surely ask ourselves is why the commentators, homilists and halachists should depart from what is the apparent *peshat* – plain meaning of the word – and adopt an alternative interpretation, one which also creates grammatical difficulties in the structure of the sentence – an awkward transition from plural to singular. (We should note that according to the understanding that *Adonai* is a *shem kodesh*, since it refers to God, even if it is a plural form, it is still understood in a singular meaning, so that there is no real transition from plural to singular in that verse.)

Perhaps this is because these authorities found the straightforward explanation to be too radical. How could one dismiss God for the sake of these transient visitors! This question was surely felt by the author of *Tanna de-Bei Eliyahu* cited above, who emphasizes the courage it must have taken for Abraham to tell God "Wait a while . . ."

It has also been observed that the Rambam appears to have been inconsistent in this matter. For in his halachic works, he follows the opinion that *Adonai* is a holy name (*Hilchot Yesodei ha-Torah* 6:9), and so too in *Beur Shemot Kodesh ve-Hol*, attributed to the Rambam, ed. M. Gaster, *Dvir* 1; (Berlin: 1923, 198). On the other hand, in his *Guide for the Perplexed* (2.42, M. Friedländer transl., [London: 1942, 237]), he seems to give greater credence to the alternative explanations:

> In such visions, a prophet either sees God who speaks to him, as will be explained by us, or he sees an angel who speaks to him, or he hears some one speaking to him without seeing the speaker, or he sees a man who speaks to him, and learns afterwards that the speaker was an angel. In this latter kind of prophecies, the prophet relates that he saw a man who was doing or saying something, and that he learnt afterwards that it was an angel.
>
> This important principle was adopted by one of our Sages, one of the most distinguished among them, R. Hiyya the Great (*Bereshit Rabbah*, 48:10), in the exposition of the Scriptural passage commencing, "And the Lord appeared unto him in the plain of Mamre" (Gen. xviii). The general statement that the Lord appeared to Abraham is followed by the description in what manner that appearance of the Lord took place; namely, Abraham saw first three men; he ran and spoke to them. R. Hiyya, the author of the explanation, holds that the words of Abraham, "My Lord, if now I have found grace in thy sight, do not, I pray thee, pass from thy servant," were spoken by him in a prophetic vision to one of the men; for he

> pass not away, I pray thee, from Thy servant."[3]

> says that Abraham addressed these words to the chief of these men. Note this well, for it is one of the great mysteries [of the Law].

It would seem to me that when the Rambam is giving halachic rulings, he follows the dominant rabbinic opinions, in accordance with the accepted guidelines for rabbinic adjudication. But when discussing philosophical issues, he nonetheless prefers that opinion which gives support to his theological position. And this, indeed, is what he says in *Shemot Kodesh ve Hol*, that though there is a difference of opinions among the commentators, we will rely on the *tradition* (*kabbalah*), i.e., as far as a halachic determination. This touches on the broader question of the relationship between his halachic and his philosophical-theological writings, which is beyond the scope of this study. See, for example, Isadore Twersky, *Introduction to the Code of Maimonides (Mishneh Torah)* (New Haven and London: 1980, sect. iv, [*Law and Philosophy*] 356–514).

3. This subject requires further examination and elaboration. For in *Tikunei ha-Zohar* 6, ed. R. Margaliot (Jerusalem: 1978), 46, we read:

> And he who receives guests in full friendship it is as though he has received the countenance of the *Shehinah*, for in that measure that a person acts, so [heaven] acts towards him. R. Eleazar [the son of R. Shimon bar Yohai] came and kissed his hand. And all the members of the group (*haverim*) bowed down before him saying: "Had we to come to this world only to hear these words, it would have sufficed."

And slightly earlier:

> And for this reason, he who welcomes a guest . . . with a joyful countenance [cf. *Avot* 3:15] and with true pleasure in this world, when the soul and spirit leave the body from this world, they will be welcomed in the world-to-come.

My grandfather, of sainted memory, R. David Sperber, in his *Michtam le-David*, vol. 1 (Jerusalem: 1965, 70), noted the difference between the formulation of *Tikunei ha-Zohar*, which suggests that there is an *equal* measure to the mitzvah of welcoming guests to that of welcoming the *Shechinah*, whereas, the Talmudic texts clearly speak of the ascendancy of hosting guests over welcoming the *Shechinah*. He offers a solution to harmonize the sources, suggesting that there may be different degrees of hosting and welcoming, wholeheartedly or less so, etc.

My father, *zt"l*, in his *Maamarot* (Jerusalem: 1978, 189–190), continues this discussion, examining whether this statement is purely homiletical, or also of halachic significance. He shows that since the homiletical source for this statement is the verse in Gen. 18:3, "And [Abraham] said, Adonai (My Lord), if I have found favor in Thy sight, pass not away, I pray Thee, from Thy servant" – and there is a question as to whether *Adonai* refers to God, or to the three angels, (depending on the vocalization of the word) this would effect the ritual sanctity of the word (how it is to be written by the Scribe, whether it can be erased, etc.). This, indeed, is a source of controversy in BT *Shevuot* 35b, where Haninah the son of R. Yehoshua holds it is secular and R. Elazar ben Azariah, in the name of R. Elazar ha-Modai, is of the view it is sacred (see preceding note).

And the Talmud links the statement of R. Yehudah in the name of Rav, that we quoted above, to the latter view, namely that this is a sacred name. And so too rules the Rambam in *Yesodei ha-Torah* 6:9, citing the statement of R. Yehudah in the name of Rav in *Hilchot Evel* 14:2. We see, then, argues my father, that this statement is not merely homiletic but also has serious halachic implications. And see further below.

He then continues, following upon the words of my grandfather (ibid., 71), to cite the statement of the Hasid of R. Yosef Yavetz, in his commentary to *Avot* 1:5 : "Yose b. Yohanan of Jerusalem said: Let thy house be opened wide, and let the needy be members of thy household . . .":

> The Holy One blessed be He is very distant from the heavenly heavens and close to the wretched destitute, and it is for this reason that the Sages said, "Greater is the hosting of guests than the hosting of the *Shechinah*"; for the *Shechinah* dwells between the shoulders of the destitute, and hosting them is a high and lofty [mitzvah], and does not intervene [i.e., contradict] between the hosting of the *Shechinah*. [Cf. *Genesis Rabbah* 48: If I see the *Shechinah* waiting on them. D.S.] On the contrary: it increases beyond measure [the mitzvah]. And if this were not the case, why would the Sages have said what they said? Surely the ultimate goal is to receive the *Shechinah*, and how could it defer to any other activity?

What R. Yosef Yaavetz is contending is that the one mitzvah does not override the other, but that welcoming the poor is the most complete and perfect way of carrying out the act of *devekut* – cleaving unto God – because, it is as though God Himself dwells with the poor, just as of Benjamin the verse says, "and He shall dwell between his shoulders" (Deut. 33:12), and the Talmud in BT *Sotah* 37a explains that he merited to become "a guest of the *Shechinah*" (*ushpozichan de-Shehinta*).

However, the Maharal mi-Prague has a different view on this issue, and in his *Hiddushei Aggadot* vol. 1 (London: 1960, 67), explains that "new faces" (*panim hadashot*), i.e., guests, are in the image of God, and in welcoming them one connects to the image of God. But "welcoming God Himself" is only honoring Him, for no one can see Him and live. Consequently, hosting guests is *greater*

And in the parallel version in BT *Shevuot* 35b, the formulation is even more forceful. For there we read not merely *gedolah*, great, but "*gedolah yoter* – greater than."[4]

---

than welcoming the *Shechinah*. "And you must understand these words, that there is a great difference between hosting guests and welcoming the Shechinah, for one may not write more on this subject."

My father elaborated in considerable depths (ibid., 191–194) on this theme, moving on to the views of Rav Kook, *zt"l*, (*Olat Re'aya*, vol. 1, 64), and R. Menachem of Chernobil (*Meor Enayim, Va-Yera*), who argues that Rav Yehudah in the name of Rav's proof is that Abraham would otherwise not have left that which was certain [*vadai*] (his hosting of God) for that which was uncertain [*safek*] (his welcoming the strangers). Clearly, then, he knew that welcoming the strangers was of greater importance. He ends by examining the view of the Netziv of Volozin, R. Naftali Zvi Yehudah Berlin, in his *Haamek Davar*, to Gen. 18:2, who explains that the Sages' statement "does not mean that welcoming a guest is greater than receiving the *Shechinah*, but that it is greater in that it supersedes [receiving the *Shechinah*], for such was His will, that a practical mitzvah takes precedence over this one," adding that "this teaches yet a greater lesson, that *even* welcoming guests, which is a mitzvah of charity, supersedes the mitzvah of boundless love of the Divine." (We might nonetheless raise the question: how did Abraham know this?)

So whatever may be the theological explanation for the rabbinic statement, according to the Netziv and the Maharal mi-Prague, the practical halachic application is that this act towards one's fellow person supersedes even the urge to ascend to a degree of cleaving to the Divine.

4. Rambam, in *Hilchot Evel* 14:2, after citing this Talmudic text, adds: "and accompanying them [as they leave town] is greater than welcoming them. The Rabbis said: 'Whosoever does not accompany them, it is as though he sheds blood.'" The Rambam (14:3) continues that "One compels to accompany [the visitor] in the same way one compels [to give] charity. And the court would appoint emissaries to accompany people passing from one place to another." His rulings are based on BT *Sotah* 46b.

There is a very instructive passage in *Seder Eliyahu Rabba*, ed. Friedman, 14–15, = *Tanna Debe Eliyyahu*, transl. W.G. Braude & I.J. Kapstein (Philadelphia: 1981, 481–482), which I shall cite in full:

> R. Eliezer said: Communities may be compelled to provide escort for travelers because the reward for such escort is limitless, [as is shown by the following account:] *The [Israelite] scouts saw a man come forth out of the city, and they said unto him: Show us, we pray thee, the entrance into the city, and we will deal kindly with thee. [And he showed them the entrance to*

Abraham receives the visit of the three angels
Gustave Doré, *Le Sainte Bible*, Tours 1866

> *the city* (Judg. 1:24–25)]. What was the kindness they did for him? *They smote the city with the edge of the sword; but they let the man go and all his family (ibid.).* And what reward did he receive? *The man went into the land of the Hittites, and built a city, and called the name thereof Luz, which is the name thereof unto this day* (Judg. 1:16). This is the Luz in which the fringes [of the prayer shawl] (Num. 15:38) are dyed blue for all Israel. Nay more! When Sennacherib came up against the Land, he did not disturb Luz. And Nebuchadnezzar did not destroy it. Even the angel of death has no permission to enter it. When old men and old women within it grow weary of life, they are taken outside the wall [of the city] and there they die.

Now, may not the matter of providing escort be strongly argued on the basis of the foregoing events? Here was a man – [in fact, a Canaanite] – who did not walk a step or utter a word, but merely pointed with his finger to guide the scouts and yet thereby brought about deliverance for himself and for all his family to the end of all generations. How much greater, then, is the reward a man will receive from the Holy One for escorting – walking along with and talking to – a disciple of the wise from town to town, from city to city, from province to province.

There is a tale told concerning a certain wealthy person in Vilna, who was known to be most hospitable to strangers, that one day his house and all his assets were burned up in a fire. The Gaon, R. Eliyahu of Vilna, was asked why a person so famed for his hospitality should have suffered such a calamity. Why did not the mitzvah of hospitality to strangers not protect him from this calamity? To which the Gaon replied: He was wont to serve them with food and drink alone (אכילה ושתיה); however, he did not accompany them on their way out (לויה). So of the initial letters of אכילה שתיה ולינה או לויה [=אש"ל] only the letters א"ש remained, i.e., אש – *esh* – fire, and as he had not fully carried out the mitzvah of pertaining to guests, it could not protect him from fire.

The Gaon himself, even though he was constantly engaged in Torah study, would interrupt in order to fulfill the mitzvah of welcoming guests – personally – serving food, drink and lodging (לינה), but also adding accompanying the guests on the way out. (See A. Tobolsky, *Olam Hesed Yibaneh*, vol. 2, [Jerusalem: 1988, 19], citing *Kol Eliyahu, Parshat Va-Yera, Ahavat Hesed* 47a, in the name of a certain great authority.)

This notion that לויה – *levaiah*, accompanying, is part and parcel of the mitzvah of *hachnasat orhim* – hospitality, and is the final component of that mitzvah, is already found in the *Mateh Moshe*, of R. Moshe of Premishle, basing himself on *Daat Zekenim mi-Baalei ha-Tosafot* to *Shoftim* ad fin., who writes that the verse in Gen. 18:16 states that "Abraham went with them [the three angels] to bring them on the way," and this is followed by (in v. 17), "And the Lord said: Shall I hide from Abraham that thing which I do?" And see *Genesis Rabbah* 48:20, ed. Theodor-Albeck, 496, on this verse, where it brings a proverb: Did you feed?

This is a remarkable statement. Because we might have thought that "the hosting of the *Shechinah*," which we may understand as expressing some sort of *devekut*, cleaving to *Ha-Kaddosh Baruch Hu*, must surely be the ultimate aim of every God-fearing person, the pinnacle of spiritual endeavors. Or as Gershom Scholem wrote in his seminal essay on *devekut*, "*Devekut*, or Communion with God" (in *The Messianic Idea in Judaism*, New York: 1977, 203):

> Throughout Kabbalistic literature, *devekut* is frequently mentioned as the *highest ideal of the mystical life* as Kabbalists see it, [my emphasis, D.S.] . . . In Kabbalism it is the last grade of ascent to God.

Surely this was clearly stated by R. Moshe Hayyim Luzzato, in his *Derech Ha-Shem* (part 1, 4:6) that "a person was created only to cleave to his Creator."[5]

(See also Moshe Idel, *Kabbalah: New Perspectives*, New Haven and London: 1988, 35–58, on "Varieties of *Devekut* in Jewish Mysticism.")

Did you give drink? Did you accompany [the guest]? And this notion is also found in *Zohar, Va-Yera* 104a. (See Tobolsky, vol. 1 [Jerusalem: 1988, 267–268.]) And on the passage in the *Zohar*, see Mordechai Spielman, *Tiferet Zvi*, vol. 2 (Brooklyn, NY: 1985, 260).

And it is interesting to note that *Shulhan ha-Tahor* 102:2, Tobolsky, 267 states that by accompanying one's guest one causes the *Shechinah* to be attached, as it were, to oneself, for *levaiah* means attachment, i.e., attachment to the *Shechinah*. And this is actually based on what we find in *Zohar Va-Yera* 104a:

> Come and see: When a person accompanies his friend, he draws the *Shechinah* to attach to himself and to come with him on his way and to save (i.e., protect) him. And it is for this reason a person must accompany his friend, because in this manner he attaches him to the *Shechinah*, and draws the *Shechinah* to be attached to him (להתחבר עמו).

The weight given to this mitzvah is expressed symbolically by the Hida (*Homat Anach, Va-Yera* 6) by noting that the words in Gen. 18:16, "[Abraham] went with them to send them off" – הלך עמהם לשלחם, have the numerical value 613, "to teach you, that he who accompanies the guest, it is as though he had carried out all [613] mitzvot of the Torah."

5. See additional references to the Rambam's view, and that of others, in R. Asi ha-Levi Even Yuli, *Shulhan Aruch ha-Middot*, vol. 2, *Halachah ve-Musar* (Jerusalem: 2009, 332). This is a vast topic, which cannot be dealt within this present framework.

Not so, we are told; welcoming the stranger, the dusty Bedouin[6] coming in from the heat of the desert, washing his feet and feeding him, overrides even the hosting of the Creator!

6. See *Genesis Rabbah* 48:2, ed. Theodor-Albeck, 486. One of them looked like a huckster, the other a Nabatean, the third an Arab. BT *Kiddushin* 32b: like Arabs. Note that the word נווטי cannot mean a sailor (from the Greek and Latin *nauta*), since this took place in the desert. סרקי may possibly represent a Saracen.

We may recall that Abraham's tent was open on all sides, so that he could welcome guests from whichever direction they came. See *Genesis Rabbah* 48:9, ed. Theodor-Albeck, 436; and cf. ibid., 54.6, p. 584. For additional sources, see L. Ginzberg, *Legends of the Jews*, vol. 1, 270–271; idem vol. 5, 248, n. 223. At the end of that note Ginzberg writes:

> Even today in the vernacular of the Jews of Eastern Europe a house with many doors is described as a "house with Avraham Avinu's (Father Abraham's) doors."

A similar tradition is found in *Lamentations Rabbah, Petihta* 23, ed. S. Buber (Vilna: 1899, 18), concerning the house of Nehushta bar Elnatan, the mother of King Yehoyachim (II Kings 24:8), which, from the context of the homily (based on Eccl. 12:4), was adjacent to the market-place and whose doors were open to hospitality.

Further on Abraham's yearning to carry out the mitzvah of *hachnasat orhim*, hospitality for strangers, see *Midrash ha-Gadol* to Gen. 18:1, ed. M. Margaliot, vol. 1 (Jerusalem: 1947, 290), and his note to line 9, Gen. 21:33, 34, and additional parallels listed in M.M. Kasher's *Torah Shelemah*, vol. 3, part 2 (Jerusalem: 1934), 739, n. 23.

12

Devekut: Cleaving to God with Mitzvot between Man and His Neighbor

Furthermore, in BT *Sotah* 14a, we read in the name of R. Hama be-R. Haninah as follows:

> What is the meaning of the verse in Deuteronomy 13:5: "Ye shall walk after the Lord your God, [and fear Him, and keep His commandments, and obey His voice, and ye shall serve Him, and cleave unto Him]?" And is it possible for a person to walk after the *Shechinah*. And surely it is said (4:24), "For the Lord thy God is a consuming fire ..."? But [it means]: Go after the attributes of the Holy One blessed be He. Just as he clothes the naked ..., so you too should clothe the naked; Just as He visited the sick ..., so you too should visit the sick; The Holy One blessed be He comforts the mourners ..., so you too should comfort the mourners; the Holy One blessed be He buried the dead ..., so you too should bury the dead.[1]

Thus, the supreme virtues of God that humans should, as it were, emulate, are all in the category of mitzvot between man and his neighbor.

Furthermore, when the Sages try to conceive of a way to "cleave to the

---

1. Compare *Sifrei Deut. Ekev*, sect. 49, ed. Friedman, 85[a] and T.Z.L. Lauterbach, *JQR OS*, 1, 1910–1911, 307.

For a discussion on "walking in His paths," see Yitzhak Blau, in the *Torah U-Mada Journal*, 9 (2000), 20–22, discussing Walter Wurzburger's *Ethics of Responsibility: Pluralistic Approaches to Covenantal Ethics* (Philadelphia: 1994). See on this also David Schatz, "Beyond Obedience: Walter Wurzburger's Ethics of Responsibility," *Tradition* 30/2 (1996), 74–95.

Lord," they again translate this into terms of deeds relating to persons. Thus in BT *Ketubot* 111a we read in the name of R. Yohanan:

> "But you that did cleave unto the Lord your God are alive, every one of you this day" (Deuteronomy 4:4) – And is it possible to cleave to the *Shechinah*? Is it not written, "For the Lord thy God is a consuming fire . . ." (4:24). But [it means to say] that you should marry your daughter to a Torah scholar, and do business for Torah scholars, and benefit Torah scholars from your properties, then the verse credits you as if you are cleaving to the *Shechinah*. Similarly it says, "to walk in His ways and to cleave unto Him" (11:22) – and is it possible for a person to cleave to the *Shechinah*? But everyone who marries his daughter to a Torah scholar, and does business for Torah scholars and benefits them from his own properties, the verse credits him as if he is cleaving to the Shechinah.

Here again, the stress is on helping one's neighbors in a variety of fashions, though, of course, the emphasis is aimed at strengthening Torah scholarship.

With the above in mind, it is surely significant that on entering the synagogue in the morning for the *Shaharit* prayer, even before beginning to pray, it was the custom in many congregations to give charity, and a special charity box was fixed at the entrance to the synagogue, on which at times was written, or engraved the verses, "As for me, I will behold Thy face in righteousness (*be-tzedek*, here referring to *tzedakah* – charity)" (Psalms 17:15), and "Righteousness (*tzedek*) shall go before Him" (85:14). The source for the practice is in BT *Baba Batra* 10a:

> R. Dostai b. R. Yannai explained: . . . Not so the Holy One blessed be He. A person gives a penny to a poor man, and he attains the merit to receive the countenance of the *Shechinah*. As it is said, "As for me, I will behold Thy face in righteousness. I shall be satisfied, when I awake, with Thy likeness" (Psalms 17:15).
>
> R. Eleazar would give a penny to a poor man and then pray. He said: "It is written, 'As for me, I will behold Thy face in righteousness'" (17:15).

It is, then, through a righteous deed to one's neighbor that we attain the merit to a spiritual encounter with the Divine.[2]

---

2. On the history of this practice and its extent, see Appendix.

Perhaps this is, as it were, encapsulated in a little-known halachah which may be seen as a metaphor for our overall theme, namely that true piety cannot admit isolation from the outside world. It is most eloquently expressed by Eugene Korn in a recent review essay he wrote.[3] Towards the end of that essay he writes:[4]

> There is an often overlooked *halakhah* that the room in which one prays must contain a window.[5] This requirement is not the result of imitating the stained-glass window décor of grand cathedrals, but reflects the healthy spiritual outlook of *Hazal*. For prayer and piety to be something significant they must connect to the world outside. They must transcend technicalities and provide a view to culture and its enduring human issue. If that is true about the single *mitsvah* of *tefillah*, it is all the more so about the entire enterprise of *shemirat ha-mitsvot* and our covenantal commitment to a life of Torah.

And, indeed, the Rabbis went so far as to assure one who gives charity that his prayers will be heard (i.e., favorably). Thus we find in *Midrash Psalms* 65:4, ed. Buber, 313, that either Ben Azzai or R. Akiva said:

> He who does righteous deeds (גומל חסדים, here meaning: gives charity), his prayers will be heard [i.e., on high], as it is said, "Sow to yourselves in righteousness . . ."; [And what is written after that?] – "for it is time to seek the Lord" (Hosea 10:12) – for he prays before the Lord and is answered.[6]

We have already noted above how careful the Arizal was to pay his workers wages on time, even if it required delay in the *Minhah* prayer.[7]

---

3. "Windows on the World – Judaism Beyond Ethnicity . . ." *Meorot* 8, 2010.

4. Ibid., p. 9.

5. BT *Berachot* 34b: Said R. Hiyya bar Abba in the name of R. Yohanan: A person should only pray in the room that has windows, as it is written, "and his windows being open in his chamber towards Jerusalem, [he kneeled upon his knees three times a day, and prayed]" (Dan. 6:11). The simple meaning is, of course, that one should direct one's thoughts to Jerusalem, and (/or) towards heaven (Rashi, etc.). This halachah is cited in the *Shulhan Aruch Orah Hayyim* 90:4, and see *Magen Avraham* ibid., sect. 4.

6. See on this R. Hayyim Palache, *Tzedakah le-Hayyim* (Jerusalem: 2000, 267–268).

7. One may further assume that he prayed individually, and not in the

The statement that we cited earlier from BT *Shabbat* 127a in the name of R. Yehudah in the name of Rav extolling the importance of hosting strangers, is not merely some kind of ethical hyperbole. It has clear halachic implications, as we see from the Mishnah in *Shabbat* 18:1:

> One may clear away [on the Sabbath] as much as four or five baskets of straw or grain to make room for guests, or [to avoid] hindrance in the House of Study.

Rashi explains the Mishnah to mean that, if one requires room to seat the guests at a meal or the students for their lesson, we do not concern ourselves with the fact that moving the bails of straw will be an effort on the Sabbath.

On this Mishnah, the Talmud (*Shabbat* 127a) comments as follows:

> Said R. Yohanan: Great is the hosting of guests as rising up early to the House of Study [of Torah, of course], as we have learned "to make room for guests or [to avoid] hindrance in the House of Study." But Rav Dimi of Nehardea said: It is greater than rising up early to the House of Study. For we have learned: "for guests," and only afterwards "to avoid hindrance in the House of Study."[8]

The *Sheiltot* to *Va-Yerah*, section 11, ed. S.M. Mirsky (Jerusalem: 1960, 73), has, apparently, a slightly different reading. For he writes:

---

quorum of a *minyan* (of ten males), since normally there would not be a *minyan* so late. This in itself is surely significant, since the dominant view among the *poskim* (decisors) is that praying in a *minyan* is an important mitzvah (see *Shulhan Aruch Orah Hayyim* 90:9; *Aruch ha-Shulhan* ibid., sect. 13; A.Y. Pfoifer, *Ishei Yisrael*, [Jerusalem: 1998, 8:1, p. 70; 11:1, p. 101; 15:1, p. 126]; for the relevant sources). Even those who do not regard prayer in a *minyan* (*tefillah be-tzibbur*) as mandatory agree that it is preferable.

8. Rav Dimi's statement is followed by that of Rav Yehudah in the name of Rav that we cited above. Rav Dimi's statement may also be seen in the light of that which we discussed above on the status of Torah study.

> And R. Yohanan says: Greater is the hosting of guests than the [avoidance] of hindrance to the House of Study.[9]

We see, once again, the paramount importance of mitzvot of a social nature.

---

9. See S.M. Mirsky's long note, 73–74. And see also *Shulhan Aruch Orah Hayyim* 333:1, in the additions of the Rema. This also requires some further halachic clarification. Moving about objects on the Sabbath within one's house is not forbidden by biblical law, as it is not considered a "*melachah*." However, Rabbis forbade it as a *shevut*, an abstention from secular occupation on the Sabbath or festivals, because they regarded it as being out of harmony with the celebration of the day. So, for example, in BT *Rosh ha-Shanah* 32b we read that one does not go beyond the *tehum* . . . or do things which are forbidden by *shevut* . . . in order to get a *shofar* on Rosh ha-Shanah. And so too the *Shulhan Aruch Orah Hayyim* 586:21 rules:

> We do not transgress the laws of Yom Tov, even that which is [only] forbidden as a *shevut* in order to get a *shofar* on Rosh ha-Shanah.

From this it appears that a *shevut* is not overridden by the requirement to perform a biblical mitzvah. See *Mishnah Berurah*, sect. 83 ad loc., who explains that "the Rabbis equated their ruling to that of a biblical one, requiring that one not override it in order to carry out a positive biblical commandment."

It would seem that this principle applies only in the case when the biblical mitzvah is a *ritual* one – e.g., blowing the *shofar*; however, when it is a social one, such as welcoming guests, this principle does not apply. That is to say the Rabbis did not intend it to apply. But what is even more remarkable is that according to this principle one desists from an act which would go against the *shevut* (שב ואל תעשה – *shev ve-al taaseh*, "sit and do not act"), despite the fact that this will not enable one to carry out a biblical injunction, whereas, in our case, the Rabbis *are permitting an active deed*, contrary to the *shevut*, in order to be able to host one's guests suitably, that is to say to carry out a socially-oriented mitzvah.

(See on this principle in detail, in R. Yaakov Hayyim Sofer, *Edut be-Yaakov*, vol. 2 [Jerusalem: 2011], sect. 35, 121–123).

13

How to Welcome Guests

AND HERE I would recall the tradition related by R. Yaakov Tavshonsky, in his *Imrei Haskel*, Vilna: 1909, 57 (cited in Dov Eliach's *Avi ha-Yeshivot*, vol. 1 [Jerusalem: 1991], 265–266), concerning R. Hayyim of Volozin:

> Once R. Hayyim Voloziner, who made it a rule to come regularly to the Beit Midrash at prayer times, was late for prayer. The beadle went to call him to come and found him seated at his table happily in discussion with a group of distinguished guests who had come to visit him. Noting the expression of surprise on the beadle's face, R. Hayyim explained himself in the form of a question: "Is the issue of the importance of hosting guests, which is said to be greater than hosting the *Shechinah*, of little importance in your eyes?!"

In a somewhat similar vein, we read concerning the great Hasidic master, Reb Yaakov Yitzhak of Lublin, the *Hozeh* ("Seer") of Lublin (died 1815), as related by Martin Buber in his *Tales of the Hasidim: The Early Masters*, New York: 1947, 316–317.

> Rabbi Jacob Yitzhak was in the habit of taking poor wayfarers into his house and waiting on them himself. Once he had served such a man with food, filled his glass, and stood beside his chair ready to fetch him whatever he needed. After the meal, he took away the empty plates and platters and carried them into the kitchen. Then his guest asked him: "Master, ... why have you taken the trouble to carry out the empty dishes?"
>
> The rabbi replied: "Is not the carrying out of the spoon and the

> coal-pan from the Holy of Holies part of the service of the high priest, on the Day of Atonement!"

We may also recall what is told by Reb Menahem Mendel of Rymanov (died 1815), recorded by Buber in his *Tales of the Hasidim: The Later Masters*, New York: 1948, 128:

> A man came and complained to Rabbi Mendel that he could not fulfil the commandment to be hospitable because his wife did not like to have guests, and whenever he brought people to the house it gave rise to quarrels which threatened his domestic peace.
>
> The rabbi said, "Our sages say: 'Welcoming guests is a greater virtue that welcoming the Divine Presence.' This may sound exaggerated to us. But we must understand it properly. It is said that when there is peace between husband and wife the Divine Presence rests in their minds. That is why welcoming guests is described as being more important than welcoming the Divine Presence. Even if hospitality destroys the peace that exists between a man and his wife, the commandment to be hospitable is still the more important."

And while we are on the subject of hosting strangers, I cannot restrain myself from relating a well-known story attributed to the great Hasidic leader, R. Levi Yitzhak of Berditchev.

> It is told that once he reached the city of Lvov, and turned to the dwelling of a wealthy and respected man, who at his request let him enter into his home. R. Levi then asked him if he would permit him to stay in his house a single night, and this he did without giving his name or identifying himself or telling from where he came. The reaction of the wealthy man was an angry refusal. "My house is not a hotel for passers-by," he shouted. "Look for an inn."
>
> R. Levi left the rich man's house and turned unto a poor children's teacher, who warmly welcomed him, fed him and saw that he would have a place to stay the night, and all this without knowing who his guest was.
>
> However, R. Levi met an acquaintance of his, who lived close to the poor teacher, and rapidly the news spread throughout the city that the great R. Levi Yitzhak of Berditchev, the "advocate and protector of Israel," was in town.
>
> Within a short space of time all the Jews of the city collected

> together before the entrance of the house of the poor teacher, and wished to seize upon the countenance of the *tzaddik*. Among those who had gathered together was the rich man, who had refused him hospitality, and sent him away shamefully. He understood that the man he had thought was a vagrant wayfarer was indeed a great *tzaddik*, and he pushed his way through the crowd to beg forgiveness. "Forgive me, Rabbenu; I did not recognize you earlier," he explained. "But now that I know who you are, please come and stay in my house. All the *tzaddikim* that come to our city stay with me," he said.
>
> R. Levi turned unto the congregation and said as follows:
>
> "Do you know the difference between Abraham and Lot? Surely, not only Abraham, but Lot too, welcomed his guests most warmly, and fed them with honor and respect."
>
> The people in the crowd looked intently at R. Levi, awaiting the continuation of his words and his response. He continued:
>
> "Concerning Lot, it says, 'And two angels came to Sodom' (Genesis 19:1). Whereas, with Abraham the verse says, 'And behold, he saw three people standing facing him' (18:2). Lot saw angels and therefore hurried to bring them into his house, because he knew he was hosting angels. But Abraham only saw people, poor travelers, covered in dust from their journey, weary and hungry, requiring food, drink, and rest. And, nonetheless, he opened his house before them.
>
> "And it is for this reason that the Sages said (in *Kiddushin* 32b): Perhaps you may contend that they looked to him [Abraham] like angels. No, they only looked like Bedouin, and even so he warmly welcomed them. So we too, offspring of our forefather Abraham, must welcome each and every person gladly. And since this poor teacher welcomed and hosted me after the manner fitting to an offspring of our forefather Abraham, so I see no reason to change my domicile."[1]

Indeed, *Tanna Debe Eliyyahu* (12) 13, transl. W.G. Braude and I.J. Kapstein, (Philadelphia: 1981, 187), extols every detail of Abraham's acts of hospitality towards his three angels-guests:

---

1. Compare further the story of the Shinyever's Rebbe's attitude towards a slaughterer (*shochet*) who would not tolerate guests. See Yehezkel Shraga Fraenkel, *Rabbenu ha-Kaddosh mi-Shinyeve* (Ramat Gan: 1991, vol. 1, 260–262).

> As a reward for the shade of the tree under which our father [Abraham] had seated the ministering angels, the Holy One had seven clouds of glory hover for forty years over Israel in the wilderness. [As a reward for the morsel of bread which our father Abraham fed the ministering angels, the Holy One fed Israel with manna for forty years in the wilderness.] And besides providing Israel with the manna, what did God do about its taste? Blessed be the Preserver of the world; blessed be He in whose presence no man is favored over another, [where every man is treated with complete fairness]. Even as our father Abraham had provided several kinds of food (cf. Genesis 18:6, 8) to the ministering angels, so [God provided for Israel]: [he] who sought the taste of bread in the manna found the taste of bread in it, he who sought the taste of meat in the manna found the taste of meat in it, he who sought the taste of honey found the taste of honey in it, he who sought the taste of milk found the taste of milk in it, he who sought the taste of butter found the taste of butter in it, as is said, "*The people went about, and gathered it, and ground it in mills, or beat it in mortars, or seethed it in pots, or made cakes of it. However it was prepared, its taste was like the taste of rich cream from the breast [of a nursing mother]*" (Numbers 11:8). And as a reward for the calf which our father Abraham had the ministering angels eat, the Holy One on two occasions provided Israel with quail – once before the revelation of the Torah and once after the revelation of the Torah, (cf. Exodus 16:13, and Numbers 11:31–35).

And cf. BT *Baba Metzia* 86b, in the name of Rav Yehudah in the name of Rav, for a similar motif. (But see also the remarks of the Hafetz Hayyim, in his *Ahavat Hesed*, Warsaw: 1888–1893, 45b, and also 46b.)

And there is a tradition in the name of the Gaon R. Eliyahu of Vilna (brought in *Divrei Eliyahu*, [Vilna: 1910], a collection of sayings attributed to the Gaon, collected by I.L. Perfel and A.D. Bloch, p. 70), according to which the Gaon proved that welcoming guests was a greater mitzvah than welcoming the *Shechinah*, noting that in *Shulhan Aruch Yoreh Deah* 242:16 it is stated that when leaving one's master one does not turn one's back on him. But Abraham ran to his guests (Genesis 18:2), obviously turning his back upon the *Shechinah*, thus demonstrating that he regarded this as a more important mitzvah. This fits in well with what we know of the Gaon's personal involvement in this mitzvah, (see A. Tobolsky, *Olam Hesed Yibaneh*, vol. 2, [Jerusalem: 1988, 19]).

14

"*Pikuah Nefesh*" and the Brisker "*Humra*"

I WOULD FURTHER SUGGEST that it is this basic principle, that social mitzvot have greater weight, as it were, than ritual ones, is behind the well-known halachic ruling that פיקוח נפש דוחה שבת, that the danger to life takes precedence over the laws of Shabbat (BT *Shabbat* 132a), and indeed over other laws of great gravitas (see BT *Yoma* 85ab).[1]

The Rambam's ruling in this regard is well-known for its forcefulness. Thus he writes (in *Hilchot Shabbat* 2:3):

> When we do these things (i.e., desecrating the Sabbath for a sick person), we do not do them not through the agency of a non-Jew, or a child, neither by slaves nor women, in order that the Sabbath be not light in their eyes. But one does so by the great ones of Israel and their Sages. And one may not hesitate (or: delay) in desecrating the Sabbath for a sick person, as it is stated, "[Ye shall therefore keep My statutes and My judgments:] which if a man do, he shall live in them" (Leviticus 18:5) – and not die by them (referring to BT *Yoma* 85ab).

---

1. See also above, section 2 that the Rabbis determined the identity of certain elements of the four species (*arba minim*) used on Sukkot – the *lulav,* etc. – as those that do not do bodily harm to him that holds them (BT *Sukkah* 30b), basing themselves on the verse in Prov. 3:17, "Her ways are ways of pleasantness." Prickly plants that might scratch the hand that holds them could not, according to the rabbinic understanding, be one of the species.

See further above, section 7 ad init., for the passage in the Rambam *Hilchot Rotzeah* 4:9.

Indeed, we learn just this from the Mishnah in *Sotah* 3:4, which talks of a *hasid shoteh*, a "foolish *hasid*," which the Talmud (*Sotah* 21b) explains as being one who when he sees a woman drowning in the river, says, "It is not proper [for me] to gaze at her and save her"; that is to say, his notion of the laws of modesty prevent him from saving her. Of just such a type of person, the Mishnah says "he is in the category of those *mevalei olam* – who wear out the world" – causes it to decay, destroy it.

It is of interest to note that when we speak of *pikuah nefesh*, according to some of the latter-day authorities, this refers not only to *physical* life-threatening situations, but also to situations where one's *spiritual* life is threatened. Thus, R. Moshe Feinstein (*Igrot Moshe Orah Hayyim* vol. 1, section 156/1) ruled, in accordance with the opinion of the *Baalei Tosafot*, that when a person is involved in transgressing a sin the punishment of which is *karet*, extinction of the soul (see Ramban to Leviticus 18:29), and he is in the process of regretting his actions, one is permitted to desecrate the Sabbath in order to save him from carrying out this sin. For he regards the damage of *karet* as *pikuah nefesh*. The specific example that he is dealing with is of less importance to us, and is beyond the scope of our discussion; it is the basic principle that he is expressing that is of interest to us. (See also his *Dibrot Moshe* to Shabbat, section 3.)

It is well-known that R. Hayyim Brisker took an extreme position of leniency in matters where he saw even a hint of a life-endangering situation (ספק ספיקא של פיקוח נפש). Thus it is related by Aharon Sorasky that:[2]

> Once a Jew from Brisk came to him with a question: His son, who had been drafted to the army, was sick and in the hospital in the nearby town of Sidlitz. On the following day, Shabbat, the doctors would examine him to decide whether or not he was fit enough to join the army. And so, asked the father, was it permitted for him to travel that night on Shabbat, to Sidlitz in order to intercede on his behalf. R. Hayyim did not hesitate for one moment, but ordered the man to do all in his power to save his son, since there was a danger to his life.
>
> The people who were present were puzzled by his unusual ruling, and after the man had left, R. Hayyim explained his response:
>
> "If this young man will have to serve five years in the army, it is not

---

2. Aharon Sorasky, *Marbitzei Torah u-Musar be-Yeshivot Nusah Lita mi-Tekufat Volozin ve-Ad Yameinu*, vol. 1 (Jerusalem: 1976, 112).

> unlikely that during this period a war will break out and he will be sent to the front and possibly killed. And even the slightest suspicion of a life-endangering situation (ספק ספיקא של פיקוח נפש) overrules the laws of Shabbat (דוחה שבת)."

R. Hayyim's position on a sick person's fasting on Yom Kippur is well-known. Sorasky relates (*Marbitzei Torah u-Musar be-Yeshivot Nusah Lita mi-Tekufat Volozin ve-Ad Yameinu*, vol. 1 [Jerusalem: 1976], 112–113) that shortly before his death R. Hayyim dwelled in Otbosk, a place near Warsaw where people sick with tuberculosis (TB) would come for treatment in the pure fresh air. On Tisha be-Av, twelve days before he died, a woman came to him weeping that her son lay sick with TB in the next-door house, in a life-threatening condition, and the doctor forbade him to fast. However, the young man refused to listen to the doctor. R. Hayyim hurried to the young man's house and entreated him to listen to the doctor's directions, but despite his entreaties the young man adamantly refused. Then R. Hayyim said: "If I eat today, will you join me?" The youth replied: "If you eat, I'll eat with you."

Such tales relating to R. Hayyim are legion (see Sorasky), and he was wont to explain his position saying: "I do not rule leniently concerning Yom Kippur (etc.), but stringently concerning the law 'Take ye therefore good heed unto yourselves.' ונשמרתם מאד לנפשותיכם (Deuteronomy 4:15)."[3]

---

3. As to the inner-halachic logic of this position, it was explained by his son R. Velvele, as related by R. Shlomo Yosef Zevin, in his *Ishim ve-Shitot*, 3rd ed. (Tel Aviv: 1966, 64). And see further the response of the Radbaz, no. 287.

See also R. Zeev Arieh Rabiner, *Gedolei Yisrael – Mekadeshei Shabbat* (Tel Aviv: 1970, 201–203). Rabiner, 133–134 also recalls that when the Hafetz Hayyim was told of a group of people who were desecrating the Sabbath, and asked to excommunicate all of them, he replied, "How do we know that within these many families, with their wives and children, there are not those who are seriously ill, and are cases of true *pikuah nefesh*?"

"While I was a *talmid*, it was told in the yeshiva, Netzach Yisrael, that the Rosh Yeshiva, Rav Yisrael Gustman, was once asked a question, without going into particular circumstances, whether a bride (before she completed counting the seven 'clean' days) could use the mikveh the day prior to her wedding, which is halachically allowed under certain circumstances. Rav Gustman confirmed that she could do this in that instance. He then received a telephone call from another Rav/Posek, heatedly inquiring how he could have approved such a decision. The story continues that the Rosh Yeshiva responded emphatically, 'You

Indeed, he may well have learned this from his great father R. Meshulam David ha-Levi Soloveitchik, (the *Beit ha-Levi*), who went so far as to rule that it was permitted to send a telegram on Shabbat to a *tzaddik* so that he pray for one seriously sick, since prayer is the most effective kind of treatment for the sick, and therefore it is included in the principle that danger unto life overrules any Sabbath strictures. And, of course, the same would be true of fasting on Yom Kippur, etc. And for much the same reason R. Hayyim's son, Reb Velvele (R. Yitzhak Zeev Soloveitchik), insisted that a certain sick person not fast on the ninth of Av, and even traveled far in Switzerland to tell him so directly, knowing that he would not do so without the Rabbi's personal intervention. And similarly, we are told that he ruled that R. Moshe Bernstein, the Rosh Yeshiva of Kamenetz, who was sick and paralyzed, eat on Yom Kippur, even if he felt good and wished to fast.[4]

---

are *machmir* on *hilchot niddah* and I am *machmir* on *mitzvat peru urevu*,' and then hung up the phone" (from a communication by Tzvi Mauer, Feb. 18, 2013).

4. See Shimon Yosef Meller, *Uvdot ve-Hanhagot le-Beit Brisk*, vol. 1 (Jerusalem: 1999, 43–44, 52–53, 67). And see further, p. 297, that once R. Velvele visited a *Talmid Hacham* who was critically ill, and he complained that due to his state he could not concentrate in his learning and his prayer. R. Velvele answered him saying, "Know that in your state of health, you are not obligated to keep any of the mitzvot, but one, and that is the mitzvah of 'take ye therefore very good heed unto yourselves'" (Deut. 4:15).

15

Human Dignity and Avoiding Embarrassing Others

AND SIMILARLY, we can well understand the rabbinic statement that גדול כבוד הבריות שדוחה לא תעשה שבתורה, that "great is the [need to] respect the dignity of individuals that it has precedence over a negative commandment of biblical authority (BT *Berachot* 19b, BT *Menachot* 36b, BT *Megillah* 3b, BT *Eruvin* 41b). I have discussed this concept in detail in my *Darkah shel Halachah* [Jerusalem: 2007], 34–43, 67–84, and again in my *Netivot Pesikah*, Jerusalem: 2008, 150–159, with numerous examples, a rich bibliography and a discussion as to the parameters of this principle. An examination of these sources will show that the principle of *Kevod ha-beriyot*, the dignity of the individual, takes precedent over mitzvot between man and his Maker, so that, for example, if one finds oneself wearing *shatnez* of rabbinic status, one need not disrobe to remove it in a public place, because one's nakedness would be shameful in public (Rambam, *Hilchot Kilayim* 10:29). Similarly, if someone suddenly realizes on Shabbat, when he is in an area called a *carmelit*, that his *tallit* is invalid, because, for example, one of the *tzitziyot* was torn off, he should not take the *tallit* off but continue wearing it until he reaches his home, since this would be shameful for him. And since "carrying" in a *carmelit* is only forbidden by rabbinic law, respect for his dignity overrides the rabbinic prohibition of carrying in a *carmelit*.[1] (See above, section 10, note 4.)

---

1. To further clarify the issue, we should explain that one is permitted to carry a kosher *tallit* on Shabbat. But if it is *pasul*, then one would be "carrying" the defective *tzitziyot* in a public place. See also *Shulhan Aruch Orah Hayyim* 13:3 the *Mishnah Berurah* ad loc., the detailed discussion of J. Davidson, in his *Hilchot*

A classic example of this is the famous ruling of the Rema. In order to understand it, we must begin with the fact that the Mishnah in *Beitzah* 5:2 rules that one does not conduct marriages on Shabbat or Yom Tov. The Gemara (BT *Beitzah* 37b) explains that this is in order to avoid any possible move towards permitting business transactions, since marriage is a sort of act of acquisition. This ruling is followed by the decisors; see e.g., *Shulhan Aruch Orah Hayyim* 339:4. However, there was a case in the time of the Rema (R. Moshe Isserles) of an orphan girl who had no relatives who was about to be married on a Friday (which was a common day for marriages), and at the last minute the parents of the bridegroom were dissatisfied with the size of her dowry, and the groom wished to retract from the marriage. Finally, after negotiations with the elders of the congregation, they came to an agreement, but by then the Sabbath had already begun. The Rema was approached with the question whether they could nonetheless complete the marriage ceremony, and he ruled positively, arguing that this is for her dignity, in order not to cause her greater shame, especially as the prohibition is only a rabbinic one, and "great is [the need] to respect the dignity of individuals that it has precedence over a negative commandment ..." And indeed this ruling is to be found in the Rema's annotations to the *Shulhan Aruch*.[2]

We see, then, how a great authority, as it were overruled a clear Mishnaic ruling to preserve the dignity of this poor orphan girl.

Yehuda Brandes, in his latest book *Aggadah le-Maaseh: Iyyunim be-Sugyot Meshulavot, Aggadah, Halachah u-Maaseh* (Jerusalem: 2011, vol. 1, 91 et seq.), reveals most persuasively how much the dignity of the individual is a key element in the mitzvah of *tzedakah*, charity. The notion of supporting people, orphans and so forth לפי כבוד, in accordance with the requirements of their dignity (M. *Ketubot* 6:5, BT *Ketubot* 67a), underscores that this is a basic requirement. "Dignity," he points out, "is a relative

Derech Eretz (Brooklyn, NY: 1999, 11–16, 141–142); and also the remarks of Tzvi Marx, *Halakha and Handicap* (Jerusalem: 1992–1993, 112–115).

2. See *Teshuvot ha-Rema*, ed. A. Ziv (Jerusalem: 1971, sect. 125, 488–495). For a detailed examination of this ruling in English, see Nissan E. Shulman, *Authority and Community: Polish Jewry in the Sixteenth Century* (Hoboken, NJ: 1986, 16–18). See further A. Ziv, *Rabbenu Moshe Isserles (Rema): Hayyav, Deotav, Haverav, Talmidav u-Tze'etzaav* (New York: 1972, 215–218), and for the further development of this ruling, see M. Raffeld, "*Me-Olamoh shel ha-Rema*," *Ha-Tzofeh* (Lag ba-Omer, 5764 [2004]). See also the astonishing story found in A. Tobolsky's *Hizaharu bi-Chevod Haverchem* (Bnei Brak: 1981, 225–227).

concept, dependant upon the social context of a person. The differences between one person and another are conditioned by his economic status, his lineage (*yichus*), position in the community, education and many and varied additional elements." He continues to develop this theme citing examples from the areas of damages and recompense for shaming a person (M. *Ketubot* 3:7, M. *Baba Kama* 8:1, M. *Arachin* 3:4: It is always according to the [status of the] shamer and the shamed).

More recently, I learned of another somewhat remarkable example of how this principle functioned in practice in the case of Rabbi Moshe Kleers, the Rabbi of Tiberias around the year 1934. It is related in A. Tobolsky's *Hizaharu bi-Chevod Haverchem*, Bnei Brak: 1981, 326–327, (citing the pamphlet *Mi-Pi Dodi: Zichronot mi-Pi R"M Kleers Shnat 1934, Meorot* 12):

> On one of the Sabbaths, Rabbi Kleers, the Rabbi of Tiberias, was informed that it appeared that the *eruv* was faulty [and, as a consequence, people could not carry things within the town], and had not been correctly organized before the Sabbath. He looked into the matter and ascertained that it had been set up by the local Sephardi Rabbi and under his directions. He turned to those who questioned its *kashrut*, and ruled that it was in order, but that he had not the time to explain his reasoning.
>
> He was on the very best of terms with this Sephardi Rabbi, and they both had the deepest respect for one another. On the following Sunday he came to the Rabbi and said to him: "I have to clarify a difficult halachic issue, and I require your help." The Sephardi Rabbi smiled and said: "Surely you do not need my help. Are you teasing me?" He replied: "I am not feeling well; am rather weak, and find it difficult to sort this issue out by myself." "Please come in," said the Rabbi, "and we will study the matter together." "No, I would prefer if we could both go together to the synagogue," which was a little further away.
>
> They both went to the local Beit Midrash which was empty, and R. Moshe pulled out a volume of the Talmud, the Tractate *Eruvin*, and they both sat at length analyzing an issue in depth, with the various commentators until finally the Sephardi Rabbi understood what this was all about. Deeply disturbed, he cried out: "I erred last Friday in the preparation of the *eruv*." Rabbi Kleers calmed him down, explaining that it was for this reason that he had come to him. "And how did you act, last Shabbat?" asked the Sephardi Rabbi. "I

> ruled that the *eruv* was *kasher*, in order," he replied. The Rabbi was astounded: "How come?" he asked. Rabbi Kleers smiled: "The laws of *eruvin* are merely of rabbinic authority, while the dignity of the Torah [i.e., the Rabbi] and the individual is of biblical authority (*mi-de-Oraita*) . . ." he replied.

And yet another very moving story in this vein is recorded by the great *Maspid* Reb Shalom Schwadron, in R. Paysach J. Krohn's *The Maggid Speaks: Favorite Stories and Parables of Rabbi Shalom Schwadron shlita, Maggid of Jerusalem*, Brooklyn, NY: 1987, 64–65:

> In a small town far away from Kovno, a local *rav* had erred in a ruling he had made on a religious question posed to him. Though not everyone realized his mistake, two devious and mischievous individuals knew that their *rav* had blundered badly. He had forgotten that the very same situation on which he had ruled was discussed in the Shach, one of the primary commentaries of the *Shulchan Aruch* (Code of Jewish Law).
>
> Seeking to humiliate their *rav*, the two miscreants sent a letter to R. Yitzchak Elchonon, [Spektor, 1817–1896], in which they posed the same question. They knew that R. Yitzchak Elchonon's answer would be in accordance with the Shach's ruling as opposed to their *rav*'s opinion. Once armed with R. Yitzchak Elchonon's letter of reply they would show it around to the community at large and this would shame and disgrace the *rav*.
>
> When R. Yitzchak Elchonon received the letter, his first reaction was one of surprise. For although he had received queries from people in this particular town before, he remembered that he had never received any from either of these men. Why would they be writing now, he wondered, and why would they be sending a question with which any *rav*, including their local *rav*, would surely be familiar?
>
> Therefore, he investigated and learned that these men were exceptionally argumentative and had a history of causing trouble in the community.
>
> R. Yitzchak Elchonon suspected at once that the two men were contemplating a plot to embarrass their *rav*, and he sought to foil their plot. First he sent a letter to the two men with the wrong answer to the question, ruling exactly as their *rav* had ruled. Then, the very next day, he sent them a telegram which would arrive before the letter, saying that he had erred in his written ruling, and that they

> should disregard the letter with the wrong ruling that would soon be coming.
>
> Thus the mischievous twosome would not be able to use either the letter or the telegram to defame their *rav*, for the letter agreed with the *rav* and the telegram clearly indicated that even the great and sainted R. Yitzchak Elchonon had erred in this matter – just as their *rav* had.

Reb Shalom heard this story from R. Isser Zalman Melzer (1870–1953) who, when he told it, his eyes would fill with tears, so deeply was he moved by the length to which Reb Yitzachk Elchonon would go to save another Jew from embarrassment.

The need for extreme sensitivity not to mortify a person, when he is mistaken, and even if he is sinful is vividly expressed in a tale told of the father of the Baal Shem Tov (1700–1760), as recorded in Martin Buber's *Tales of the Hasidim: The Early Masters*, New York: 1947, 35–36:

> Rabbi Eliezer, the Baal Shem's father, lived in a village. He was so hospitable that he placed guards at the outskirts of the village and had them stop poor wayfarers and bring them to his house for food and shelter. Those in Heaven rejoiced at his doing, and once they decided to try him. Satan offered to do this, but the prophet Elijah begged to be sent in his stead. In the shape of a poor wayfarer, with knapsack and staff, he came to Rabbi Eliezer's house on a Sabbath afternoon, and said the greeting. Rabbi Eliezer ignored the desecration of the Sabbath, for he did not want to mortify the man. He invited him to the meal and kept him in his house. Nor did he utter a word of reproof the next morning, when his guest took leave of him. Then the prophet revealed himself and promised him a son who would make the eyes of the people of Israel see the light.

(See also above, section 13, "How to Welcome Guests.")

We may also point to another expression of this basic concept of the dignity of the individual, as it is reflected in rabbinic and post-rabbinic exegesis. The last verse of *Parshat Yitro* (Exodus 20:26) is, "Neither shalt thou go by steps unto mine altar, that thy nakedness be not discovered thereon." This verse is clearly speaking of the need for great respect and modesty when approaching the Temple – or Tabernacle – altar. The following verse, at the beginning of *Parshat Mishpatim* (21:1) is, "Now these are the judgments which thou shalt set before them." The verses, in the next two chapters, list commandments relating to the relationship between man and his neighbor. But the Rabbis of the Tannaitic period linked the last and the first verse of these two consecutive chapters. Thus in BT *Sanhedrin* 7b, Bar-Kappara asks from where do we learn that judges have to be careful, or considerate and patient in judgment. (M. *Avot* 1:1). And his reply is from the proximity of these two verses, the first reinterpreted as meaning do not go up in haughtiness (ולא תעלה במעלות), where dealing with "judgments" (משפטים) of the following verse. Thus a verse already referring to a need for *ritual* respect is reinterpreted homiletically to refer to the requirement for *interpersonal* respect – a midrashic transfer from the realm of the ritual to that of the social-ethical.

And so too in yet another such Tannaitic statement on the same couplet of verses. For in BT *Sanhedrin* 7b, R. Eliezer inquires:

> From whence do we know that a judge must not step over the heads of the holy people (שלא יפסע על ראשי עם קודש)?[3]

And again the reply is from the proximity of these two verses, namely that he, the judge of *mishpatim*, should not haughtily step over the heads of the litigants. The author of *Torah Temimah*, R. Baruch Halevy Epstein, to this verse (223, note 3) further explains (in contradistinction to Rashi's explanation ad loc.):

> That the Rabbi or judge should not look disparagingly upon the common folk as though they are not considered worth anything in his eyes, so that he brushes them aside from his thoughts as unworthy of his consideration, and does not treat them with any form of respect.

Here we find a total interpretative transferal from the simple plain meaning of the ritual requirement in the Temple to that of the area of decency and respect even to people who one might regard as being of a lower class.[4]

The subject of human dignity was discussed very clearly by Samuel

3. On this, see A. Büchler's classic article in *Disserationes in honorem Dr. Eduardi Mahler* (Budapest: 1937, 379–405).

4. We may also note the very fascinating and deeply significant statement of the great medieval commentator, R. Avraham ibn Ezra, to that same verse at the beginning of *Parshat Mishpatim*. He writes as follows:

Belkin, in his illuminating volume, *In his Image: The Jewish Philosophy of Man as Expressed in Rabbinic Tradition*, London, New York, Toronto: 1960, 107–108. Here I can do no better than to quote him in full:

> In cases of indignity, the Mishnah does consider the standing or place in the community of the humiliator and the one whom he humiliates. Where humiliation is concerned, the rabbis admitted a relation between the sensitivity of the individual, the place of his humiliation, and the station and intention of the one who brought the indignity upon him. The same mishnah, therefore, says that if a man slips off a roof and injures someone, he is liable for the injuries but not for the indignity inflicted because there was no intention to inflict injury. A distinction is also made between an indignity suffered by an ordinary person or a minor, and an indignity suffered by a dignitary of a mature person (Tosefta *Baba Kama* 9:12). Consideration is also given to the fact that a man is more deeply hurt when he is humiliated in the street than when he is humiliated in a public bath (B. *Baba Kama* 86b).

> After the people of Israel said to Moses [on hearing the first two of the Ten Commandments], "speak thou with us, [and we will hear; but let not God speak with us, lest we die]" (Exod. 20:19), the Lord said to Moses as he drew right unto the cloud, "Thus thou shalt say unto the children of Israel" (v. 22), and he began to caution them against [making] gods of gold (v. 23), and that he would make a covenant with them when he descended [from the Mount], namely, that God alone would be their God, and He taught them the Commandments and the mitzvot, that he should tell them, that if they would keep them, He would make with them the covenant. And at the end He set them these conditions, namely the sections beginning with v. 20 in chap. 23, "Behold, I send an Angel before thee [to keep thee in the way and to bring thee unto the place which I have prepared]." And the main thrust of that chapter is to uproot idolatry from their land when they entered it. And so Moses explained [this] to them *before* the making of the covenant.

According to our understanding of Ibn Ezra's statement, the acceptance of all the social mitzvot listed in *Mishpatim*, and, of course, the destruction of idols and idolatry, constituted a condition prior to the finalization of a covenant between God and Israel. This surely indicates Ibn Ezra's valuation of social mitzvot, alongside with the required expurgation of idolatry.

The great concern of our Sages with the exact definition of indignity and humiliation is not surprising, for they were deeply conscious of the dignity of man who was created in the image of God. For them, to inflict indignity on any man, be he a freeman or a Canaanite slave (M. *Baba Kama* 8:3), was one of the most serious offenses. Whoever humiliates his fellow man in public, the Talmud declares, is as if he had shed blood, for "the red disappears and the white comes," making the infliction of indignity akin to an act of murder (B. *Baba Metzia* 58b). Rabbi Eleazer of Modiin included those who humiliate a fellow man in public among those who have no share in the world to come, (M. *Avot* 3:11). We can, therefore, understand why the relative status of the injured and the humiliator plays a great part in determining the seriousness of the offense. A man must compensate his neighbor whom he humiliates, primarily because by inflicting an indignity on his fellow he commits a crime against the dignity of man.

Rabbi Akiba and some of his disciples were of the opinion that it is impossible to determine the relative worth of human personalities. Rabbi Meir, therefore, said that for purposes of indemnity even the most insignificant persons are regarded as "freemen who lost their possessions, for they are all equally the children of Abraham, Isaac and Jacob" (B. *Baba Kama* 86a). Rabbi Akiba, too, strikingly expressed the respect which our Sages had for the dignity of man. The Mishnah states:

> This is the general rule: All is in accordance with the person's honor. Rabbi Akiba said: Even the poorest in Israel are looked upon as free men who have lost their possessions for they are the sons of Abraham, Isaac and Jacob. It once happened that a man unloosed a woman's hair in the street and she came before Rabbi Akiba and he made him liable for four hundred *zuz*. Said the culprit: Rabbi, extend for me the time, and Rabbi Akiba extended him the time [for payment]. He [the culprit] watched her standing at the entry of her courtyard and he broke before her a cruse that held an *issar* worth of oil. She then unloosed her hair and scooped up the oil in her hand and laid her hand on her head. He set up witnesses against her and came before Rabbi Akiba and said to him: Rabbi, should I give to such a one [who has no regard for her own dignity] four hundred *zuz*? Rabbi Akiba answered: Thou has said naught at all. For he who inflicts wounds upon himself, even though he is not permitted to do so, is not culpable; but if others wound him they are culpable (M. *Baba Kama* 8:6).

Rabbi Akiba here taught two profound lessons. First, that one cannot set relative standards for human dignity; that all upon whom indignity is inflicted are judged to be freemen, for human rights are not bestowed upon men in proportion to their worldly possessions. Second, that even if one does not stand upon his dignity, and even if he demeans his own dignity, it is forbidden to others to inflict indignity on him. Human dignity is not determined by one's personal attitude toward it or himself. Dignity graces man because he is made in the image of God and no man has the right to inflict indignity on his fellow being.

See further Nachum Amsel, *The Jewish Encyclopedia of Moral and Ethical Issues*, Northvale, New Jersey and London: 1996, 112–115 (no. 28, "Human Dignity"), especially p. 113a.

Not only the dignity of the individual may take precedence over ritual mitzvot, but so too the convenience of the congregation, in rabbinic parlance *tircha de-tzibbura* (or *torach ha-tzibbur*, in Hebrew). Under this rubric the Rabbis permitted the shortening of liturgical prayers (*Response of the Rashba*, vol. 1, no. 215, based on a *baraita* in BT *Berachot* 31a), hastening certain Torah readings (BT *Yoma* 70a; Rambam, *Hilchot Tefillah* 12:23; *Shulhan Aruch Orah Hayyim* 133:3, etc.), cutting out certain Torah passages from the liturgy (BT *Berachot* 12b; JT *Berachot* 1:5), reducing the number of *tekiyot* on Rosh ha-Shanah (*Rif* Rosh ha-Shanah ad fin.; Rambam, *Hilchot Shofar* 3:10; *Shulhan Aruch Orah Hayyim* 592:1), and others.[5] All these measures, related to ritual mitzvot, were taken for the convenience of the congregation. For even the slightest delay in the service can be considered sufficiently vexing to the congregation or the individual as to affect a ritual mitzvah. Thus, even though the *Shulhan Aruch Orah Hayyim* 8:9 requires a person to examine the threads of his *tallit* before he makes the blessing over it, if he is called up to the Torah reading and he is wearing his *tallit* he need not check it out, since this would constitute an inconvenience for the congregation by causing a delay (*torach ha-tzibbur*), (*Taz, Orah Hayyim* 13:3; cf. *Shaarei Teshuvah*, sect. 10).[6]

---

5. See in detail *Encylopedia Talmudit*, vol. 20 (Jerusalem: 1991, 662–678). See also my *On Changes in Jewish Liturgy: Options and Limitations* (Jerusalem, New York: 2010, 72); and cf. below, sect. 23, n. 4.

6. See on this R. Jacob Davidson, *Hilchot Derech Eretz* (Brooklyn, NY: 1991), 15–16; and 8–9 with regard a single individual, where he shows that the principle of ברוב עם הדרת מלך – "the greater number of people the greater the honor to the King," meaning that there is importance in having many people attend a prayer session, nonetheless, if this requirement causes even a slight delay to an

I think that the principle התורה חסה על ממונם של ישראל, namely that the Torah shows concern for peoples' financial state, and indicates methods of avoidance of impoverishment, especially if they might result from observing mitzvot, comes under the same rubric. For poverty is one of the most degrading situations (see *Leviticus Rabbah* 34:6; BT *Baba Batra* 137b, etc.). The biblical sources for this principle have been laid out by Rabbenu Behaye in his commentary to Exodus 12:4, and are found in early rabbinic sources such as the *Torat Kohanim Metzora* to Leviticus 14:36:

> On what did the Torah show concern? On his pottery and his jug.

The meaning is that one who sees a sign of suspected leprosy in his house, should remove the pottery jars from the house, i.e., even the cheapest utensils he has, before the Cohen comes to examine it. For up to that time everything remains pure. However, after the Cohen's examination, if he finds it to be leprous, all the contents of the room will become unclean. And, as is well-known, pottery, when it becomes unclean – impure, cannot be purified, but must be broken up and thrown away. So the verse tells us:

> Then the priest shall command that they empty the house, before the priest goes into it to see the plague, that all that is in the house be not made unclean: and afterwards the priest shall go in to see the house. (Leviticus 14:36)

(See above section 2, ad fin.)

In BT *Rosh ha-Shanah* 25b, and BT *Menahot* 76b and 85a, additional biblical sources for this concern are brought. It is for this same reason that we are told in M. *Keritot* 1:7, that Rabban Shimon ben Gamliel brought down the price of the bird-offerings that women brought to the Temple after giving birth.

And here I can do no better than quote extensively from an important essay by the late Prof. Marvin Fox, entitled "The Mishna as a Source for Jewish Ethics," (*Marvin Fox: Collected Essays on Philosophy and Judaism*, ed. J. Neusner, vol. 3, *Ethics, Reflections*, New York: 2001, chapter 26, 87–88):

---

individual, disturbing him in some way, the above-mentioned principle which is *God*-directed, is overridden by the *human* requirement. (See *Orah Hayyim* 8:5, and *Mishnah Berurah* ad loc. sect. 11; *Shaarei Teshuvah* sect. 7 in the name of the *Mabit*.)

In some other cases we find rulings which appear to depend on value preferences, but without any explicit statement. The Torah sets forth extensive rules concerning one who is afflicted with *nega*, a skin eruption which requires that the person be examined by a priest and then quarantined if he has the disease. A treatise of the Mishna is devoted to an exposition of the details of these laws. In M. *Negaim* 3:2 we find a striking exception to the Torah rule that when a person shows the symptoms of this skin eruption he should be brought immediately to the priest for examination. The Mishna text rules that if the eruption appears on a bridegroom, we delay until the end of the seven days of the marriage feast before bringing him to the priest. Similarly, for any person, if what appears to be a *nega* erupts during a festival, the examination by the priest is delayed until the end of the festival. No explanation is given here, or in the parallel tannaitic source in *Torat Kohanim* for this delay, but the reason seems obvious. The decision is to spare the bridegroom and his bride the pain of interrupting the festive celebration of their marriage, and to spare the householder and his family the pain of interrupting the celebration of the festival if it should turn out that they must be quarantined. Here we have a case where nothing is explicitly stated in the texts before us in justification of the value decision which gives priority to the completion of the festive celebrations. In fact, we can only infer that this is the reason. In any case, however, a choice had to be made as to whether the Torah's rules about quarantining the person suffering from this skin eruption should be immediately enforced, or to give prior status to the Torah's rules concerning the celebration of a marriage or a festival. Here again, even if we conjecture that the decision is based on humane moral considerations, we should remember that these considerations are not imposed from without, but reflect a choice between competing values in the Torah itself. (Cf. above, section 2.)

In another setting, and in a different mode of response, the Mishna advises us, in certain cases, how to benefit a householder by evading the stringencies of the law. In M. *Maaser Sheni* 4:4 the text begins with the permissive statement, מערימים על מעשר שני, "We may circumvent the laws of the second tithe." The situation here is that the householder is required by the Torah to bring the second tithe to Jerusalem and eat it there. If it is difficult for him to bring the actual produce to Jerusalem, he is permitted by the Torah to redeem it for its monetary value and bring the money of redemption to Jerusalem to spend there.

> In this case the Torah requires that he add one fifth of the value to the sum of redemption. Our Mishna goes on to teach us how to circumvent the duty to pay this added fifth. The technical details of the procedure are of no direct interest for our purpose. What matters is that we have an open invitation to evade the law, and a detailed procedure outlined for doing so legally. Here we seem to have a case in which the Sages gave preference to their concern for the protection of the farmer's financial interest against the explicit teaching of the Torah. Understandably, they sought and found a technically legal method, but even they themselves call it הערמה an evasion or circumvention of the law.
>
> We have a similar case in M. *Temurah* 5:1, which opens with the question, "How can we circumvent [or evade] the law of the first-born animals?" – כיצד מערימים על הבכור. The concern is to evade the restriction which the Torah imposes against dedicating a first-born animal for sacrificial use other than that specified. The owner would like to use it for a sacrifice which he already owes, and thus save himself added expense, since the first-born animal must be given to the priest in any case, and the owner will derive no personal benefit from it. The text before us outlines a procedure for evading the law so as to benefit the owner of the animal. As in the former case, no direct justification is given for this legalized circumvention of a Torah-given obligation. These are cases where it would appear that the *Sages gave priority to their concern for the financial interests of the farmers*, even if it had to be achieved by designing a legal mode of evasion. In an unusual move, they sacrifice straightforward honesty and fulfillment of duty to the desire to save expense. We may well have here cases in which *the value of saving money is given priority in the legal system* without any justification in the system itself. [My emphasis, D.S.]

Even this somewhat random selection of examples – and there are many more such in rabbinic sources[7] – underscores the concern for the finan-

---

7. Another example of this principle may be found in BT *Berachot* 35b, where we read: "The earlier generations used to bring fruits in [to their houses] over roofs and through courtyards . . . in order not to have to separate their tithes." In my booklet *Legitimacy and Necessity: Scientific Disciplines and the Learning of Talmud* (Jerusalem, 2006: 24–25), I pointed out that though the Hazon Ish expressed his reservations from the use of manuscript testimony in determining halachic rulings (ibid., 23–24), and was loathe to suggest textual emendations of

cial well-being of the individual, and in the above cases despite apparent *ritual* requirements, demonstrates how the human concern as it were override the ritual one. And in this connection we might call attention to a responsum by R. Yosef Shaul Nathansohn (Galicia c. 1808–1875) in his *Shoel u-Meshiv, Mahadura Tlitaah* (part 1, Lemberg 1870, no. 104), who in order to save a family from great personal financial loss and shame ruled leniently using both these principles and intertwining them.

As we stated earlier on, poverty is one of the most humanly degrading social forces, and hence, התורה חסה על ממונם של ישראל. This leads us on directly to the issue of charity.

Talmudic and rabbinic sources on the basis of manuscript evidence, nonetheless:

> Paradoxically enough, one of the Hazon Ish's very daring emendations in the Talmud is actually born out by the Munich manuscript he so denigrated. Thus in B. *Berakhot* 35b we read: "The earlier generations used to bring the fruits in [to their houses] over roofs and through courtyards . . . in order not to have to separate their tithes." The Hazon Ish writes: "The word 'courtyards' is clearly an error, for the main way of entry is through the courtyards" (*Ma'asrot*, 5:15). He bolsters his emendation with suitable references. B. *Gittin* 81a, B. *Bava Metzia* 88a, B. *Menahot* 67b, and Rambam *Ma'asrot* 4:1 – in all of which this word is missing. And so, indeed it is in the Munich manuscript, as cited by Rabinovicz in his *Dikdukei Soferim* to *Berakhot* (p. 193). Furthermore, Rabinovicz, in long note (n. 4, ad loc.), discussed this matter, proving that since the Talmudic statement in *Berakhot* "is that of Rabbi Yohanan, and he holds that a courtyard obligates tithes, and everyone agrees that a courtyard obligates tithes [at least] by rabbinic ruling," the word should indeed be deleted. He also notes that the *Tzelah* already pointed this out. (And see the continuation of his lengthy note, with additional comments of the Av Beit Din of Lvov.) The Hazon Ish, then, could have gained an additional verification of his emendation from the manuscript, and added argumentation from Rabinovicz's comments.

See also my *Netivot Pesikah* (Jerusalem: 2008, 31–34). See most recently for an analysis of the Hazon Ish's position on this issue, in Benjamin Brown, *Ha-Hazon Ish: Ha-Posek, ha-Maamin u-Manhig ha-Mahapecha ha-Haredit* (Jerusalem: 2011, 384–397); and see further S.Z. Havlin's critical review of Brown's book in "Katharsis: A Critical Review" in the *Humanities and Social Sciences* (18, 2012: 43–49), for a somewhat different perspective on this issue.

16

The Overriding Importance of Charity

THE GENERAL THESIS in the earlier chapters, namely the ascendancy of social over ritual mitzvot, is reflected in yet a different halachic area. The *Sheiltot* (to *Terumah*, *Sheilta* 62) writes:

> The house of Israel is obligated to give charity from their monies to whosoever is in need thereof. And he who shows pity for the impoverished is likened by the Holy One blessed be He as if he did good deeds to God himself, as it is stated (Exodus 25:2), "that they should bring *to Me* an offering," (i.e., if they give charity to the poor, it is as though they are giving it to God himself).

And in BT *Baba Batra* 10a we read in the name of R. Yohanan:

> What is the meaning of the verse in Proverbs 19:17, "He who hath pity upon the poor lendeth unto the Lord"? If it were not written, it would be impossible to say it, namely that "the borrower is servant to the lender" (22:7).

Rashi explains that he who has pity for the poor it is as though he is lending to God, and "the borrower" – God – becomes, as it were, "servant to the lender."

And the Netziv, returning to the *Sheiltot* (in his *Haamek Shealah*, 413) notes, that the author of the *Sheiltot* derived his ruling from a biblical verse relating to donations made to the tabernacle, and nonetheless, he learned from it that charity given to the poor is of greater virtue than money given to the temple itself. (And we have seen above [section 4 *Ha-Osek be-Mitzvah Patur min ha-Mitzvah*: The case of prayer and Torah] that one interrupts Torah study to give charity.) (Cf. above, section 4.)

And this too is the view of the Tosafot in BT *Baba Batra* 9a, who learn this from Rav Asi's statement, that: "Charity may be weighed against all other mitzvot, as it is said (Nehemiah 10:33), 'Also we made ordinances (mitzvot) for us to charge ourselves yearly with the third of a shekel for the service of the house of our God.'" And though this verse is talking of money for the Temple, Rav Asi learned from it – and from the plural "mitzvot" – that charity is even weightier than donations to the Temple.

This triggered off a discussion among the decisors, summarized in *Shulchan Aruch Yoreh Deah* 249:16:

> There is an opinion that the mitzvah [to give to] the synagogue is greater than the mitzvah of charity, and the mitzvah of charity to youths or to the sick is greater than that of the synagogue. (*Mahri Kolon, Shoresh* 128, in the name of the *Tashbetz* in the name of the *Rash* to Yerushalmi *Zeraim*.)

But the Gaon of Vilna (252:2) stated explicitly that charity is greater than the building of a synagogue.

This also seems to be reflected in a passage in *Pesikta Rabbati*, chapter 6 (25b), where the question is raised: Why did Solomon not build the Temple with his father David's treasures? For the verse in 1 Kings 1:51 states:

> "So was ended all the works that King Solomon made for the house of the Lord. And Solomon brought in the things which David his father had dedicated: even the silver, and the gold, and the vessels, did he put among the treasures of the house of the Lord." – There are those who explain this . . . negatively . . . For there was a famine in the days of David for three years, and David had several treasure houses of silver and gold that had been dedicated to the building of the Temple. And he should have used them to save lives, and he did not do so. God said to him: My children are dying of starvation and you are hoarding money to build a Temple. Should you not have [used it to] save lives? Since you did not do so, by your life, your son Solomon will make no use of it [when building the Temple].

Hence the verse states that only when "was ended all the works" did Solomon bring these treasures to the house of God. So charity, and certainly saving the lives of the hungry, have greater priority even than building God's Temple.

And in Yerushalmi *Shekalim*, chapter 2 ad fin., we read that Rabbi Avun (=Avin) made these gates for the great synagogue (in Tiberias). Rabbi Mana (mid-fourth century C.E.) came to him, and he said (boastingly): "See what I have done." To which Rabbi Mana responded by quoting the verse in Hosea 8:14: "'For Israel hath forgotten his Maker, and buildeth Temples ...' Are there no [poor] people who are studying Torah?" And the *Tashbetz* has an additional reading: or sick people who lie among the rubbish. The *Korban ha-Edah* further elaborates: He should have used his money to help people's livelihood ... It would be better to give to poor Torah scholars who are involved in mitzvot at all times than for building edifices. And the Rambam summarizes thus in *Hilchot Matnot Aniyim* 1:2:

> One is obligated to be more careful with the mitzvah of charity than all other mitzvot, for charity – *tzedakah* – is a sign of the righteousness – *tzedek* – of the offspring of Abraham our forefather.

In view of all that has been said above, it is surely clear that charity, as a mitzvah towards one's fellow man, must be seen as preferential to building a synagogue or even the Temple, which are mitzvot between man and his Maker. And this, indeed, is the view of the Tosafot as mentioned earlier.

Indeed the Shinyever Rebbe, R. Yehezkel Shraga Halberstam, (the author of *Divrei Yehezkel*, Podgorze: 1901), is reported by his son as having said in the name of the Baal Shem Tov, that the city of Brody would always be protected, because there hang on the gates of the city two charity boxes, one of general charity, and one for free loans (*gemilut hesed*).[1]

And here I believe we may add another example which demonstrates the special status of charity. The Talmud in BT *Ketubot* 50a teaches us that:

> In Usha they made a ruling that one may not give away (המבזבז) more than one fifth [of his assets], lest one fall a burden on the community. And it once happened that a certain person wished to give away more than a fifth, and his fellows did not let him do so. And who was this person? R. Yeshevav. And who did not let him do so? R. Akiva. Said Rav Nahman, and some say R. Aha bar Yaakov, "What is the biblical

1. See Yehezkel Shraga Fraenkel, *Rabbenu ha-Kadosh mi-Shinyeve* (Ramat Gan: 1992, vol. 1, 262). And see below Appendix.

> source [for this ruling]? [Jacob's vow that] 'and of all that thou shalt give me, I will surely give the tenth unto thee'" (Genesis 28:22).

This biblical verse reads עשר אעשרנו, *aser aasrenu* – usually translated "I shall surely give a tenth." But from the doubled use of the root *aser* (tenth), the Rabbis learned that one may only give up to twice one-tenth, i.e., a fifth.

This ruling was followed by the decisors. And indeed the Rambam at the end of *Hilchot Arachin ve-Haramim* uses very sharp words, declaring that one who gives away all his possessions – this is not an act of piety but of foolishness, and he is considered a *Hasid shoteh*, a "silly Hasid." Similarly, Rema to the *Shulhan Aruch Orah Hayyim* 656 tells us that one shouldn't waste one's money on a splendid *etrog*, etc. However, there are other texts that suggest that a person may give away more than a fifth in order to carry out certain mitzvot. Thus, in BT *Pesahim* 49ab we read that a person should give away *all* his wealth in order to [be able to afford] marrying the daughter of a *Talmid Hacham*, or to marry off his daughter similarly. And, so we are told in BT *Ketubot* 53a, did Rav Papa, while Kalba Savua gave *half* his belongings to R. Akiva (63a). And so, indeed, rules the Rambam in *Hilchot Issurei Biah* 21:32, and this also is the ruling in *Shulhan Aruch Even ha-Ezer* 2:6.

There is, however, no contradiction between the various rulings, even the two apparently contradictory rulings of the Rambam. In the one case, he is talking about dedications to the Temple, to sacrifices, to *hekdesh*, etc. – i.e., to ritual obligations. On the other hand, he is talking of interpersonal mitzvot, such as making the right kind of marriage. Jacob's vow was to give his tithes to God, and as such they could not exceed a fifth. But a careful reading of the relevant sources makes it clear that charity to *poor people* may exceed that amount. (However, see JT *Peah* 1:1, and M.M. Kasher, *Torah Shelemah*, vol. 5, Jerusalem: 1935, 1151.) Of course, one must not act in an excessive fashion, which might ultimately have negative results, such as impoverishing oneself which will lead one to become a burden upon the community.

In view of the above, I think we can have a deeper understanding of the halachah regarding charity on Shabbat. For the Talmud in BT *Shabbat* 150a rules in the name of R. Elazar that one assigns, or apportions (פוסקין) charity to the needy on Shabbat. In this he follows the view of Beit Hillel in Tosefta *Shabbat* (16 [17]:22, ed. Lieberman, 79–80), as opposed to that of Beit Shammai. (See Tosafot *Shabbat* ibid., ad loc.) And, indeed, this is the ruling in the Rambam (*Hilchot Shabbat* 24:5), and *Shulhan Aruch Orah Hayyim* 306:6. The other examples of permitted activities, such as to watch over public affairs (לפקח על עסקי רבים) etc., which are listed in these sources, are all interpersonal *mitzvot,* and, of course, those concerned with the public have the additional component that we mentioned earlier on, when discussing the needs of the community (צרכי רבים and צרכי ציבור). And here we may add a revealing point made by the author of the *Mishnah Berurah* (ibid., 27). He writes as follows:

> Assigning charity: To poor people or the synagogue. And indeed to give an object to the synagogue – this has been an accepted practice, even though we say one does not take upon oneself to donate the value of someone (ערך פלוני עלי), and one does not consecrate on Shabbat, as we see below 339 [4] (see *Mishnah Berurah* 23), that is consecration to the altar or the upkeep of the Temple. But our consecrations (הקדשות) are permitted, because they are not sacred but profane (חולין) . . . . [i.e., they are to other *people* and not to the *Temple*].

We seen, then, that charity and other interpersonal mitzvot can override certain Shabbat restrictions, while in other cases these restrictions are in force.

Indeed, it appears that in certain aspects charity is weightier even than Shabbat, as noted by R. Eliyahu ha-Ithmari, in his *Meil Tzedakah*, Izmir 1731, section 501, 216, and other later authorities, (though this too is a point of controversy). See the as yet unpublished *Nefesh ha-Yefeh* by R. Rahamim Palache, ed. Hezki Sofer, 394, and note 445. (I am grateful to him for making his work available to me.)

This notion expresses itself in a variety of folkloristic motifs. Thus, for example, in *Zichron Tov*, by R. Yitzhak Landau (Pietrokov 1892, *Inyanei Emunah* 2, p. 7), we read that R. Yitzhak of Naschiz (1789–1868), by his son R. Mordechai, the following story (from the year 1867):

> My father, of blessed memory, told me the following. He was engaged in trading and after each journey he would put aside a small amount of his earnings until he collected enough to purchase an *etrog*. Once he managed to collect six silver rubles, and he set off to Brody to buy an *etrog*, for he was still in the city of Leshno. And on the way he met a water-carrier who was transporting water with his horse, but his horse had died, and he was weeping and groaning. The Rabbi [i.e., my father] said to him, "Why are you crying?" The water-carrier explained to him [that his horse had died]. The Rabbi immediately gave him his six silver rubles, and brought with them another horse. The Rabbi remarked, "And what difference is there

> between the different mitzvot for God? This too is a mitzvah for God (מצות ה')." (The writer – probably R. Yitzhak Landau – added: We have heard that he said in a jocular manner, "All the world makes a blessing over an *etrog*, and I shall do so over a horse!") However, in the end, through his merit they brought him to his house a very beautiful *etrog*.

This tale has recently been analyzed and discussed in detail by Admiel Kosman, in an article published in *Kabbalah* 10, 2004, 238–248, entitled "*Ha-'Yad' ha-Mushetet ve-ha-'Regel' ha-Oleh*." He referred us to other versions of this story (238, note 45) and similar such motifs (239, note 53), to which much more can be added. (See, e.g., Haim Schwarzbaum, *Studies in Jewish and World Folklore*, Berlin: 1968, index s.v. Charity, 512b, especially, 277–280.) Setting aside his interpretation, we would see the main thrust of this tale as teaching us that he considered charity to the poor water-carrier as more important a mitzvah than having a splendid *etrog* (even though the beauty of the *etrog* is an essential part of the mitzvah, since it is derived from the biblical commandment to take a "*pri etz hadar*," literally "a beautiful fruit" [Leviticus 23:40]).

And there is a remarkable homily in *Leviticus Rabbah* 31:1, ed. Margaliot, 714–715:

> "Thy charity (צדקתך) also, O God, is very high" (Psalms 71:19) – R. Ami asked R. Shmuel bar Nahman [as follows]: Since I have heard of you that you are a master of *aggadah*, what is [the meaning of the verse] "Thy charity also, O God, is very high"? He replied: "Just as the people of this world require charity the one from the other, so too those in the celestial world require charity the one from the other. That is what the verse in Ezekiel 10:2 means, "And he spoke unto the man clothed with linen . . ."

To understand the connection with the verse in Ezekiel, we must see the continuation of the homily in *Leviticus Rabbah* 26:8, which has a fuller version:

> God said to the angel, and the angel said to the Cherub, "The Lord has decreed that I may not enter into your realm. Therefore, do unto me a charitable deed and give me two of your embers that I may not be instantly burned." And he lifted them up and gave them to the man clothed in linen.

(See the whole chapter 10 in Ezekiel for a fuller understanding of this homily.)

What I believe we have here is a symbolic parallelism between human interpersonal righteousness and charity and, as it were, an equivalence in the celestial realm, indicating that what one does below has a sort of celestial importance, and consequently a primary status.

There can surely be no clearer and more powerful expression of the primacy of the mitzvah of *tzedakah* – charity, than that which the Rambam wrote in *Hilchot Matnot Aniyim* 10:1:

> One is obligated to take care in the [practice of the] mitzvah of *tzedakah* more than all other positive commandments. For charity is the characteristic of the righteous of the seed of Abraham our forefather, as it is said, "For I know him, that he will command his children and his household after him, that they shall keep the way of the Lord, to do *tzedakah* and judgment . . ." (Genesis 18:19). And the throne of Israel will not be established and the religion of truth will not stand fast but through *tzedakah* [a reference to Proverbs 16:12], as it said, "In righteousness (*bi-tzedakah*) shalt thou be established" (Isaiah 54:14). And Israel will not be redeemed but through *tzedakah*, as it is said, "Zion shall be redeemed with judgment, and her converts with righteousness (*bi-tzedakah*), (Isaiah 1:27).

And although the term *tzedakah* has many meanings, and may be translated in several ways, the context in which it appears here in *Hilchot Matnot Aniyim* ("The Laws of Charity to the Poor"), makes it clear that the Rambam is referring to "charity" in its various manifestations.

A very extreme, and even dangerously provocative, formulation of what we have discussed above, is to be found in a statement of the great Hasidic Rebbe R. Moshe Leib of Sasov (died c. 1876), as documented by Martin Buber, in his *Tales of the Hasidim: The Later Masters*, New York: 1948, 89:

> Rabbi Moshe Leib said:
>
> "There is no quality and there is no power of man that was created to no purpose. And even base and corrupt qualities can be uplifted to serve God. When, for example, haughty self-assurance is uplifted it changes into a high assurance in the ways of God. But to what end can the denial of God have been created? This too can be uplifted through deeds of charity. For if someone comes to you and asks your help, you shall not turn him off with pious words, saying: 'Have faith

> and take your troubles to God!' You shall act as if there were no God, as if there were only one person in all the world who could help this man – only yourself."

Furthermore, there is a special quality to charity given personally, both educationally and spiritually. We have elaborated on this below in Part III ("Practical and Educational Implications"), recording the opinion of the Hafetz Hayyim on the subject of "mendicants." He notes that one may not restrain itinerant beggars from soliciting alms, and substitute municipal funds for the poor. The beggars must be allowed to continue to ply their trade. We see from his treatment of the subject of how the social, educational and spiritual arguments came into play in this significant halachic ruling.

And in this connection, we may call attention to a tale recorded by Jerome R. Minz, in his *Legends of the Hasidim: An Introduction to Hasidic Culture and the Oral Tradition in the New World*, Chicago and London: 1968, 220–221 (related by a Slonim Hasid):

> One of the students of the Baal Shem Tov went to a city and became the rabbi there. And he wanted to change the custom of the city. Instead of the poor people going around begging, he thought they should have a fund to which everyone should donate once a year and they would distribute it among the needy. But in the town there was a *tsaddik nistar* [hidden righteous man] who did not take from the fund, and since his source of income was cut off – people did not donate privately anymore – he was left penniless. This aroused a judgment in heaven against the rabbi, and as a punishment they decreed that he should want to convert to Christianity.

We shall not bring the continuation of this tradition which tells of the dire consequences of his initiative and its final resolution, for the above will suffice to highlight this powerful message.

At the same time we may recall that the Rambam, in listing the eight gradiated degrees of merit in giving charity (*Hilchot Matnot Aniyim* 10:7 et seq.) from the highest downwards, states that the "second down" (10:11) is:

> One who gives charity to the poor and does not know to whom he has given it, and the poor man does not know from whom he has received it . . . For pious people would give secretly and poor people from a wealthy family would receive it covertly. And close to this is placing charity in an alms box.

However, here too there is the element of personal giving on a regular basis, rather than a community organized tax. And, of course, this *matan be-seter* (giving overtly) is in order to avoid the embarrassment of the recipient.

Recalling the Rambam's statement quoted above, charity may be seen as one of the premier mitzvot of the "social" category, and is given the highest possible "ranking," or perhaps "rating," in the "mitzvah hierarchy," if one can coin such a phrase. This despite the fact that we are cautioned that we do not know the reward for mitzvot, be they "light" or "grave" (*Avot* 2:1).

We have thus far discussed rather extensively the premise that people-directed mitzvot have a preferential status over God-directed mitzvot. And this view was found to be among numerous authorities, as referred to in the *Klei Hemdah* mentioned above, section 1 (and cf. *Sdei Hemed*, vol. 3, 164–177, and vol. 5, 233). (Cf. section 2 ad init.)

But perhaps the most remarkable testimony to the superior status of charity is to be found in BT *Sanhedrin* 103b, where we read as follows:

> Why was Michah not listed [among the evil kings]? Because his fare (שפיתו) was available for wayfarers ... R. Natan taught us: From Gereb [Michah's temple] to Shiloh is three miles, and the smoke of the altar [at the Temple of Shiloh] and the smoke from the idol of Michah would intermingle with one another. The angels wished to harm (לדחפו) him (i.e., Michah). But the Holy One blessed be He said to them: "Leave him alone, for his fare is available for wayfarers."

Rashi adds (ad loc.) that everyone would be welcomed and hosted by him.

In the parallel text in *Pesikta Rabbati* (ed. Friedmann-Ish Shalom, Vienna: 1980, 137a):

> And note: the idol of Michah was placed in the West, and the Temple was standing in Shiloh. And he (Michah) would offer incense to his idol ..., while in Shiloh they would sacrifice morning and evening. And the two smokes would intermingle rising up to the heavens. And the Holy One blessed be He said: "Which one [i.e., which offering] should we accept, this one or that one?!"

This is a truly remarkable tradition, in that it places charitable hospitality on such a high level, as to diminish even the sin of Michah's idolatrous practices. (See above, sections 7 ad fin. and 13.)

17

Who "Eats of Their Fruits" in This World?

PERHAPS WE CAN LINK this associatively with an interesting observation made by R. Yosef Hayyim Sofer (in his *Menuhat Shalom*, Part II, Jerusalem: 2003, 22):

> It is very clear that the Tanna of [Mishnah] *Peah* 1:1, who listed "those things [mitzvot] that a man eats their fruits in this world . . . ," only listed those acts which serve well both to God and to man, where human beings also have real material benefit therefrom, such as honoring one's parents, righteous deeds to one's fellows; but those which are only good towards heaven, such as sending away the mother bird [Deuteronomy 22:7], are not listed.

He bases his comments on the passage in BT *Kiddushin* 40a, which elaborates on the verse in Isaiah 3:10, "Say to the righteous, that it shall be well with him: for they shall eat the fruits of their doings." The Talmud homiletically understood the verse to mean "Say to the righteous for [he is] good" (אמרו צדיק כי טוב), and then asks:

> And is there a righteous person who is not good? It means one who is good towards heaven and good to humankind – he is a good righteous person. Good to heaven and bad to humankind – this is a righteous person who is not good. And so similarly you may say [on Isaiah 3:11]: "Woe unto the wicked! It shall be ill with him: for the reward of his hands shall be given him." And is there a wicked man who is bad, and one who is wicked and not bad? Yes, if he is bad towards heaven and towards humans, this is a bad wicked person.

> But if he is bad towards heaven, but good towards humans, then he is a wicked person who is not bad.

Furthermore, elsewhere (*Lecha Naeh le-Hodot*, Jerusalem: 2010, 80–81, 84–85), referring to Rambam's commentary to Mishnah *Peah* 1:1, he notes that a person can get a reward in this world for interpersonal mitzvot, while the principle brought in BT *Kiddushin* 39b that "reward for mitzvot is not [received] in this world" refers primarily to ritual mitzvot. He quotes numerous additional sources to support this contention, such as the Hida's *Hasdei Avot*, Warsaw: 1872, 2:1, who cites the Maharit (=R. Yosef di-Trani), Responsa *Tirosh ve-Yitzhar*, by R. Yehezkel Michelson, Bilgurai 1937, section 1, 123:3, etc. He also (on p. 84) refers us to Maharal mi-Prague's explanation for this difference in his *Tiferet Yisrael*, Warsaw: 1886, chapters 58 and 62; and see further R. Moshe of Trani's *Beit Elokim*, Warsaw: 1873, *Shaar ha-Hasidut*, chapter 42. However, he also lists a number of exceptions to this rule, such as "Love of God" (28), *Sefirat ha-Omer* (92), *Eruv Tavshilin* (92–93). However, these (with the others not here mentioned) are the overwhelming minority of the eighty categories he lists, as will be clear from a cursory perusal of his list (76–109).

So here again, from all of the above, we see that a greater preference is given to one who is virtuous both to his God and his fellow men, the inference being that piety towards God alone is not sufficient, and makes for a righteous man who is nonetheless not considered a good man.[1] Or in the

---

1. Cf. above (sect. 2) on one who is exempt from something and does it is considered an ignorant man. A less extreme formulation of this motif may be found in *Genesis Rabbah* 48:2, ed. Theodor-Albeck, 486, which states that when Abraham saw the three angels, whom he thought were itinerant Bedouin (see above, sect. 6), he said to himself:

> If I see the *Shechinah* awaiting then I will know that they are great people, and if I see they are respectful to one another I will know that they are decent people.

(Here I have followed the regular edition and some manuscript readings.) And on this R. Hayyim Shmuelevitz, the Rosh Yeshiva of Mir, said that although it may be that people are great enough to have the *Shechinah* wait on them (or awaiting them), it is still not certain that they are decent people. And Abraham only ran towards them when he noted how they behaved towards one another; for then he knew that they were both "great" and morally decent. (See A. Tobolsky, *Hizaharu be-Chevod Haverchem* [Bnei Brak: 1981, 48–49].)

words of R. Samson Raphael Hirsch, in his *Nineteen Letters on Judaism*:[2]

> A life of seclusion devoted only to meditation and prayer is not Judaism. Study and worship are but paths which lead to action. "Great is study, for it leads to the practical fulfillment of the precepts," say our Sages, and the flower and fruit of our devotions should be the resolve to lead a life of action, pervaded with the spirit of God. Such a life is the only universal goal. (See above, section 4.)

It is therefore both relevant and meaningful to point out the custom of giving charity upon entering the synagogue, before beginning the morning prayer. (See above, section 4 near note 1, and below Appendix, with accompanying illustration.)

2. Ed. J. Breuer (New York: 1960, 99–100), cited by S.Z. Leiman, in his article "Rabbinic Openness to General Culture in the Early Modern Period," apud *Judaism's Encounter with Other Cultures: Rejection or Integration?* ed. J.J. Schachter (Northvale, N.J. and Jerusalem: 1997, 188). Leiman (189, n. 109) notes that: "Breuer's translation ... is based upon S.R. Hirsch, *The Nineteen Letters of Ben Uziel*, transl. B. Drachman (New York: 1899, reissued: New York: 1942). He also refers us to the new translation by Karin Paritzky, with commentary by R. Joseph Elias, in *The Nineteen Letters* (Jerusalem: 1995).

18

The Sinful Nazirite

I BELIEVE THAT in this way we may understand more fully the view of R. Eleazar ha-Kappar in BT *Nedarim* 10a. We should preface our explanation by first quoting the verse in Numbers 6:11:

> "And the priest shall offer the one for a sin offering, and the other for a burnt offering, and make an atonement for him, for that he sinned by his soul, and shall hallow his head that same day."

This clearly suggests that the Nazirite is sinful.[1] But in Numbers 6:5 it is stated that:

---

1. The primary Tannaitic source for this view is in BT *Nedarim* 9b (=BT *Nazir* 4a) where Shimon ha-Tzaddik declares that he never ate of the sin offering of a Nazirite, except on one occasion:

> Once a young Nazirite came from the South, and I saw he had beautiful eyes and handsome looks, and he had curly locks. I said to him: "My son, why do you wish to destroy your curly hair (i.e., cut off the locks)? He answered me [saying]: "I was a shepherd for my father in my village, and once went to draw water from the spring, and I saw my reflection in the water, and my [evil] spirit welled up in me and threatened to drive me out of this world (i.e., by leading me astray). I said to myself: O wicked one, why do you find pride in a world that is not yours, in one who is destined to end up [being devoured] by worms and maggots. I swear that I shall shave off my hair to heaven! Immediately, I stood up and kissed him on his head and said: "My son, may there be many Nazirites like you in Israel."

> "All the days of the vow of his separation there shall no razor come upon his head: until the days be fulfilled, in which he separateth himself unto the Lord, *he shall be holy*, and shall let the locks of the hair of his head grow."

And again in verse 8:

> "All the days of his separation *he is holy unto* the Lord."

The Talmud in *Nedarim* 10a quotes a *baraita* of R. Eleazar ha-Kappar on verse 11, "and make an atonement for him, for that he sinned . . .":

> And what manner of sin is this? In that he distressed himself by distancing himself from wine.

And this is said to be consonant with the later statement of the Babylonian Samuel, who stated "that anyone who sits in fasting, sins."[2] And in the Yerushalmi *Nedarim* 9:1, Rav Dimi, in the name of R. Yitzhak says: "Is it not sufficient what the Torah forbade you, and you wish to forbid upon

---

We see here the somewhat ambivalent attitude of Shimon ha-Tzaddik. He himself did not encourage the asceticism of Naziritism. But he did appreciate a genuinely pious person who is moved to some sort of ascetic penance.

The parallelism with the Greek Narcissus theme has been noted by scholars. See Urbach, cited below, sect. 19, and also A. Büchler, *Studies in Sin and Atonement in the Rabbinic Literature of the First Century* (London: 1928), and idem, *Types of Jewish-Palestinian Piety from 70 B.C.E. to 70 C.E.* (London: 1922). (On the Narcissus legend, see Ovid, *Met.* 3.341; Pausanias 9.31.6; Eustathius, *ad Hum.*, 266.) Here again this subject is too broad for the scope of this study.

However, see meantime William Hansen, *Ariadne's Thread: A Guide to International Tales Found in Classical Literature* (Ithaca and London: 2002, 257–261), and Stith Thompson, *Motif-Index of Folk-Literature* (revised and enlarged edition, Copenhagen, 1955, A 26665.1 and 115.1). Neither of these scholars referred to the Jewish version. Thompson only referred his readers to Wolfram Eberhard, *Chinese Fairy Tales and Folk Tales* (London: 1937, 131 no. 87).

2. How different this is from the position of the 12th and 13th centuries' Hasidei Ashkenaz, the so-called "pietists," who encouraged fasting, and introduced a variety of new extended periods of fasting. See what I wrote in my *Minhagei Yisrael*, vol. 2 (Jerusalem: 1991, 130–132). Of course, they had their early sources to serve as precedents for their behavior. See, e.g., BT *Baba Batra* 60b:

yourself other things."[3] The passage there continues: "Had you known

---

> We have learned, that when the Temple was destroyed there were many *Perushim* (lit., separatists, but here meaning: ascetics) in Israel who would not eat meat neither would they drink wine.

This was because they were no longer able to bring meat sacrifices, nor make wine libations. This is the main source for the subsequent stream called the *Aveilei Tziyyon*, "the mourners of Zion." (On them see Y. Gertner's study in *Bar-Ilan* 20–21 (1983), 130–144, and in *Milet* 2, (1984), 201–224. Much has been written about this movement, but this is not the place to expand on the subject.) However, the continuation of that Talmud passage tells us that R. Yehoshua (late 1st cent. C.E.) chastised others as follows:

> If so, let us not eat bread, for the meal offerings can no longer be brought. Let us not eat fruit, for we can no longer bring first-fruits. Let us not drink water, because there can no longer be water libation.

The *Perushim* had no answer to his arguments, and he "compromised" with them saying:

> We cannot desist from mourning ... but we may not do so too much ... The Rabbis said: A person, when he white-washes his house should leave an area unpainted ...

(See what I wrote in *Minhagei Yisrael*, vol. 1, [Jerusalem: 1989, 141, n. 13].) See further, S. Lowy, "The Motivation of Fasting in Talmudic Literature," *JJS* 9 (1958), 19–38; M. Beer, "On Penances of Penitents in the Literature of *Hazal*," *Zion* 46/3 (1981), 159–181 [Hebrew]; I.G. Marcus, *Piety and Society: The Jewish Pietists of Mediaeval Germany* (Leiden: 1981); *Minhagei Yisrael*, vol. 2, 106–108, etc.

An additional early source that they could draw upon is the statement in *Masechet Soferim* 21:1, ed. M. Higger (New York: 1937, 354), which later appears in the *Tur* and the *Shulhan Aruch* 580:3, as:

> There are those who say that they [i.e., the Rabbis] instituted that one should fast every Monday and Thursday because of the destruction of the Temple and the desecration of the [divine] name, and in the future [these days] will be turned into [days of] joy and rejoicing.

See further R. Yaakov Hayyim Sofer, *Kaf ha-Hayyim, Orah Hayyim* 580, 151a, nos. 25–30, that some would only eat bread and salt on those days, and others would desist from meat and wine, etc.

3. See R. Ovadiah Yosef in a diatribe against those who do not bathe from Rosh Hodesh Av until Tisha be-Av, (*nrg hadashot* Aug. 3, 2008), where he is said to have stated that "he who acts so stringently (*mahmir*) is an ass (*hamor*), not

that in taking upon yourself this vow, [and] it is as though you are seizing a sword and piercing yourself, would you have done so?" Similarly, the Tosefta *Taaniyyot* 2:12 (BT *Taanit* 22b) says in the name of R. Yossi: "The individual is not permitted to mortify himself in fasting, lest he fall a burden on the community, and they will need to support him." Indeed, the Yerushalmi at the end of chapter 1 of *Kiddushin* warns us "that a person will have to give account of all that his eye saw and he did not partake thereof." (See further Tosefta *Nezirut* 4:7.)

This overall negation view of asceticism[4] is accepted by Maimonides in

---

a human being. Why? If the Torah permitted it! You wish to be Abu Ali and be more stringent than the Torah?!" (See above, sect. 10.)

Yet another example of the strictures and limitations on taking the stringent position may be seen from Rambam's ruling in *Hilchot Maachalot Asurot* 17:22, where he writes:

> The oil of gentiles is permitted, and he who forbids it is committing a great sin, because he is rebelling against the [authority of the] court which permitted it.

This is based on Mishnah *Avodah Zarah* 2:6, BT *Avodah Zarah* 35b. And in Yerushalmi *Avodah Zarah* 2:8 we read:

> Yitzhak ben Shmuel bar Marta came down to Netzivin (Nesbis). He met Simlai the Southerner. He sat and expounded: Rabbi [Yehudah ha-Nasi] permitted oil [of gentiles]. He said: Shmuel ate [of it], and Rav did not accept this ruling [permitting him] to eat. Shmuel said to him: "Eat, or I will announce [lit., write concerning you] that you are a rebellious Elder (זקן ממרה)." [Shmuel] pressured him, and he ate.

It is on the basis of this Yerushalmi text that the Rambam rules that forbidding gentile oil, i.e., taking the stringent halachic position on this issue – as did Rav – is a great sin (חטא גדול).

4. See on this the classic essay of E.E. Urbach, in *Sefer Yovel le-Yitzchak Baer* (Jerusalem: 1961, 48–68) republished in his collected essays, *Me-Olamam shel Hachamim* (Jerusalem: 1988, 437–458), [Hebrew].

More recently this subject has been dealt with in depth by Eliezer Diamond, in his *Holy Men and Hunger Artists: Fasting and Asceticism in Rabbinic Culture* (Oxford: 2004), where, inter alia, he seeks to identify a difference between the Palestinian and Babylonian approaches to fasting (128–132). He also makes a strong case for fasting having taken the place of Nazirism after the destruction of the Second Temple (106 et seq.).

See preceding two notes. The pietists – Hasidei Ashkenaz – had, of course,

Hilchot Deot 3:1, and in *Arachin ve-Haramin* 8:13, where he states explicitly:

> A person shall never sanctify all his possessions, and he who does so sins, going against the sense of the biblical verse ... And this is not piety (*hasidut*) but idiocy (*shtut*), for he loses all his possessions and will fall a burden on others ... (See above, section 16.)

However, R. Eleazar in BT *Taanit* 11a says that "he is called holy."

Some commentators (such as the Rema) explained this apparent contradiction between the verses and between these early authorities in the following manner:

> The *Nazir*, or the ascetic, had virtuous intentions, and his holiness will express itself *after* his period of asceticism, when he refrains from following his base instincts and follows the median path. But at the time of his *nezirut*, he is sinning.

So his sinfulness is in that he afflicts his body, and will probably afflict himself upon the community which affects his בין אדם לחברו relationships and mitzvot, and this, even though his intentions are most virtuous, in that he wishes to distance himself from sin and bring himself closer to his Maker.

Apparently, the sin of self-mortification, which is in the category of a sin

---

a totally different view, and encouraged extreme forms of asceticism, as forms of penance. See, e.g., *Minhagei Yisrael*, vol. 2 (Jerusalem: 1991, 128–130); A. Ruker, *JJS* 16 (1965), 168–172. The classic essay on this subject is still that of Yitzhak Baer, "*Ha-Megamah ha-Datit-Hevratit shel 'Sefer Hasidim'*," *Zion* 3/1 (1938), (special publication, 1–50 + 2). A very important essay was published by Hayyim Soloveitchik, entitled "Three Themes in *Sefer Hasidim*," *AJS Review* 1, (1976), 311–357. More recently he published an essay calling into doubt the centralized degree of influence of the Hasidei Ashkenaz: "Piety, Pietism and German Pietism: *Sefer Hasidim I* and the Influence of *Hasidei Ashkenaz*," *JQR* 92/3–4 (2002), 455–493. Of related interest is Rella Kushelevsky's *Penalty and Temptation, Hebrew Tales in Ashkenaz, Ms. Parma 2295 (de-Rossi 563)*, (Jerusalem: 2010, [Hebrew]). There is a very considerable literature on the various aspects of the Hasidei Ashkenaz, (mysticism – G. Scholem, Y. Dan; pietism – I.G. Marcus, referred to above; liturgy, D. Sperber, *On Changes in Jewish Liturgy* [Jerusalem: 2010]), but, here, again this is beyond the scope of this study.

of man against fellow man – even though the fellow man is himself, for he is not master over his own body, but only has stewardship over that which God granted him[5] – overrides the virtues of seeking excessive piety. And such excessive piety may at times be regarded not as *hasidut*, but as *shtut*, as we learned from the Rambam referred to above. So such a righteous man is not always considered a good man.[6]

5. R. Aharon Lichtenstein, in an essay entitled "Beyond the Pale? Reflections Regarding Contemporary Relations with Non-Orthodox Jews," apud *The Relationship of Orthodox Jews with Believing Jews of Other Religious Ideologies and Non-Believing Jews*, ed. Adam Minz, (New York: 2010, 32, n. 41), wrote as follows: "The notion that a person is *not* master of his own being, while anathema to secular modernists, is, of course, a linchpin of classical religious thought. It served to negate a possible legal right to sell oneself, and, from Plato to Spenser, as a rationale (unlike Camus) for rejecting suicide." The subject is too broad to be discussed here.

6. See Eliezer Diamond, *Holy Men and Hunger Artists: Fasting and Asceticism in Rabbinic Culture* (Oxford: 2004, especially 133–136). See further R. Yosef Karo in *Kesef Mishnah* to *Hilchot Terumot* 1:11, and what I wrote in *Minhagei Yisrael*, vol. 4 (Jerusalem: 1995, 285–286).

19

Again to the Righteous Man Who Is Not Necessarily Considered Good

INDEED, THIS CONCEPT, of a righteous man who is not necessarily good, is found in the Netziv's introduction (*Petiha*) to Genesis. There he writes that:

> There were *tzaddikim* and *hasidim*, righteous and virtuous men, who toiled in the learning of Torah, but who had no integrity in the ways of the world (אך לא היו ישרים בהליכות עולמים).... And the Holy One blessed be He, who is integrity personified, cannot bear righteous people of this nature, but only those who walk the paths of integrity in the ways of the world, and not in a distorted manner . . .

Admittedly, here we do not clearly see the relative weight of the two categories of mitzvot, but this aspect of the issue has already been discussed above.[1]

And here I would recall a personal memory of many years ago. It was when my late father, of blessed memory, was in the hospital, recovering from an operation, and in the next bed was an elderly gentleman who had had a stroke and could no longer speak. He could only make unintelligible

1. See further the discussion of R. Aharon Lichtenstein, in his *By His Light: Character and Values in the Service of God*, adapted by R. Reuven Ziegler (Yeshivat Har Etzion: 2002, 113–118), section entitled "Frumkeit Devoid of Goodness." And see the passages cited by A. Tobolsky, in his *Hizaharu bi-Chevod Haverchem* (Bnei Brak: 1981, 95–97, especially the statement of R. Yehezkel Sarna, the Rosh Yeshiva of Yeshivat Hevron, under whom I had the privilege to study for several years).

noises. His wife and children took turns in sitting by his bed, and as I also spent many hours with my father, we got to be talking to one another. His wife told me that the family was Moroccan, and that she had married at the age of fourteen or fifteen, and that her husband was considerably older than her. She had brought up the family, supported it by working as a maid in various houses, while her husband sat and learned Torah. He would get up at about three-thirty in the morning,[2] go to the synagogue, sit in his corner and learn all day,[3] interrupting only for the prayers. After *Shaharit*, the members of the *shul* would give him some breakfast, and at midday his wife, or a child, would bring him some lunch. In the evening he would come home, and his wife would give him supper, and he would go to bed early, so as to be able to get up at three-thirty. He never gave a lesson in the synagogue, nor even a sermon; in fact he never talked to the other congregants; he just sat in his corner and studied. He never taught his children, and no one really knew what he was studying or how much he really knew. And now he was incapable of speaking, or even communicating in an understandable fashion, so that his "Torah" could serve no one else. The members of the synagogue held him in awe as a supremely righteous person; his family held him in great respect. But I remember wondering all the while, and being not a little troubled by my thoughts, that perhaps he was not really a good person – a righteous man who, in fact, was not good;

---

2. I might here remark that my grandfather, Rabbi David Sperber, of blessed memory, used to get up every night at about three in the morning to begin learning. This was in accordance with the kabbalistic view that at the middle of the night, when the sun begins to come close to sunrise, that is the time when the attribute of Mercy (מידת הרחמים) comes into force (the Arizal, cited in *Shaar ha-Mitzvot, Birkei Yosef, Orah Hayyim* 236:1, based on Zohar, *Hayyei Sarah* 132b). In the morning, he would make a cup of hot milk for my grandmother, when she got up.

3. I presume that he learned in the synagogue, not only because it was more convenient, and he would not be troubled by the children, etc., but because in Yerushalmi *Berachot*, ch. 5 ad init., it says: "R. Yohanan said: 'There is a ratified covenant (ברית כרותה) that he who studies intensely (היגע תלמודו) in the synagogue will not readily forget [what he has learned].'" And this is quoted (almost verbatim) by the Rambam in *Hilchot Talmud Torah* 3:12, except that he alters "synagogue" to "*beit ha-midrash*" (academy), while in the *Tur* and the *Shulhan Aruch Yoreh Deah* 246:22, the reading returns to "synagogue." On these various changes, see R. Yaakov Hayyim Sofer's very scintillating explanation, in his *Drupteki de-Oraita*, vol. 1 (Jerusalem: 1987, 63–65).

and that it was his wife, a single illiterate woman, who had shouldered the burden of educating and maintaining the whole family for so many years, who was really the righteous person, righteous and good!

At any rate, measuring him up to the requirements of the Djikover Rebbe, cited above (section 6), he may have been a *tzaddik*, but he certainly did not incorporate the element of the *hacham* in his *tzidkut* (righteousness).[4]

Here, we should bear in mind what the Hafetz Hayyim said (as recorded

---

4. Maybe I am doing him a profound injustice, in which case I can but crave his pardon. After all, of the Gaon of Vilna it is stated (in the introduction to *Beur ha-Gra* to *Shulhan Aruch Orah Hayyim*):

> He never inquired of his sons and daughters regarding their occupation or economic well-being. He never sent them a letter inquiring about their well-being. When any of his children came to visit him, even though he rejoiced greatly, for often they had not seen him for a year or two, he never inquired about the well-being of their family or regarding their occupation. After allowing his son to rest for an hour, he would urge him to return immediately to his studies, saying: "You must make amends in my house for the study time forfeited during your journey here."
>
> Throughout his lifetime, he never slept more than two hours in any twenty-four hour period. He never slept for more than a half-hour at a time, and during that half-hour his lips recited *halakhot* and *aggadot* in a whisper. When the half-hour elapsed, he gathered strength like a lion, ritually cleansed his hands, and began learning in a loud voice, after which he went back to sleep for a half-hour. It was his practice to sleep three half-hours in the evening and one half-hour during the day.

See also the description of Rav Elyashiv's relationship to his wife, daughter, and grandchildren, in Avraham (Rami) Reiner's article "*Kavim Rishonim le-Darko ha-Hilchatit shel HaRav Yosef Shalom Elyashiv*," *Netuim* 17, 2001, 102–103 (with references).

However, I would hesitate to compare my Moroccan gentleman with the Gra or with Rav Elyashiv. (See S.L. Leiman, apud *Judaism's Encounter with Other Cultures: Rejection or Integration*, ed. J.J. Schachter [Northvale, N.J. and Jerusalem: 1997, 14.].) See also the comment of R. Aharon Lichtenstein concerning his father-in-law R.J.B. Soloveitchik, who, apparently never kissed his son. See *Mevakshei Panecha* by H. Sabato and A. Lichtenstein (Tel Aviv: 2011, 237).

I am also reminded of the somewhat perplexing passage in BT *Rosh ha-Shanah* 18a:

by Arieh Leib Pupko, *Michtevei ha-Rav Hafetz Hayyim*, Warsaw: 1937, vol. 2, 45):

> We read in Genesis 18:26: "And the Lord said: if I find in Sodom fifty righteous men within the city, then I will forgive all the places for their sake." From this we learn that the righteous persons were expected to be within the city sharing its regeneration, if they were to be effective in the effort to save it from perdition. If they, the *tzaddikim*, separate themselves in their way of life from civic affairs, they can exercise no influence whatsoever, even if they exist.

> Rava and Abbaye were of the house of Eli. Rava who was engaged in Torah lived forty years. Abbaye who was engaged in Torah and charitable deeds lived sixty years.

See Tosafot ad loc., and cf. BT *Moed Katan* 28a, according to which Rava states that the length of one's life-span is not so much dependent upon merit as upon luck (*mazal*), for Rabbah and Rav Hisda were both righteous people, and the one lived forty years and the other ninety. Nonetheless, Tosafot to *Rosh ha-Shanah*, referred to above, concludes that though Rava also must have been involved in charitable deeds, and he certainly taught others, nonetheless, Abbaye must have been more active in charitable activities.

See further the Hafetz Hayyim's discussion of this passage in his *Ahavat Hesed* (Warsaw: 1886–1893, 53b note, and also his note 23a–24a), that a person who throughout his whole life was connected (דבוק) to "truth" (*emet*), which is Torah, and not with *hesed*, mercy, charity, benevolence, cannot connect with *tzedek*, justice. This can only happen if he was involved in both *emet* and *hesed*. He is interpreting the verse in Psalms 85:10, "Mercy (*hesed*) and truth (*emet*) are met together; righteousness and peace have kissed each other."

Perhaps here we should also consider that which we have learned from BT *Hagigah* 5a, commenting on the verse in Eccl. 12:14 that states that God brings to judgment all deeds, "even hidden ones, whether good or bad." Upon which R. Yannai explains that this could refer to one who gives a poor man charity in public, perhaps one who is not asking for it, for by doing so he puts the poor man to shame. The Talmud continues that once R. Yannai saw someone giving a *zuza* (a small coin) to a poor man in public, and he said to him, "It were better had you not given him anything, than having given him and shamed him." From this we learn that sometimes one thinks one is doing a good and virtuous deed, and unknowingly – "even hidden ones" – one is doing something bad and harmful. R. Yannai teaches us that we will be judged also for such unintentioned hurt carried out as intended piety. That is to say, even deeds of apparent righteousness need care and aforethought and extreme sensitivity as to their possible ramifications.

A further radical formulation of this concept is found in the following folkloristic tale, which is an adaptation of a parable by the great Lithuanian preacher, Rabbi Jacob ben Wolf Kranz, better known as the Dubner Maggid (1740–1804):

> A rich man, who was a profligate, a souse and a lecher, died in a certain town. The entire community mourned his death and followed his hearse to his last resting place. What a wailing, what a lamentation, was heard as his coffin was lowered into the grave! In the recollection of the oldest inhabitant, no rabbi or sage had ever departed this life amidst such general sorrow.
>
> It chanced that on the following day, another rich man died in the town. He was just the opposite of the first in character and manner of living. He was ascetic and dined on practically nothing but dry bread and turnips. He had been pious all the days of his life and sat all the time in the House of Study poring over the Talmud. Nonetheless, no one except his own family mourned his death. His funeral passed almost unnoticed, and he was laid to rest in the presence of only a handful.
>
> A stranger, who happened to be visiting in the town at the time, was filled with wonder, and asked: "Explain to me the riddle of this town's strange behavior. It honors a profligate yet ignores a saint!"
>
> To this, one of the townsmen replied: "Know that the rich man who was buried yesterday, although he was a profligate and a drunkard, was the leading benefactor of the town. He was easy-going and merry, and loved all the good things in life. Practically everybody in this town profited from him. He'd buy wine from one, chickens from another, geese from a third, and cheese from a fourth. And, being kindhearted, he'd pay well. That's why he is missed and we mourn after him. But what earthly use was that other one, the saint, to anybody? He lived on bread and turnips and no one ever made a kopek on him. Believe me, no one will miss him!"
>
> (From Nathan Ausubel, *A Treasury of Jewish Folklore*, New York: 1948, cited in Bennet Muraskin, *Humanist Readings in Jewish Folklore*, Farmington Hills, Michigan: 2001, 68–69.)

Of course, the fact that "no one will miss him" does not necessarily mean that that is how the Heavens will judge him. Nonetheless, the gist of the message is clear, strengthening the fact that the strictly ascetic "saint" is a less positive personality even than a reprobate who helps others. (And cf. above, section 4 ad fin.)

20

An Interesting Comment on the Literary Structure of Leviticus

IT IS INTERESTING to note what Rashi writes in his commentary to the book of Leviticus. This book, as is well-known, deals to a large extent with ritual laws, i.e., with laws relating to man's relationship to his Maker and indeed begins with them. The first verse in this book reads as follows:

> "And the Lord called unto Moses, and spake unto him out of the tabernacle of the congregation, saying . . ."

On these first words "And [the Lord] called unto Moses," Rashi comments as follows:

> All oral communications of the Lord to Moses, whether they are introduced by דבר or by אמר or by צו, were preceded by a call (to prepare him for the forthcoming address). It is a way of expressing affection, the mode used by the ministering angels when addressing each other, as is said, "And one called unto another [and said Holy, Holy, Holy is the Lord of hosts]." (Isaiah 6:3)[1]

Rashi, basing himself on the Sifra ad loc., is teaching us that before one begins to shower a spate of commandments (upon a community or an individual), one must prepare the recipient with words of affection – חיבה.

It is surely significant that Rashi begins his commentary on this book

---

1. Rosenbaum and Silbermann translation; see also their n. 1 in the Appendix on p. 136.

of ritual with words of advice on matters of etiquette and decent behavior towards one fellow man.

And from these same initial words of that verse, the Talmud in BT *Yoma* 4b comments as follows:

> Tanya: Why did He "call" before he "spoke"? The Torah teaches us *derech eretz*, good behavior, that a person should not speak to his neighbor without first calling (i.e., preparing) him.

The *Torah Temimah* ad loc. elaborates as follows:

> The reason for this is so that the audience can prepare itself to listen [to the commandments]. And this is similar to what we have learned from BT *Niddah* 16b, that the Holy One blessed be He hates a person who enters his neighbor's house suddenly (i.e., without knocking). And in Tractate *Derech Eretz* [*Rabbah*], chapter 5 we read: And all people should learn good behavior from God, who stood at the gate of the garden (of Eden) and called unto Adam, as it is said, "And the Lord God called unto Adam and said unto him, where art thou?" (Genesis 3:9). And the reason that our Gemara (in *Yoma*) did not cite that verse, may be explained as follows: to teach us an additional lesson, that even in the case of one who one knows intimately and loves with a deep love, even so one should not speak to him suddenly. And it is for this reason that [the Talmud] brought its proof from Moses, concerning whom God Himself testified, "[My servant Moses is not so], who is faithful in all Mine home. With him I speak mouth to mouth, even apparently, and not in dark speeches . . ." (Numbers 12:7–8) – And even so God prepared him before he actually spoke with him (and gave him commandments).

Here too, the Talmud teaches us lessons in decency and good behavior from the first words in the book of Leviticus. Perhaps this is yet another indication that דרך ארץ קדמה לתורה, as R. Yishmael ben R. Nahman said: *Derech eretz* came twenty-six generations before Torah . . .[2] (*Leviticus*

2. See further *Seder Eliyahu Rabbah* (14) 15, ed. Ish Shalom, p. 71=*Tanna Debe Eliyyahu*, transl. W.G. Braude & I.J. Kapstein (Philadelphia: 1981, 199):

> My questioner further said to me: "My master, Israel has been banished twice, once in the days of the First Temple, and once again in the days

Rabbah 9:3, ed. Margaliot, 179).[3]

> of the Second Temple. Why was the period of Israel's banishment [after the destruction of the First Temple] specified, but not specified after the destruction of the Second Temple?" I replied: "My son, though those who lived during the days of the First Temple were certainly idolators, right conduct – *derech eretz* – characterized them. And what was the right conduct which characterized them? Charity and loving kindness.

3. See also *Avot* 3:16: R. Elazar ben Azariah says: "If there is no [study of] Torah there is no seemly behavior – *derech eretz*; if there is no seemly behavior there is no Torah."

On which R. Yonah Girondi remarks:

> He wishes to say that one must first improve one's moral behavior, and then the Torah will dwell in him, for it never does so in a person who has no fine moral qualities (מדות טובות), and not that he should study Torah and afterwards improve his moral behavior, for that does not work.

(See also Benedict Thomas Viviano's somewhat questionable interpretation, in his *Study as Worship: Aboth and the New Testament,* [Leiden: 1978], 82–86, 105–110.) Accordingly, R. Yaakov Hayyim Sofer, in his *Drupteki de-Oraita*, vol. 1, (Jerusalem: 1987, 44–45) explains that strange order, at first blush, in Rambam's *Mishneh Torah*, where he brings *Hilchot Deot before Hilchot Talmud Torah*. For one would have expected the laws concerning the study of Torah to come first, since study of Torah seems to have the primary position among the mitzvot. (See M. *Peah* ad init.) However, in view of the above, the order in the Rambam is explained.

On moral behavior, see R. Eliyahu, ha-Gaon mi-Vilna's commentary to the *Book of Esther* 10:3:

> Moral behavior is supreme above all else, and [therefore rules] of moral behavior are not formulated in the Torah, because they encompass the whole Torah.

And compare his commentary to Canticles 1:5, that they are the *ikar ha-Torah* – the primary basis of Torah. And see also R. Hayyim Vital's *Shaarei Kedushah* part 1, sect. 2, ad init., that they are the necessary preparation for the 613 commandments. See *Drupteki de-Oraita* vol. 2 (Jerusalem: 1993, 56). (R. Sofer, however, has doubts as to the authenticity of the Gaon's commentary to the *Book of Esther*, and other works attributed to him, which, most likely were written by his disciples. See his comments in his *Zechut Yitzhak*, vol. 2 [Jerusalem: 1992, 266], with additional references.) Cf. above, sect. 13 ad fin.

Here I shall permit myself a somewhat cynical observation. In the last several decades there has been a considerable volume of hagiographic publications, biographies of *tzaddikim*, saintly personalities, and Rebbes. And of late, there have appeared several series of volumes of such biographies, arranged by the date of their decease, i.e., *yahrzeit*, sometimes in a volume per month (i.e., the works of Perlov and Schiff, etc.). Some of these are well-indexed, with lists of personalities mentioned, verses and sources cited, and a subject index, which include such notions as *tzedakah* (charity), *hachnasat orhim* (hosting of guests), *limud Torah* (learning Torah), etc. I have examined a great number of such volumes, and noted that the term *derech eretz* hardly ever appears in these subject indices. Perhaps the authors understood the phrase "*derech eretz kadmah le-Torah,*" – *derech eretz* came before Torah – to mean that it is now antiquated, altmodisch and defunct, and its place has been taken over by Torah. Hence, it does not merit mention.

21

On the Primal Nature of "*Derech Eretz*"

AND HERE LET US recall the words of the Maharal mi-Prague, in his *Netivot Olam, Netiv Derech Eretz*:

> Therefore, a person should not view lightly those matters which are *derech eretz*, for *derech eretz* came before *Torah* . . . and it is impossible to read a Torah situation (מציאות של התורה) without *derech eretz*, as they said, "If there is no *derech eretz* there is no Torah" (*Avot* 3:17), for *derech eretz* is the basis of Torah which is the way of the Tree of Life.[1]

And to this we may add the remarkable statement of R. Simlai in BT *Sotah* 14a:

---

1. It is well-known that R. Samson Raphael Hirsch developed this notion as a central theme in his Jewish *Weltanschauung*. So central was the theme of *Torah and derech eretz* in his thought that it was embedded in the foundation stone of his synagogue. The text of the scroll buried in the foundation's scroll read:

> May we merit to raise up together our sons and daughters to *Torah and derech eretz*, as we were instructed by the founding fathers of our nation, the true sages.

Similarly, emblazoned in gold letters on the banners of the Jewish day school founded by Hirsch was the phrase: "*Yafeh talmud Torah im derech eretz.*" See S.Z. Leiman in *Judaism's Encounter with Other Cultures*, p. 191, referring us to Mordechai Breuer, "'*Torah and Derech Eretz*' according to the Teaching of R. Samson Raphael Hirsch," *Ha-Maayan* 9:1, 9, [Hebrew], and cf. Herman Schwab, *The History of Orthodox Jewry in Germany* (London: 1950, 43).

> The *Torah* begins with an act of righteousness (גמילות חסדים), and ends with an act of righteousness. It begins with an act of righteousness, as it is written, "Unto Adam also and to his wife did the Lord God make coats of skins, and clothed them" (Genesis 3:21). And it ends with an act of righteousness, as it is written, "And He buried him (i.e., Moses) in a valley." (Deuteronomy 34:6)[2]

Finally, we may again recall the classic statement of Hillel in BT *Shabbat* 31a, who, when asked by a gentile who wished to be converted that he teach him all the Torah [while standing] on one leg, replied with his famous statement, "That which is hateful to you, do not do to your friend. That is the whole Torah (כל התורה כולה) and, as for the rest, it is commentary. Go and study it."[3] What a powerful statement this is, and it reverberates throughout the ages. Thus, as a random example, we read in Sebastian Brant's fifteenth century *Narrenschiff*, or *Ship of Fools* (Edwin N. Zeydel's translation, New York: 1944, 232, no. 69):

> You are silly if you do
> What others should not do to you;
> Before you would abuse another,
> Reflect if you would like it, brother.

And more recently, George Bernard Shaw in his *Man and Superman* (1903), (*Maxims for Revolutionists*, 227) writes:

---

2. And see what I wrote on this in my *Darkah shel Halachah* (Jerusalem: 2007, 62, nn. 78, 79).

3. It is interesting that we find an almost identical formulation in the ancient Indian epic (*Mahabharata, Santi Parva* CCLI 19–21, 24–25):

> Do not treat others in a way in which you would not want to be treated by others . . .

See Saral Jhingran, *Aspects of Hindu Morality* (Delhi: 1989, 194). It is difficult to date this section of the *Mahabharata*, which is a very long and complex document, parts of which go back possibly to sometime in the early first millennium B.C.E., while others may be dated to as late as 500 C.E. However, I am not suggesting any influence in either direction, just a moral parallelism. See below, section 32 ad fin. See my forthcoming study on *The Halachic Status of Hinduism*.

> Do not do unto others as you would [wish that] they should do unto you. Their tastes may not be the same.

But how much paler are these formulations compared to that of Hillel.

Elsewhere, I have further elaborated on this theme, and brought additional sources to underscore this premise, and to show how it is borne out in a variety of different halachic contexts.[4]

---

4. Perhaps we may link this to what the *Torah Temimah* comments on the verse in Exod. 24:12, n. 30 (p. 358):

> Already in the writings of the *Rishonim* and the *Aharonim* the question was raised why we do not make a blessing over a number of mitzvot, such as charity, *gemilut hasadim*, returning lost objects, visiting the sick, and so forth. And many suggestions and reasons were offered. But in my opinion the reason is simple: Because the formula of a blessing "who has sanctified us with his *mitzvot* and commanded us . . ." teaches us that with this mitzvah that we are doing we are becoming sanctified and separated from the rest of the nations of the world who do not act thus. And this is not the case for mitzvot between man and his neighbor, such as those we listed above. For they are also practiced by non-Jews, and consequently it is not relevant to say with regard to them "who has sanctified us with this mitzvah," i.e., who has distinguished us [from them], because in this regard we are no different from the nations of the world.
>
> And it would appear that this was the intention of the Rambam, when he wrote in *Hilchot Berachot* 11:2, "All positive commandments between man and his God, be it a non-obligatory one, or an obligatory one] one makes a blessing over it before carrying it out. And the *Kesef Mishnah* ad loc. writes: And our master was careful to write "between man and his God," to teach us that mitzvot between man and his neighbor, such as charity and likewise, over them one makes no blessing. But he did not expound on the reason. But in view of what we have suggested, the issue is clear . . .

Indeed, we find the same reasoning in the response of the *Rashban*, R. Shlomo Tzvi Shik (Satmar: 1900), to *Even ha-Ezer* sect. 1, basing himself on BT *Menahot* 42a: We do not need to make a blessing over any mitzvah which is acceptable (כשרה) to a non-Jew. And Rashi ad loc. explains: For one cannot say "and sanctified us with His mitzvot," since this mitzvah is acceptable (i.e., practiced) also by non-Jews. (But see above, sect. 3.)

I believe much the same notion is to be found in Ramban's commentary to Exod. 15:25. On the words in that verse, "there He made for them a statute and an ordinance" he writes, after rejecting Rashi's interpretation, that:

> The simple straightforward meaning is that when they entered the great and terrifying wilderness with its awful thirst [as it was] without water, He set out for them practices that they should abide by until they reached the settled land, for their survival and needs . . . Because custom is called statute . . . and rules that they should live by, to love one another and to behave in accordance with the advice of the Elders, and to act with modesty in their tents with regard women and children, and relate peaceably with those who enter their camp to tell them things, and ethical exhortations that they be not like those negative hordes who carry out all manner of abominations shamelessly . . . [all of which] are not the statute of the Torah, but practices for the well-being of the states. (See above, sect. 6 ad fin.)

And much the same concept is to be found in the Rambam's *Commentary to Mishnah Avot*, sixth of the "Eight Chapters" (see *Ethical Writings*, transl. Raymond Weis and Charles Butterworth [New York: 1983, 79–80]), where he states that:

> The bad things to which the philosophers referred when they said that someone who does not desire them is more virtuous than someone who does desire them and restrains himself – *these are the things generally accepted by all people as bad*, such as murder, theft, robbery, fraud, harming an innocent man, repaying a benefactor with evil, degrading parents, and things like these. They are the laws about which the Sages, peace be upon them, said, "If they were not written down, they would deserve to be written down" (BT *Yoma* 67b). [My emphasis, D. S.]

(And see on this passage, Menachem Kellner, *Maimonides' Confrontation with Mysticism* [Oxford: 2006, 64–65].)

In other words, these kinds of practices belong to a category of "natural morality," i.e., *derech eretz*. This homiletically suggests yet another meaning for דרך ארץ קדמה לתורה in the Rambam, that *derech eretz preceded Torah*, namely that rules and customs of *derech eretz* , i.e., morality preceded the giving of the Torah at Sinai.

Further on this question, see my *Netivot Pesikah*, 187–188, nn. 273–274.

Part II

Halachic Practice

So far, our main discussion has been largely theoretical, though interspersed with occasional instructional tales. How then do these ideas translate themselves into everybody life, and what may we learn from the behavior of pious sages of bygone years, who may serve as role models for us in the present day?

22

The Brisker Rav (1853–1918)

UNDOUBTEDLY, ONE OF THE great role models among the latter-day *Gedolim* was Reb Hayyim Halevy Soloveitchik, the Brisker Rav. I learned of an example of his exemplary behavior from an article by R. Aharon Hersh Fried, published in *Hakirah* 6, 2008, 49–50:

> Late on a Wednesday night, a traveling Jew arrived in Brisk. The lights were out in all the homes, and he did not want to awaken the people with whom he had meant to be staying. Noticing one house in which the lights were still on, he decided to knock on the door and ask whether he could possibly stay the night. The homeowner opened the door and graciously welcomed him to stay the night. The homeowner remarked that coming from the road, the traveler must also be hungry, and went into the kitchen to prepare him something to eat. While the בעל הבית was in the kitchen, the guest got a chance to look around and he noticed that he was in a בית מלא ספרים, a house filled with *seforim*, and quickly surmised that he was in the home of a *rav* or at least a *dayan*. At this point he became uncomfortable with this revered personage preparing a meal for him, and he voiced his protestations, saying to the בעל הבית, "You needn't trouble yourself" (איר דארפט אייך ניט מטריח זיין), and repeating it. The בעל הבית did not answer him, continued preparing the meal, and served it to him, amidst his continued protestations. The בעל הבית then began to prepare a bed for the guest, who again protested, "You needn't trouble yourself. Just put the bedding down and I'll arrange the bed myself. Please, you needn't trouble yourself." Again, the בעל הבית did not answer, but continued to make the bed. The next morning, the

> בעל הבית (i.e., the Brisker Rav) took the man to *shul*. Being that it was Thursday morning and there was קריאת התורה, Reb Chaim told the *gabbai* to give the guest הגבה. As the guest was about to lift the *Sefer Torah*, Reb Chaim tapped him on the shoulder and said, "You needn't trouble yourself."

The author writes of R. Hayyim that his "*gadlus* in *chesed* was possibly even greater than his *gadlus* in learning," and that this anecdote encapsulates the point beautifully.

Reb Hayyim Halevy Soloveitchik – The Brisker Rav

23

Reb Yisrael Lipkin Salanter (1810–1883)[1]

We have already mentioned above (section 2 ad fin.) that Reb Yisrael Salanter did not distinguish between the two categories of mitzvot, and, if anything, gave preference to those between man and his neighbor. We can now continue by quoting a passage from Rabbi Yehudah Leib Maimon's *Sarei ha-Meah*, vol. 2, Jerusalem: 1961, 272–273; relating to Reb Yisrael:

> And it once happened that Reb Yisrael Salanter, during his stay in Kovno, lived for a while in the house of a wealthy pious man, Reb Yaakov Karpas, and would dine at his table. Members of the household noted that when he washed his hands before the meal, he would do so with a minimal amount of water, even though a bucket full of water was prepared for him. They wondered in amazement: Should not a *tzaddik* like Reb Yisrael rule more stringently (*mehadrin*) to wash his hands with a plentiful amount of water! They went and spoke to Reb Karpas, who examined the matter and found that indeed Reb Yisrael would wash his hands with no more than a *reviit ha-log* and no more. He too was most surprised, and when they sat together at a meal, he asked Reb Yisrael: "Forgive me, our Master, but this is a matter of Torah and I must learn about it. Why then does it suffice you to wash your hands with a *reviit*? Surely, it is a clear

1. A full treatment of this deeply influential personality will be found in Dov Katz, *Tenuat ha Musar*, vol. 1 (Tel Aviv: 1952, 137–386); and see below for additional bibliography.

ruling in the *Shulhan Aruch* (*Orah Hayyim* 155:10), 'even though the amount (for handwashing) is a *reviit*, one should wash more plentifully.' Why then do you, sir, not do so?"

Reb Yisrael answered as follows:

"I have seen that the maid brings the water from afar, from a well in the valley. Your house is situated high on the hill, and the maid almost collapses under the weight of her burden, when she brings up the pail of water on her shoulders. *And it is forbidden for a person to be overly religious* (להדר) *at the expense of others*" [my emphasis, D.S.].[2]

---

2. In order fully to appreciate the nature of R. Karpas's question and Reb Yisrael's answer, one must add the following information. The source for the *Shulhan Aruch*'s ruling that one requires a *reviit* of water for handwashing is in Tosefta *Yadayim* 1:5, ed. Zukermandel, 681. (On the exact reading see S. Liebermann, *Tosefeth Rishonim*, vol. 4 [Jerusalem: 1939], 144, and M.M. Kasher's comments in his *Torah Shelemah*, vol. 21 [*Ki Tisa*, 18–19, 163–164].) And from the context it is understood to be the minimum amount required. In BT *Sotah* 4b we read in the name of R. Zerika in the name of R. Eleazar: Anyone who scorns, or makes light of [*mezalzel*] handwashing will be uprooted (*ne'ekar*) from the world. In *Derech Eretz Zuta* 8:9: Any scholar who makes light of handwashing is despicable (*meguneh*). (See my extensive commentary on this passage in my *A Commentary on Derech Erez Zuta, Chapters Five to Eight* [Ramat Gan: 1990], 163–168.) And in BT *Shabbat* 62b and BT *Niddah* 14a we are told that three things lead a person to poverty: one being the making light of handwashing. And in BT *Eruvin* 21b we read of R. Akiva (died c. 135 C.E.), who while imprisoned was ministered by his loyal disciple R. Yehoshua ha-Garsi. On one occasion R. Yehoshua ha-Garsi brought him a little water, and he used it to wash his hands. The disciple asked in perplexity, "There is not enough to drink, and you use it to wash your hands!" The reply was, "What can I do? For one is guilty of death over [not washing one's hands]. Better that I die my own death rather than transgress the views of my colleagues." (See Tosafot ad loc.) We see then with what gravity the Rabbis viewed the enactment of handwashing. It would therefore be expected that so saintly a personality as Reb Yisrael would go beyond the minimal amount required for handwashing, thus demonstrating its importance, and to allay any suspicion of any form of negligence in the performance of handwashing. This is what troubled R. Karpas, and hence his probing question. Reb Yisrael's response is, therefore, all the more significant given the halachic background of handwashing.

I heard a very fine *vort* from a former student of mine. In the story of Abraham and the three angels (discussed earlier on), we find Abraham preparing a lavish meal for his guests. "And Abraham ran unto the herd, and fetched a calf tender

Indeed Reb Yisrael was wont to say:

> "At times, out of excessive zeal to carry out a mitzvah between man and his Maker, people err and transgress a much more serious mitzvah between man and his neighbor, as for example is the case of the days of *Selichot*: If someone rises very early to recite the *Selichot* in the synagogue, and in doing so causes discomfort to the maid in his house, who, generally speaking, is a poor orphan girl who hires herself out to serve in the house of strangers, and she has to get up early in order to prepare a hot drink in the morning, then the sin of 'distressing an orphan' outweighs all the mitzvah of reciting the *Selichot*."[3]

---

and good, and gave it to a young man; and he hastened to dress it" (Gen. 18:7). "And he took butter and milk, and the calf, which he had dressed, and set it before them" (v. 8). Furthermore he requested of his wife Sarah to make "three measures of fine meal, knead it and make cakes upon the hearth" (v. 6). But at first the verse (4) states: "Let a little water, I pray you be fetched, and wash your feet." Why, then, did he offer them only "a little water?" Surely, they were hot and dusty and would have welcomed more than "a little water." Why then was he so sparing with the water, while he was so generous with their fare? The answer lies in the Bible's careful formulation: "*Let* a little water be *fetched*," meaning that he did not bring it from the well himself, but required that it be brought by someone else. (See Rashi ad loc.) When requesting that someone else do something for him, he made a minimal demand, so as not to make his request burdensome.

This story reminded me, in a somewhat oblique fashion, of a passage in the *Mishnah Berurah* to the first *siman* of the *Shulhan Aruch*. There (n. 2) he writes concerning the ruling that as soon as one wakes up one must immediately wash one's hands and not walk four cubits without doing so, because of the "spirit of uncleanness" (רוח הטומאה) which is on them on awakening. However, he adds, one must not do anything forbidden in order to overcome the lack of handwashing water, as, for example, "to take the water which his friend prepared for himself, unless it is clear to him that he will supply him with other water in its place, and many err in this issue." Clearly, the *Mishnah Berurah* is not regarding such action as theft; for it is obvious that one may not steal another person's property. Rather the situation is such that taking the water, probably from a communal water source, would cause additional effort on the part of his friend, and unless he makes certain that he is not causing such additional work, he may not take this water. It should be borne in mind that at times one had to go a considerable distance in order to reach a water source, such as to draw water from a well. See *Mishnah Berurah*, ibid., on how to walk or run when the water is far away.

3. Much the same concern, in a different set of circumstances appears in a story told in A. Tobolsky, *Hizaharu bi-Chevod Haverchem* (Bnei Brak: 1981,

Indeed, in his own synagogue, he ruled that the Friday-night and festival services should begin early, even before the true time of reading the *Shema*, justifying this as follows:[4]

159–160). These tales, and similar ones attributed to him, are to be seen within the context of R. Yisrael's *Mussar* methodology. See M. Gottlieb, "Mussar: A Jewish Psycho-Ethical Model for Our Time," *Conversations* 8 (2010), 43, citing his own article, "R. Yisrael Salanter and Therapeutic Values," *Tradition* 15 (1975), 112–129. See further, Hillel Goldberg, *Israel Salanter: Text, Structure, Idea: The ethics and theology of an early psychologist of the unconscious* (New York: 1982); Immanuel Etkes, *Rabbi Yisrael Salanter ve-Reishitah shel Tenuat ha-Mussar*, (*Rabbi Israel Salanter and the Beginning of the 'Musar' Movement*) (Jerusalem: 1982, [Hebrew]).

A somewhat similar tale is told of him as follows:

> Once he entered a small synagogue in one of the alleyways of Vilna to pray the afternoon prayer. He was accompanied by one of the great authorities of the time. The great authority washed his hands [as one should before prayer, (see *Shulhan Aruch Orah Hayyim* 92:5; A.Y. Pfoifer, *Ishei Yisrael*, 2:38–40, pp. 23–24; 10:19, p. 93; 27:30–34, pp. 292–293, with full references)] using the water from the synagogue urn [very generously], whereas R. Yisrael merely wetted his hands, hardly using any water. The great authority asked him in surprise: "Are you not accustomed to wash your hands before praying?" R. Yisrael replied: "Indeed, I am accustomed to do so, and with much water. However, here I see that there is a rather fixed number of congregants, and apparently guests are unusual. The beadle no doubt prepares in advance the amount of water required for that number of congregants. [At that time there were no taps with running water, but an urn that had to be filled from a well.] And if we waste much water, the regulars will not find enough for themselves and may well complain about the beadle and refrain from giving him the few pennies he is wont to receive. And thus we will be depriving him of his livelihood.

See *Shaarei Tziyyon* (1913, 56); A. Tobolski, *Hizaharu be-Mamon Haverchem* (Bnei Brak: 1981, 246), and see further episodes. On handwashing before prayers, see *Shulhan Aruch Orah Hayyim* 92:4. For an example of such an urn, see *Beit ha-Kenesset She-be-Belza: Tzurat Tavnito, Hilchotav u-Minhagav*, (Brooklyn: 2008, 98–99). In Belz, it was filled once a week.

4. See on the issue of early *Maariv* service the seminal essay of Yaakov Katz, in *Zion* 35, 1970, 35–60, reprinted in his *Halakhah ve-Kabbalah* (Jerusalem: 1984, 175–200). Cf. above sect. 4. See Etkes, 178, on shortening the service on Yamim Noraim by omitting various *piyyutim*, in order to enable the cantor to have an

The maid in your house, just as other women, are not obliged to say the *Shema*, but they are obligated to hear the *Kiddush*, (see BT *Berachot* 20ab), and they will not eat until they have partaken of the *Kiddush* – wine. Therefore, one should not take the stringent position (להדר) to recite the *Shema* at the right time, thereby causing distress to the maid, who after a long day's work with much toil in preparing for Shabbat, waits eagerly to eat and satisfy her hunger.[5]

---

opportunity to rest. He refers us to Yaakov Mark, "Rabbi Yisrael Salanter," apud *Bi-Mehitzatam shel Gedolei ha-Dor* (Jerusalem: 1958, 68). We also did so on the second day of Rosh ha-Shanah which fell on a Friday, in order to enable the women to prepare for Shabbat. See A. Tobolsky, *Hizaharu bi-Chevod Haverchem* (Bnei Brak: 1981, 258). See also above sect. 15, n. 5.

5. His concern for the hungry and his sensitivity to them expresses itself more powerfully in his sermon (published in *Even Yisrael* [Warsaw: 1883, Jerusalem: 1954, 1969], sermon 3), cited and analyzed by Etkes, 173–174. He begins by asking why Abraham, when inviting in the guests from the desert (mentioned above), first *rushes* off the demand of Sarah that *quickly* she produce bread for them (Gen. 18:6: "And Abraham *hastened* into the tent unto Sarah, and said: *Make ready quickly* three measures of fine meal, knead it, and make cakes upon the hearth,") whereas, when it came to the meat, the verse (7) states: "And Abraham ran unto the herd, and fetched a calf tender and good, and gave it unto a young man, and he hasted to dress it." But he did not tell the "young man" to hasten and prepare it. His reply is that there are two categories of feeding the hungry. The one, for a poor man who has nothing of his own to eat and to drink – for him feeding him is an act of "charity" – *tzedakah*. But for a wealthy person, who has much of his own, if he is passing by in a strange land, it is a great mitzvah to welcome him into one's house and to feed him, and this is called "hosting guests" – *hachnasat orhim*. For the poor man, one must rush to give him some sustenance, for he may not have eaten for several days, and not to do so might lead to his death. But for the wealthy person, we need not, or even should not rush, since this might offend him as if he were an impoverished person. He should get a fine meal, in accordance with his status. Therefore, Abraham's first concern was to hurriedly give some basic sustenance – bread. After that he prepared a more sumptuous meal with meat. Here too, he did not tarry, but there was not the same rush. And in this way, he concludes, he carried out two mitzvot, *tzedakah* – charity and *hachnasat orhim* – hosting the guests. See Etkes's further discussion and analysis on loaning money (175), and further on his sensitivity to the poor, 180–181. (See above, sects. 11, 13, and 16.)

It is further related of R. Yisrael Salanter that he once visited the *Hiddushei ha-Rim*, R. Yitzhak Meir Alter, the Gerer Rebbe. The latter paid him great respect and accompanied him to the nearby synagogue. It quickly became known to the *Hasidim* that R. Yisrael was in town, and as he came to the synagogue a huge crowd thronged around waiting to see how the great visitor prayed. How deep was their disappointment when they saw, that, rather than praying lengthily as expected of a *tzaddik*, he prayed very briefly. At the end of the service, R. Yisrael sensed the peoples' disappointment and bewilderment at his unexpected behavior. He explained to them as follows:

> I saw that because of my presence so many people have interrupted their work: the tailor – his cutting; the shoemaker – his last; the blacksmith – his bellows. They left their work in order to see me. I therefore felt that if I would pray at length I would be causing them a financial loss. And therefore I prayed speedily.

(*Maaseihem shel Tzaddikim*, by Ma-Tov Getz, Jerusalem: 1986, vol. 3, 191–192.) And cf. above, section 16.

An additional story told of R. Yisrael (Etkes, 181; Mark, p. 70) concerns his supervision over the preparation of *matzot* for Passover in the city of Salant. For on one occasion he found himself too busy to be able to stay present during the actual baking of the *matzot*. His disciples asked him with what should they be most concerned in order to receive his approbation (*hashgahah*). His reply was, "The only thing I request of you is to be most careful lest through your being overly stringent in your inspection, you will cause pain and anguish to Tzipah who kneads the dough. She may fear that she is not kneading it quickly enough. Do not forget she is a widow, and one may not cause grief to a widow."

Another version of this tradition tells that he was asked to certify the *kashrut* of a certain *matzah* factory. The owner had recently opened the factory and proudly led Rav Salanter through his factory, showing off his highly efficient, scrupulously regulated *matzah* baking operation. At the end of the tour, the owner asked Rav Salanter, "So? Will you give us your *hashgahah*?" Rav Salanter said quietly, but firmly, "No." "No?" The owner asked, "But everything here is so clean, so efficient, *mehadrin min hamehdrin*! What's the problem?" Rav Salanter replied, "You have created a very efficient plant, but the women producing the *matzot* are strained beyond their limits under the burden you have placed on them. Your workers are suffering. We have been accused of using the blood of Christian children in our *matzah*. While this is clearly untrue, in this case the blood of your workers is in these *matzot*. I cannot, therefore, give my *hashgahah*."[6]

But perhaps one of the most remarkable tales told of Reb Yisrael is that related by R. Yishayah Steinberger, in an article (in the *Makor Rishon* newspaper, January 28, 2011, Shabbat Supplement, 10):

> When Reb Yisrael was on his death bed, there was a simple person who remained with him to minister him during his last hours. And after his decease, the great disciples, who were not with him at that time, the Saba of Kelm (R. Simchah Zissel mi-Kelm), the Saba Novardok (R. Yosef Yoizel Horowitz), Reb Naftali Amsterdam, Reb Itzele Blazer and others, all sought to hear from the attendant what were his last words, his last acts, his final communications. Surely at such a crucial juncture of his life, he must have expressed deeply meaningful statements. Did he say the *vidui* (confession at the death-bed)?, they asked. "Certainly," replied the attendant. "Did he say it at length?" "He seemed to murmur some such prayers," was the reply. The disciples remained dissatisfied with these neutral responses. They were convinced he must have done something of much greater significance, on the eve of giving up his soul to his Creator. So they continued to press the attendant, until suddenly he remembered something else. "Several times before his death the Rabbi repeated a strange statement," said the attendant. "Dead people are not dangerous. There is no reason to be afraid of them." The disciples instantly understood what was Reb Yisrael's intention with this statement. He knew that this simple person would have to spend a long night alone

---

6. *Food & Justice: Haggadah Supplement,* Uri L'Tzedek (New York: 2011, 22). Cf. the version in Katz (ibid., 358), and see below Part III ad fin. For the workers' conditions in matzah-baking factories in the mid-19th cent., see the detailed description in *Kuntres Bitul Modaah*, ed. Y.S. ha-Levi Natansohn (Lemberg: 1859, 23b), which describes the cramped conditions, the sweaty heat and the blistered fingers of the workers involved in hand-baking the *matzot*. On the polemic over machine-made *matzot* as opposed to hand-baked ones – the subject of *Kuntres Bitul Modaah* – see the fine comprehensive article by Meir Hildesheimer and Yehoshua Lieberman, "The Controversy Surrounding Machine-made *Matzot*: Halakhic, Social, and Economic Repercussions," *HUCA* LXXV (2004), 193–262, especially 247–248, with a full bibliography, to which one should now add Y. Mundshein's article, "*Ha-Pulmus be-Devar 'Matzot Mechonah'*", *Zechor le-Avraham* (2002, part 2, 849–877).

> with a dead corpse, and very likely he would have an attack of panic. He wished to assure him that there was no reason for fear.

Thus at the very last moments of his life, his main concern was for the mental and emotional well-being of his attendant.

Earlier on we cited one of his aphorisms, namely that:

> Even at the hour when one stands in fear and trembling before the awesomeness of judgment, one is not free from the obligation of taking care not to tread on one's neighbor's foot.

And here it should be stressed that all R. Yisrael's *musar* ideology was fully embedded in his understanding of the halachah.

24

Reb Yisrael Meir ha-Cohen of Radin – the Hafetz Hayyim (1838–1933)

WE SHOULD TAKE NOTE of the Hafetz Hayyim's ruling in his *Shaar ha-Tziyyun* to *Shulhan Aruch Orah Hayyim* 639, subsection 67. The issue under discussion is whether one waits until midnight to take one's meal in the *sukkah* when it is raining, hoping that it might stop raining (see *Shulhan Aruch* 639:5). The *Mishnah Berurah* (ibid.) writes in the name of some latter-day authorities that, at least on the first day, one should wait to midnight. But in the *Shaar ha-Tziyyun* (66) he adds:

> If by waiting he is distressed by his hunger or (lack of) sleep (and especially when he invites poor guests, and in all probability they have not eaten the whole day long and are ravenously hungry and distressed), he should not wait . . . , and especially for poor people it is sinful to delay their meal . . . , etc.

Here, several halachic considerations are brought to bear on the issue: (a) the fact that a sufferer (מצטער)[1] is not duty bound to sit in the *sukkah* (see, e.g. *Orah Hayyim* 639:2, *Rema*, on not sleeping in the *sukkah* when it is cold, etc.); (b) the importance of welcoming guests (discussed above); (c) feeding the hungry; (d) delaying giving them food may constitute a sin (BT *Rosh ha-Shanah* 4ab). However, what is noteworthy in the Hafetz Hayyim's parenthetical note is (a) that he takes it for granted that one is

---

1. On the concept of "*mitz'taer*," and whether, for example, one in such a state is not obligated to wear *tefillin*, see R. Yitzhak Yosef's *Ein Yitzhak*, vol. 3 (Jerusalem: 2009), 377. (See above, sect. 10, n. 1, and sect. 2.)

hosting poor people in one's *sukkah*, and (b) his sensitivity to their painful plight.[2]

---

2. There is a very considerable bibliography on the Hafetz Hayyim. For a sampling, for example, Dov Katz, *Tenuat ha-Musar*, vol. 4 (Tel Aviv: 1957, 17–175); *Ha-Hafetz Hayyim: Hayyav u-Poalo*, by R. Moshe Meir Yashar, 3 vols. (Tel Aviv: 1959–1961); Lester Samuel Eckman, *Revered by All: The Life and Works of Israel Meir Kagan – Hafetz Hayyim, (1838–1933)*, 2nd ed. (New York: 1974). His son, R. Aryeh Leib ha-Cohen, published his letters: *Michtevei ha-Rav Hafetz Hayyim*, 2nd ed. (New York: 1953), which included *Derachav, Nimukav ve-Sihotav Shel ha-Hafetz Hayyim zt"l* (reprinted Tel Aviv: 1968).

The Hafetz Hayyim

25

Rav Aharon Leib Steinman

IN THIS CONTEXT, it is worth retelling what I saw related to Hannukah 2008 in the *Be-Sheva* newspaper: A group of Yeshiva students came to Rav Steinman and asked him whether it was right that they should take the strict path of eating their meals on Hannukah in their dormitory rooms, so that the place they lit their candles would also be the place of their meals. His reply was that they do not need to do so, for their eating outside of the Yeshiva canteen would create additional work for the Yeshiva's kitchen staff. Their counterclaim was that they would use disposable dishes which they themselves would clear and clean up after their meals. But he answered, rejecting this argument, that "One cannot rely on the boys to clear away the food," and, therefore, if their eating in their rooms would cause extra work for the kitchen staff, it would be better for them not to take the stringent path (שלא להחמיר).

26

Reb Yisrael Salanter Again

AND YET ANOTHER wonderful testimony about that great Torah luminary and paragon of true piety, from Rabbi Dov Katz's *Rabbi Yisrael Salanter*, Jerusalem: 1975, 45–46:

> While he was living in Salant, it once happened that Reb Yisrael did not appear in the synagogue on Yom Kippur night.[1] The congregation waited for the *Kol Nidrei* prayer, and after a while they again waited for the *Maariv* service. They looked for him in his house; they sent out people to search for him throughout the town, but they could not find him. People were greatly surprised, and the congregation in the synagogue began to be worried about him.
>
> After they finished citing all the *piyyutim* and were about to end the *Maariv* service, he suddenly appeared in a crumpled coat, straggly beard and with his hair full of feathers. He wrapped himself in his *tallit* and began to pray. After he finished praying, he related innocently that on his way to the synagogue he heard a child crying. When he entered the house from which the crying was heard, he found a baby, some two months old lying in a cradle and weeping while next to it was a bottle of milk. By the baby on the bed slept a young girl of about six. He understood that the baby's mother

1. A somewhat similar story is told of him in A. Tobolsky, *Hizaharu bei-Chevod Haverchem* (Bnei Brak: 1981, 258), when a group of Jewish soldiers turned up at the last minute and he had to arrange for them kosher meals.

> had wished to go to hear the *Kol Nidrei* prayer and had prepared milk for it, and left it under the care of his little sister, who in the meantime had fallen soundly asleep, and heard nothing of the baby's cries. Reb Yisrael took the bottle, fed the baby and put it to sleep, and afterwards woke up the sister, so he could leave for the synagogue. But the young girl entreated him not to leave her, for she was afraid to remain alone. So he agreed, and stayed with her until her mother came back from the synagogue, and then left them and went to pray.
>
> After Reb Yisrael finished his story, he expressed great joy that on this holy night he was privileged to carry out a great mitzvah of benevolence (חסד) towards these children. Reb Yisrael regarded the act of benevolence as a means to cling to the ways of God, who is רב חסד, "abundant in goodness" (Exodus 34:6), and we have been commanded to walk in his ways: Just as He does deeds of benevolence, so too must you do deeds of benevolence."

We see then how Reb Yisrael's extreme sensitivity to the needs of the poor, the orphan maids, and small children, overrode any ritual requirement of a more formal nature, and any more stringent attachment to halachic requirements. The needs of his fellow creatures were far more committal to him than toward Maker.

A similar tale is told of Reb Moshe Leib of Sasov (died 1807; Buber, 87):

> On the eve of the Day of Atonement, when the time had come to say *Kol Nidre*, all the Hasidim were gathered together in the House of Prayer waiting for the rabbi. But time passed and he did not come. Then one of the women of the congregation said to herself: "I guess it will be quite a while before they begin, and I was in such a hurry and my child is alone in the house. I'll just run home and look after it to make sure it hasn't awakened. I can be back in a few minutes."
>
> She ran home and listened at the door. Everything was quiet. Softly she turned the knob and put her head into the room – and there stood the rabbi holding her child in his arms. He had heard the child crying on his way to the House of Prayer, and had played with it and sung to it until it fell asleep.

(See also the versions in Jerome R. Minz, *Legends of the Hasidim*, Chicago and London: 1962, 176; and Elie Wiesel, *Somewhere A Master: Further Hasidic Portraits and Legends*, New York: 1982, 98–99.)

Whether these be hagiographic legends of questionable historicity or accurate documentation of real events is, for our purposes, of secondary importance. For their message is clear and meaningful in the extreme.[2]

2. And, of course, many of us have heard Isaac Leib Peretz's "If not higher," *Oib nisht noch hecher*, which is to be found in many English translated versions.

27

Reb Yaakov Stein and Reb Menahem Mendel of Kosov (1759–1834)

In a somewhat similar vein, Agnon[1] records the following:[2]

> The Gaon Rabbi Yaakov Stein was head of the rabbinical court in Lvov, and it was his wont to deal leniently in matters of *issur ve-heter*, i.e., ritual matters, while Rabbi Herzel, the decisor of Lvov ruled most stringently in such matters. Once, on the eve of Yom Kippur the two met at a *brit milah*. When they left one another, Rabbi Herzel wished Rabbi Yaakov a *gemar hatimah tova* and *selichah u-mechilah*, forgiveness and expiation on this holy day for both of us for the best. Rabbi Yaakov answered him that he did not need to request this. "For if I declared the non-kosher kosher, that would constitute a sin against one's Maker and Yom ha-Kippur would expiate it. But you, most honorable Sir, are unnecessarily stringent, and declare not kosher in vain, and this causes monetary loss to those who came to you with questions of this nature, and the Torah sought to minimize Israel's financial loss (התורה חסה על ממונם של ישראל);[3] hence, you are transgressing a sin against your fellow men, which Yom ha-Kippurim will [in itself] not expiate.

(Cf. above section 3 ad fin. on R. Avraham Abush.)

---

1. In his *Yamim Noraim – Days of Awe* (Jerusalem: 1938, 8).
2. He cites R. Hayyim Eliezer Deitchman, *Sefer Shemuot Tovot ve-Razin de-Oraita* (Warsaw: 1890).
3. On this principle, see what I wrote in *Darkah Shel ha-Halachah* (Jerusalem: 2007, 93–99, 140). (See above, sect. 15.)

And here we can add yet another very instructive tale told of Reb Menachem Mendel of Kosov (see Buber, 96):

> A deputation came to Rabbi Mendel of Kosov to complain of a certain slaughterer in their town. After they had enumerated a long list of misdeeds the people asked the Zaddik to relieve this objectionable person of his office. But one who had come along with the rest disputed their testimony, saying that it was slander and sprang from hatred. Rabbi Mendel decided in favor of the slaughterer. The others reproached him bitterly because he had believed the words of one single man and ignored the majority.
>
> "The Scriptures relate," he said, "that God bade Abraham offer his son as a burnt-offering, and Abraham prepared to obey. But an angel stopped him and instantly he heeded the angel's voice even though God had not himself revoked his command. What the Torah teaches us thereby is this: None but God can command us to destroy a man, and if the very smallest angel comes after the command has been given and cautions us: 'Lay not thy hand upon . . .' (Genesis 22:12) we must obey him."

And here again we may recall yet another Hasidic tale, this time told of Reb Zvi Hirsh of Rymanov (died 1846; Buber, 141):

> A woman once came to Rabbi Hirsh, her eyes streaming with tears, and complained that she had been the victim of a miscarriage of justice in the rabbinical court. The Zaddik summoned the judges and said: "Show me the source from which you derived your verdict, for it seems to me that there has been some error." Together they looked up the passage in the book Breastplate of Judgment [*Hoshen Mishpat*, a section of the *Shulhan Aruch* dealing with civil matters. D. S.] on which the verdict had been based, and discovered that there had indeed been a misinterpretation.
>
> One of the judges asked the rabbi how he had known beforehand that there had been an error. He answered: "It is written: 'The law of the Lord is perfect, restoring the soul,' (Psalms 19:8). Had the verdict been in accordance with the true law, the woman could never have wept as she did."

28

Reb Yisrael Salanter versus the Hafetz Hayyim

A FASCINATING CONTROVERSY between these two giants of both halachah and *musar* is recorded by R. Yisrael Dendrovitch, in his article in *Moriah* 31:7–8, 2011, 170–173.

It is known (and has been mentioned above in section 3, ad init.) that before Yom Kippur one must appease one's neighbor and ask his forgiveness for wrongs done him. However, the question was raised whether one was required to do so if the neighbor was unaware that he had been wronged or somehow offended. R. Moshe Sternbuch in his *Moadim ve-Zemanim* (vol. 1, Jerusalem: 1958, sect. 54) writes that he heard from the great *Mashgiah*, Reb Eliyahu Dessler, that Reb Yisrael Salanter expounded that at times begging forgiveness for a wrong done from a friend can actually be sinful. For if he was unaware of having been wronged and is now made cognizant thereof, he may be seriously hurt, whereas previously he suffered no hurt. Therefore, in his opinion, in such a case it is preferable to make no mention of the incident, but merely to state, "If I in any way hurt or offended you, I request your pardon."

This, however, was not the opinion of the Hafetz Hayyim. In his volume *Hafetz Hayyim*, (*Hilchot Lashon-Hara, Klal* 4, sect. 12) he ruled as follows:

> Even if his neighbor does not at all know [of the wrong done him], he must reveal to him how he wrongly acted against him and request his forgiveness, since he knows that through his actions this [wrong] was committed.

He was basing himself on Rabbenu Yonah's *Shaarei Teshuvah* 3:207.

R. Avraham Aba Kassovsky, the Rabbi of Yanovah and an intimate friend of the Hafetz Hayyim revealed to the Hafetz Hayyim's son, R. Aryeh Leib ha-Cohen, that which he heard from the Hafetz Hayyim himself, namely that this was a point of deep controversy between the Hafetz Hayyim and Reb Yisrael Salanter. For so writes the son in his *Michtevei ha-Rav Hafetz Hayyim*, Warsaw: 1939, 8):

> By the way I shall write to you what I heard from his holy mouth when he brought the book *Hafetz Hayyim* to the great Gaon ... R. Yisrael Salanter so that he could examine it. Afterwards he [R. Yisrael] said to him that he had a tremendous question regarding what was written in that book (*Hilchot Lashon-Hara* 4:12) that "even if his neighbor does not at all know ... he must reveal to him ..." Surely, if he did not know, informing him would only cause him pain and anguish, and why should the neighbor suffer merely so that he could atone for his misdeed." The Hafetz Hayyim replied, "But surely I was only basing myself on Rabbenu Yonah's *Shaarei Teshuvah*!"

The tale has a continuation as related by R. Aharon Soloveitchik (in his *Perah Mateh Aharon*, on the Rambam, *Mada*, Jerusalem: 1997, *Hilchot Teshuvah* 2:9, 187), in the name of R. Yitzhak Hutner, who related that:

> R. Yisrael Salanter replied to the Hafetz Hayyim, that he too knew that this ruling is found in R. Yonah's *Shaarei Teshuvah*, but we have to understand that passage differently ..., and to reveal the wrong would be to add a sin to a crime. To which the Hafetz Hayyim replied that the simple understanding of the R. Yonah passage is in accordance with his interpretation.

The Hafetz Hayyim added that he requested a *haskamah* – approbation – to the book from Reb Yisrael, in which he could state explicitly that on this issue he (Reb Yisrael) did not agree. But Reb Yisrael's reply was that he could not give such a *haskamah*, because many people would read the whole book but not the *haskamah* with care. Hence, if he were to do so, he would be transgressing the prohibition of "not to put a stumbling block before the blind" (Leviticus 19:14), i.e., he might be the cause of misleading people to do what he regarded as forbidden.

We have here evidence of how two great masters struggled with an ethical challenge: the Hafetz Hayyim, following, in his opinion, a classical authority required complete honesty and what nowadays we call "transparency," while Reb Yisrael Salanter's sense of sensitivity overcame that requirement for transparency. And his own sense of honesty, and responsibility for his words, actions and their possible repercussions did not allow him to write an approbation for the Hafetz Hayyim!

See further on this subject R. Ovadiah Yosef, *Hazon Ovadiah – Yamim Noraim*, Jerusalem: 2005, 244, referring to R. Benyamin Yehosua Zilber's *Az Nidberu*, vol. 8, Bnei Brak: 1976, sect. 66, 135–136, who brings a different tradition in the name of R. Eliyahu Dessler concerning Reb Yisrael Salanter's position (without reference to the Hafetz Hayyim). R. Ovadiah also, following R. Yisrael Salanter's view, cites R. Shlomo Zalman Auerbach as following the same line of thinking.

This controversy may also be related to yet another one. The Rambam, in *Hilchot Teshuvah* 2:3, refers that when confessing one's sin, one must enumerate them in detail (צריך לפרט את החטא), whereas, the *Shulhan Aruch Orah Hayyim* 607:2, states that one does not need to do so, following the view of R. Akiva, who bases himself on the verse in Psalms 32:1, "Blessed be he whose transgression is forgiven, whose sin is covered (כסוי חטאה)" – i.e., undisclosed (see BT *Yoma* 86b, as opposed to the view of R. Yehudah ben Baba, basing his view on Exodus 32:33). R. Yosef, *Hazon Ovadiah*, ibid., also adds that if one confesses silently one should enumerate the sins [since this will not offend anyone else].

It may further be noted that in BT *Yoma* 86b, Rav Nahman draws a distinction between sins against one's neighbors and sins against God, namely that those against God need not be disclosed, but those against humans should be disclosed. And indeed this view is followed by the Rambam in *Hilchot Teshuvah* 2:5:

> It is highly praiseworthy in a penitent to make public confession, openly avow his transgressions and discover to others his sins against his fellow-men; he should say to them: "Truly, I have sinned against so and so, and did thus and thus to him; and lo, this day, I repent and feel remorse." He, however, who is proud and does not publicize his trespasses but conceals them, has not achieved complete repentance, as it is said, "He who covereth his transgressions shall not prosper" (Proverbs 28:13). This only applies to transgressions in matters between man and man. But sins committed against God, the penitent need not publicize. Indeed, it is a mark of effrontery on his part if he does so, but he should repent of them before the Almighty, blessed be He, declaring in detail his sins before Him, and make public confession in general terms; and it is well for him that his iniquity has not become known, as it is said, "Happy is he whose transgression is forgiven, whose sin is covered" (Psalms 32:1).

29

Reb Aryeh Levin (1885–1969)

RECENTLY I CAME UPON a beautiful story that, in a sense, encapsulates all that we have been talking about. Rabbi Shlomo Riskin, the Rabbi of Efrat and chancellor of Ohr Torah Stone institutions, quoted it in his article in the *Jerusalem Post*, October 14, 2001, 42, and I cite his formulation in verbatim. It is about Reb Aryeh Levin, the saintly Jerusalem authority who lived between 1885–1969, and who was memorialized by Simcha Raz in his two biographical volumes, *Ish Tzaddik Hayah*, Jerusalem: 1978, and *Tzaddik Yesod Olam*, Jerusalem: 1996 (although I have not found this tale in either of them):

> Two days before the advent of Sukkot, he went to the Geula district of Jerusalem to choose his Four Species. Immediately, word spread and a large crowd gathered around him. After all, the *etrog* is referred to in the Bible as a beautiful fruit (*etz hadar*), and since we are enjoined to "beautify the commandments," observant Jews are especially careful in purchasing a most beautiful and outstanding *etrog*.
>
> Everyone was interested in observing which criteria the great *tzaddik* would use in choosing his *etrog*. To the amazement of the crowd, however, Reb Aryeh looked at one *etrog* and put it down, picked up a second, examined it, and then went back to the first and purchased it together with his three other species. The entire transaction took less than five minutes. The crowd, rather disappointed, rapidly dispersed, imagining that perhaps the great rabbi had a very pressing appointment.
>
> One person decided to follow Reb Aryeh to see exactly where he was going. What could be more important than choosing an

etrog the day before Sukkot, the Jerusalemite wondered? Reb Aryeh walked into an old-age home. The individual following him waited outside and 90 minutes later the great sage exited. The Jerusalemite approached him, and said, "Revered rabbi, please don't think me impudent, but I'm anxious to learn a point of Torah, and therefore I'm asking the question. The great mitzvot of Sukkot include the waving of a beautiful *etrog*. I am certain that visiting the elderly individual or individuals in the old-age home is also an important mitzvah, but they will be in the old-age home during Sukkot as well as after it. The purchase of the *etrog* is a once-a-year opportunity. I would have expected the revered rabbi to have spent a little more time in choosing the *etrog*."

Reb Aryeh took the man's hand in his and smiled lovingly. "My dear friend," he said. "There are two mitzvot [regarding] which the Torah employs the term *hidur* [beautification]; one is the mitzvah of a beautiful *etrog* [*pri etz hadar*, Leviticus 23:40] and the second is beautifully honoring the face of the aged [*vehadarta pnei zaken*, Leviticus 19:32]. However, the *etrog* is an object and the aged individual is a subject, a human being and not a fruit. Hence, I believe one must spend much more time in beautifying the commandment relating to the human being than beautifying the commandment relating to a fruit."

Reb Aryeh Levin
From the book *Ish Tzaddik Hayah* by Simcha Raz

30

The Feast on the Fast of the Seventeenth of Tammuz

HERE I SHOULD LIKE to bring an albeit somewhat questionable tale that belongs to the sphere of popular folklore, but which, I believe, reflects clearly the basic notion we have been trying to promote. It is found in a small pamphlet, entitled *Jewish Folk-Stories from Hungary*, by Gershon Bribram, edited by Otto Schnitzler, and published by the *Ethnological Museum and Folklore Archives: Israel Folklore Archives (IFA)*, no. 10, Haifa: 1965, [Hebrew], 22–24, and there entitled "A sin that comes of a Mitzvah." Here is my rough translation:

> A certain Hasid would come regularly every year to visit his Rebbe. He would try to arrange these visits on the three festivals and/or the High Holidays . . . so that he could celebrate them in his presence.
>
> And behold, it once happened, that unlike his normal practice, he came on a regular day, actually the eighteenth of Tammuz. His Rebbe received him warmly, asking after his welfare and what good news he brought with him. The Hasid replied, "Unfortunately I have no good news, for a great sin is troubling my conscience, for yesterday – the Seventeenth of Tammuz – I did not fast."
>
> "Woe am I that I hear such a thing," responded the Rebbe in deep shock. "Surely even the simplest Jew fasts on this day. What happened to you, you who always are so punctilious in your mitzvot, that you failed on this occasion?" And the Rebbe did not limit himself to these words of surprise, but went on to expound the nature of the fast, how five different tragedies struck the Jews on that day... "And how could you, a pure and honest Jew, not fast on this special day."
>
> "Indeed, this was a most serious sin that I sinned," declared the

> Hasid, "but I also fulfilled a great mitzvah on this same day. For I took care of a young bride, covering the cost of her wedding (*hachnasat kallah*)." "Indeed, that is a great mitzvah," intoned the Rebbe. "It is one of the very important mitzvot listed in M. *Peah* 1:1, for which the reward is in the World to Come. May you be blessed for this." The Hasid was overjoyed to hear his Rebbe's praise, but before he could leave to go on his way, his Rebbe stopped him, and asked him, "I have known you for quite a while, and I know you are not a wealthy man. How come suddenly you were able to carry out this mitzvah, which involves considerable expenses?"
>
> "Truth to tell," began the Hasid, "what happened is as follows. On the Seventeenth of Tammuz I got up early and asked my dear wife to prepare some food for me for my journey, so that I would have something on which to break my fast. I kissed the *mezuzah*, prayed the morning prayers, and a prayer for the journey, and went off on my way. My path led me to the bank of a certain river, and under the bridge I saw some Jewish maidens bent over doing their washing in the river. I knew I would hear no words of Torah from them, but nonetheless the evil inclination, which never sleeps, pushed me into listening to their conversation. And behold, I hear how Esther is asking Rachel, "Do you know that today is the Seventeenth of Tammuz, and every good Jew is obligated to fast on this day?" "Certainly I know," answered Rachel. "But would that the Lord grant me gold coins for my dowry equal to the number of Jews who eat on this day" (i.e., meaning even if only a few). And here Rachel sighed a deep sigh, for she came from an impoverished family, and from whence would come the money for her dowry?
>
> As soon as I heard these sighs, I was filled with pity for poor Rachel. I immediately hurried home, called together all the members of my household, my neighbors and acquaintances, and requested that they all join me in the mitzvah of *hachnasat kallah*. I asked them to dine and sate themselves on this day of fasting, so that Rachel's prayerful request be heard in the Heavens, and let it be granted to her that as many people as dined on that day, so would be the number of gold coins she would have for her dowry.

Now while this tale may be halachically questionable, I understand the theme that it contains to expose the understanding that helping the poor maiden through the mitzvah of *hachnasat kallah* was of greater importance, and hence overrode even the obligation of fasting on that day. The social mitzvah overpowered, as it were, the ritual one.

This, as I stated above, is my understanding of this popular folkloristic tale. There is, I believe, something very positive, and even charming, in the literal efficacy of wholesome naivité of the Hasid, and his uncomplicated belief in the literal prayer even when possibly unintended by the supplicant. (Compare the discussion in Tamar Alexander-Friser, *The Heart in a Mirror: The Sephardic Folklore*, Detroit: 2008, 264–266, 278 et seq.) Or you might suggest that this is a satirical narrative, parodying the Hasid as a simpleton with a primitive belief in the unnatural. If this tale came from Lithuania, one might possibly argue that it was meant as a critique of the errant beliefs of the ignorant and ingenious Hasidim. But coming as it does from Hungary, I believe that the narrator fully intended to give us a fine example of the simple, unsophisticated belief of a pious Hasid as an example of true and pure faith. Indeed, that this is the correct interpretation seems evident from the editor's preparatory remarks, on p. 19, and see his comments ad loc. Here I may add that Prof. Dov Noy, the preeminent Jewish folklorist of our generation, remarks in his introductory article "What is Jewish about a Jewish folktale?" (Foreword to *Miriam's Tambourine: Jewish Folktales around the World*, ed. Howard Schwartz, New York: 1986, xviii) that "there is an ubiquitous instructional element in literally all Jewish folktales." Here too I am convinced there is a clear instructional message.

Finally, I would call attention to Elie Wiesel's beautiful foreword to Peninnah Schram's *Jewish Stories One Generation Tell Another*, Northvale, New Jersey and London: 1989, xi–xvii, entitled "The Storyteller's Prayer." Inter alia, he writes (xvi), "Our tales try to show that the roads to God must go through man, just as God's link to His Creation and Himself is assured by man."

Incidentally, we may call attention to yet another famous tale with the theme of eating on the Seventeenth of Tammuz, though it is completely different in character. It is in R. Yisrael Ber Odesser's *Michtav Mi-Rabbi Nachman* (Jerusalem: 1984), which begins with the fact that once by mistake R. Odesser ate on the Seventeenth of Tammuz. He was so upset that he even contemplated suicide. But then, before doing so he decided to open a book at random to see if he could find any reason to live. He closed his eyes, took down a book from off the shelf, and when he opened his eyes a page fell out of it. It was a letter from R. Nachman that spoke to him directly and transformed his life. In it was written as follows:

> It was very hard for me to descend to you. My dear disciple, be strong and courageous. My fire will burn until the Messiah will come. As a sign that this letter is true, on the Seventeenth of Tammuz they will say that you are not fasting.

(See Howard Schwartz, *Leaves from the Garden of Eden*, Oxford: 2009, 22.) The inner meaning of this tale is not altogether clear to me. Doubtless, each reader will be able to find his own interpretation and a personal message to himself.

31

The *Tzaddik*'s Unexpected Companion in the World to Come

AND SINCE we have been drawn into the field of folklore, I cannot restrain myself from bringing in extenso these very moving stories to be found in Nathan Ausubel's *A Treasury of Jewish Folklore*, New York: 1948, 503–506. They are, in a sense, variations on one single theme, the surprising individual who will be the *Tzaddik*'s companion in the World to Come. They both bear the same clear message.

> 1. Rabbi Joshua was very pious and learned in the Law. Once, in a dream, a voice spoke to him: "Rejoice, Joshua, because you and Nenes, the butcher, will sit side by side in Paradise and your reward will be the same."
>
> When Rabbi Joshua awoke he cried, "Woe is me! Even since childhood I have devoted myself to the service of the Lord, studied the Torah without end and illumined the minds of eighty disciples. Now see the reward I will be getting for all my good deeds! It seems I'm no better than Nenes, the butcher!"
>
> He then sent for his disciples and said to them, "I will not enter the House of Study with you until I find Nenes the butcher and learn from him what it is that he has done to deserve being my companion in Paradise.
>
> From town to town Rabbi Joshua went with his disciples in search of Nenes the butcher, but no one had ever heard of him. At last, after much wandering, they came to the village where Nenes lived. Rabbi Joshua then began to make inquiries about him.
>
> "O learned Rabbi!" the townsfolk asked him. "How is it that a

man of your eminence should be asking after such an ignoramus and insignificant person?"

But Rabbi Joshua persisted: "Tell me what kind of man is he?"

"Don't ask us, Rabbi," they replied. "You'll see for yourself."

So they sent for the butcher, saying, "Rabbi Joshua is here and would like to see you."

Nenes was astonished.

"Who am I," he exclaimed, "that a great man like Rabbi Joshua should wish to see me? I'm afraid you've come to make sport of me! I will not go with you!"

Chagrined, the townsfolk returned to Rabbi Joshua and said, "O light of Israel! Light of our eyes and crown of our head! Why have you sent us to such a boor? He has refused to come with us."

"I will not go from here," cried Rabbi Joshua, "until I have seen Nenes, the butcher! In fact, I will go to him myself."

When the butcher caught sight of Rabbi Joshua, he became frightened. "O crown of Israel!" he exclaimed, "why do you wish to see me?" "I wish to put to you some questions," answered Rabbi Joshua. "Tell me, what good have you done in your life?"

"I am an ordinary butcher. I have a father and a mother who are old and weak. I've given up all my pleasures to attend to their needs. I wash and dress them and prepare their food with my own hands."

When Rabbi Joshua heard these words he bent down and kissed the butcher on the forehead, saying, "My son – blessed are you and blessed is your good fortune! How happy am I to have the distinction of being your companion in Paradise!"

2. Rabbi Simeon once prayed to the Almighty to show him the place reserved for him in Paradise. God answered his prayer, and he found out that his neighbor in the World to Come would be a butcher. Hearing this, Rabbi Simeon was filled with amazement.

"How can that be?" he asked himself in vexation. "All the days and nights of my life I have devoted to the study of the Torah – all my efforts I have directed to the greater glory of God. Why, then, do I deserve the humiliation of being placed next to a common butcher in Paradise?"

Rabbi Simeon thought: "I will call on this butcher and find out what manner of a man he is."

He did so and learned that he was very rich. The butcher was hospitable, and Rabbi Simeon lived in his house for eight days. He was accorded all the honors due his illustrious rank.

One day Rabbi Simeon invited him for a walk in the fields. On the way he asked him, "Pray tell me – to what ends have you devoted your life?"

And the butcher replied, "I know I am a sinner. I've neglected to study the Torah and have spent all my thoughts to the affairs of my shop. At first I was poor, but in time I began to prosper. However, in my good fortune I never forgot the needy. I distributed alms, and for every Sabbath I provided all the poor of the town, and even those of the surrounding towns, with goodly portions of meat."

Still Rabbi Simeon remained unconvinced. Was the giving of charity enough to place a common butcher on the same level with him, the Light of the Age?

"It seems to me you must have done something more meritorious that that!" he exclaimed.

"I really cannot think of anything," replied the butcher, "except one unusual thing that once happened to me. At the time I was the customs collector of this city. Whenever a ship arrived in the harbor I would go aboard to examine the cargo and to collect the customs.

"Once a ship arrived and I went aboard. The captain said to me, 'I am carrying a valuable cargo in the hold of my ship. Possibly you might wish to buy it.'

"'Show it to me,' I replied.

"He then brought up on deck two hundred Jewish slaves in chains. 'How much do you want for them?' I asked. 'I want ten thousand gold pieces for them. If you won't buy them I'll cast them all into the sea and let them drown."

"I had compassion for my Jewish brothers. I bought them and led them ashore. I fed and clothed them and provided them with lodgings. Then I paired the marriageable youths and girls among them, provided dowries for them, and married them off according to the Laws of Moses.

"Now it happened that among them was a beautiful girl. She awakened the deepest sympathy in me, so I gave her as a wife to my son.

"I had invited to the wedding feast all the people of the town, among them the Jewish slaves I had redeemed. But I noticed an extraordinary thing: amidst all the rejoicing, a youth, one of the former slaves, sat alone and shed tears.

"'Why do you weep?' I asked him.

But he did not answer.

"I then led him into a private room and this is what he told me:

> On the very day that he and his comrades had been seized as slaves he was to have married the beautiful girl who had now become my son's wife. So I said to him 'Renounce all thought of her and I will give you a large sum of money!'
>
> "He answered, 'Far better than all the gold and silver in the world would I have for my wife this girl whom I love! But now, alas! It is too late! She is already married to your son!'
>
> "When I heard these words and saw his grief I went to my son and told him of all this.
>
> "'I will divorce her,' cried my son, 'so that she can marry the youth she loves.'
>
> "And this he did. I gave her a dowry and she married the youth."
>
> When Rabbi Simeon heard the butcher's words he exclaimed, "Praise be the Lord on High who has decreed that I shall sit next to you in Paradise!"

(Perhaps this should also be related to the motif of "There are some who gain their place in the World to Come in one moment" – a statement of R. Yehudah ha-Nasi in BT *Avodah Zarah* 10b, 17a, 18a; and see the cycle of stories in JT *Taanit* 1:4, especially that of Pentakaka [or perhaps Pantakaka, see S. Lieberman, *Greek in Jewish Palestine* (New York and Jerusalem: 1994), 31, n. 13].) On the mitzvah of honoring one's parents, see BT *Kiddushin* 30b, and most recently Y.Y. Fuks, *Halichot Bein Adam le-Havero* (Jerusalem: 2008, 82–110).

32

Abba Tahnah Hasida

FINALLY I WOULD LIKE to bring the remarkable passage in *Ecclesiastes Rabbah* 9:4 (*Resh Sidra Tlitaah*):

> Abba Tahnah Hasida entered into a city on the eve of Shabbat just as it was getting dark with a package on his shoulders, when he saw someone covered in boils lying at the crossroads. He said [to himself]: "If I [take off] my package and leave it, how will I maintain myself and my family? And if I leave this boil-covered person I shall endanger my soul!" What, then, did he do? He overcame his evil inclination and brought the sick man into the city, and then returned to take up his package, and [re-]entered [the city] with the setting of the sun. And all the town dwellers were astonished, saying: "This is Abba Tahnah Hasida!" And he too was conflicted in his heart, saying: "Perhaps I desecrated the Sabbath?" At that moment the Holy One blessed be He raised up the sun, as it is written (Malachi 3:20), "But unto you that fear My name shall the sun of righteousness arise." At that hour he thought to himself: "Perhaps I have forfeited my reward [in the World to Come]." A voice came down from Heaven, declaring to him, "Go thy way, eat thy bread with joy, and drink thy wine with a merry heart; for God now accepteth thy works" (Ecclesiastes 9:7) – "Your reward is accepted" (i.e., ratified).

Admiel Kosman expands on this laconic report, interpreting it in multileveled depths.[1] I quote his eloquent analysis in parts, omitting the deeper

1. See most recently the analysis of this story on the part of Admiel Kosman,

levels of interpretation which, in my opinion, he offers conjecturally:

> Abba Tahnah the pious returns to his town, apparently after having spent the entire week working hard to provide for his family. The time when the narrative begins is an extremely significant transitory, liminal time, between weekday and holy, close to the Sabbath.
>
> The narrator begins with a close-up of Abba Tahnah's troubled face that clearly shows his weariness from the entire week. He carries his wages, his family's livelihood, in the heavy burden of a "bundle" on his shoulder. Now, as the Sabbath enters, he and the members of his household are to enjoy the fruits of his labor.
>
> The location of the opening scene, as well, is charged with meaning: it takes place in a transitional location between the field (=nature, the wild and remote space where Abba Tahnah worked the entire week) and the settled and orderly city, where God and His Presence also have a time and place that are well-defined, with a specific day and hour.
>
> But now, before the entry to the city, just before Abba Tahnah fulfills his dream of Sabbath rest, a new obstacle suddenly lies in his path, in the image of a person afflicted with boils who lies stretched out at the "crossroads."
>
> This "crossroads," where the sick person waits, is the key word, the inner code of the entire narrative. As in other Talmudic narratives, the sufferer might be Satan (the "Accuser") in disguise, waiting to test the pious hero of the tale: will his piety withstand this difficult trial?
>
> Two difficult possibilities lie before Abba Tahnah, each of which is fraught with danger. If he cares for the sick man in the little time that remains before the Sabbath, he risks not being able to return and bring in his "bundle" because of the Sabbath violation that this would entail; but if he tends to his "bundle," the sufferer who cries out for help might die in the meantime . . . The radical meaning of this choice is the risk of slightly sliding into the "sunset" (*dimdumei ha-hamah*, literally, the stilling of the sun) that ushers in the Sabbath, with its consequent violation of the inflexible norms of custom, or

---

in his *Man's World: Reading Masculinity in Jewish Stories in a Spiritual Context* (Würzburg: 2009, 101–106).

> perhaps even of halakhah. This twilight hour, when time is uncertain and almost touches the Sabbath, is quite reflective of the doubts that assail Abba Tahnah and the peril inherent in his actions.

Apparently Abba Tahnah Hasida, after his conflicted soul-searching, was willing to risk desecrating the Sabbath in order to help the poor sick man, presumably, because he thought that helping the sick overrode even the risk of the desecration of the Sabbath.

Perhaps we can compare with this what is told of Reb Shalom Shakhna of Probishtah (died 1803; see Martin Buber, *Tales of The Hasidim: The Later Masters*, [New York 1948, 50]):

> Once when Rabbi Shalom Shakhna happened to be staying in a small town of the district of Kiev, the old Zaddik Rabbi Zev of Zhytomir arrived to spend the Sabbath there. On Thursday evening Rabbi Shalom prepared to leave and went to bid Rabbi Zev farewell. The Zaddik inquired when Rabbi Shalom expected to reach his destination. "Tomorrow, around three in the afternoon," was the reply.
>
> "Why do you plan to be on the road after the noon hour on the day before the Sabbath?" Rabbi Zev asked in surprise. "At twelve o'clock I usually put on my Sabbath clothes and start singing the Song of Songs, which is Solomon's, king of peace. By that time the Sabbath peace has already begun for me."
>
> "And what am I to do," replied Rabbi Shalom, "if a tenant farmer comes to me toward evening and tells me his troubles, tells me that his calf has fallen sick, and from his words I gather that he is saying to me: 'You are a lofty soul, and I am a lowly soul; lift me up to you!' What am I to do then?" From off the table the old man took the two candlesticks with the lighted candles, and grasping them in his two hands, he accompanied his young guest through the long corridor to the outer door. "Go in peace," he said. "Go in peace."

Admittedly, this is by no means an exact parallel, and the situation for Reb Shakhna was far less extreme. Nonetheless, for a deeply pious person to go rushing off to some farmer because of his sick cow some short hours before the Sabbath, a time normally dedicated to practical and spiritual preparation to meet the Sabbath Bride – this is surely a powerful statement!

However, I believe the most powerful formulation reflecting this very primary ethical directive, is the statement of Hillel, the great early first century Sage. For when a gentile came to him requesting that he convert him to Judaism while he stood on one foot (*al regel*[2] *ahat*) he gave his famous reply as follows: "That which is hateful to you, do not do unto others – that is the whole Torah and all else is interpretation. Go learn."[3] He did not tell him to go and pray, to bring sacrifices – this took place during the latter days of the Second Temple; he did not tell him to keep kosher and keep the Sabbath. He directed his attention to the plight of his fellow people, how best to relate to them, how not to hurt or offend them, but to treat them as he would wish to be treated himself by others.

Similar such stories are legion, and we could fill many folios with such *maasei hesed*, and *musar* tales. However, I believe the above will suffice to make our point about how to relate to others clear and meaningful.

---

2. Some have seen this as a pun on the Latin *regula* – principle; i.e., teach one the whole Torah encapsulated in one basic principle. See R. Jospe, "Hillel's Rule," *JQR* 81, 1/2 (1990), 45–57, (reprinted in his *Jewish Philosophy: Foundations and Extensions*, vol. 1, ([Lanham: 2009], 191–201). And see above, section 29.

3. I.e., go learn the rest. See Rashi's second interpretation ad loc. This is the kernel of Hillel's ethical thinking, as it appears in numerous other statements and rulings of his. So, for example, *Avot* 1:12, 2:4; BT *Ketubot* 67b, etc. Paralleling this is R. Akiva's statement to Lev. 19:18, "'Love thy neighbor as yourself' – this is a most basic principle of Torah (כלל גדול בתורה)." See *Genesis Rabbah* 24:7 (where Ben Azzai also makes this same statement); JT *Nedarim* 9:4, etc. See above section 21 ad fin.

PART III

Practical and Educational Implications

33

Practical and Educational Implications

EARLIER ON I referred to an article published in *Hakirah* by R. Aharon Hersh Fried, entitled "Is there a Disconnect between Torah Learning and Torah Living?" He argues persuasively that in our education a greater stress must be put on בין אדם לחבירו. On pp. 48–49 he writes:

> The *Sefer HaBris* [*Sefer ha-Brit*, part 2, section 13, chapter 3] too, at the start of a chapter that he calls "דרך הקודש", writes that "the love of friends and the *mitzvot* and behaviors between man and his neighbor (בין אדם לחבירו) are the main facets of the 'holy path' and the foundation of the entire Holy Torah":
> והנה מה שצריך לי להזכיר בזה המאמר הנקרא דרך הקודש הוא אהבת רעים והמצות וההנהגות אשר בין אדם לחבירו כי זה עיקר דרך הקודש ושורש כל התורה הקדושה.
>
> The Alshech [*Sefer Torat Moshe*, *Shemot* chapter 19, verses 1–2] writes similarly that the reason the High Court, the Sanhedrin, had its seat in the *Beit HaMikdash*, close to the *mizbeach* (altar), was to show that in *Hashem*'s eyes the *mizbeach*, which represents the peace between G-d and man, and the Sanhedrin, which represents the law bringing peace between Man and his fellow, were both equal:
> ומן הטעם הזה אחשוב צוה הוא יתברך לשים דיינים אצל המזבח, כמאמרם ז"ל (מכילתא סוף יתרו) על סמיכות אלה המשפטים אצל מזבח אדמה. כי למה שהמזבח משים שלום בין אדם למקום, כן הדיינים בין אדם לחבירו. הורה לנו הוא יתברך כי לפניו שני הדברים שוים.

He continues in this vein, as follows:

> The words of the *rishonim* and the *sifrei mussar* are thus clear. And there's more where they came from, much more. Unfortunately, they

> receive little "press" in our homes and/or our schools. Thus, as far as our children are concerned, being nice and being *frum* are not related.
>
> In some circles I have heard it said that "there is too much talk about *Ahavat Yisroel*," and they suggest that those who talk about אהבת ישראל and בין אדם לחבירו are being motivated by secular humanism rather than Torah. This is a sure way to kill the message. It also places those who advocate doing more about *middos* on the defensive. The bizarre and twisted message becomes, that the true חרדי, the true בן תורה, and the "real" Jew would not be overly concerned about מדות and מצוות שבין אדם לחבירו. In a reversal of his usual role, the truly committed בן תורה is found pointing to היתרים and קולות in this area, showing us how all the איסורים in בין אדם לחבירו need not be taken so seriously. Thus, the same person who will go to great effort and expense to build his *succah* without even one nail in it, so as to be able to fulfill even the strict interpretation of Halacha by the Rashba (even when the *Shulchan Aruch* ruled it to be unnecessary), is now looking for היתרים for various איסורים that are, at the very least, questionable according to the *Shulchan Aruch*.

In seeking to explain this phenomenon, he directs our attention (44–45) to an article by Reb Shlomo Wolbe, published in *Ha-Beer* 15 (1977), which he calls "a *shmuess*." The article is entitled "On *Frumkeit*" (על הפרומקייט):

> In this *shmuess* he puts forth the thesis that there is a basic instinct, inborn in all creatures, each according to its level of נשמה, to be "*frum*," i.e., to want to come close to one's Creator. *Frumkeit* is not יראת שמים, it is not a מדת חסידות, nor is it דקדוק במצוות. It is simply an instinct, and like all instincts it is egotistical, i.e., concerned only with its own satisfaction, unthinking, and given to satisfaction through fantasy. The satisfaction of this instinctual drive, he writes, serves as the force behind many people's *mitzvah* activities, and in a positive way, serves to help us carry out *mitzvot* in spite of hardships. However, because of its egotistical and unthinking nature, one cannot build one's service to *Hashem* on this instinct. The *frum* instinct, no less than any other instinct, must be harnessed, and must be guided by rational thought, i.e., by Torah knowledge and halachah. If not, it will seek satisfaction in inappropriate ways. A person driven by the need to satisfy this instinct will engage in activities that he imagines will lead to a "spiritual high," even if in the process he transgresses very real

> Torah prohibitions (עבירות). He will push his way through a throng in a *shul* to get close to a visiting *tzadik*, pushing one person, jabbing another, and tearing off a button from a third person's jacket, all in the pursuit of attaining imagined proximity to קדושה, i.e., attaining a *frum* "high." He does not consider that his violation of בין אדם לחבירו may remove him from קדושה. Nor does the performance of *mitzvos* בין אדם לחבירו attract him; it does not make him feel more spiritual or holy, it does not satisfy his instinctual need for a *frum* "high."

He summarizes as follows:

> Yes, this is an age-old, deeply ingrained and intractable problem, but we cannot declare ourselves free of the obligation of trying to tackle it, and change it. If we don't, we will not succeed in changing the attitudes and behaviors of our children in the area of מצוות שבין אדם לחבירו. The only way we can do this is by concerted and unrelenting educational programs aimed at the entire community. Parents need to learn the sources with their children, *rabbeyim* and teachers with students, *rabbonim* with their congregants, and each one of us with our *chavrusos* and friends.

In other words we must educate ourselves and our children to a greater degree of awareness and sensitivity to the needs of the other.

This is very forcefully expressed in an episode described in detail by Rabbi J. David Bleich, in his *Contemporary Halachic Problems*, vol. 1 (New York: 1977, 185–186), which I shall cite in full:

> *Mendicants*
>
> The 5730 issue of *Shanah be-Shanah* contains a short item from the pen of the octogenarian scholar, Rabbi Shlomo Yosef Zevin, who in addition to his many and varied scholarly pursuits serves as general editor of the *Encyclopedia Talmudit*. An official of the Israeli Ministry of the Interior referred a proposal of the Tel Aviv Municipal government to Rabbi Zevin, in the latter's capacity as a member of the Chief Rabbinate Council, for his evaluation of the request from the point of view of Halakhah.
>
> As every tourist is painfully aware, Israel has an inordinate number of paupers who openly solicit alms not only in synagogues but on the public streets as well. There is no gainsaying that such practices are socially undesirable and do not reflect creditably upon a country in

> which they are so widespread. The municipality of Tel Aviv therefore requested the Minister of the Interior to initiate legislation which would effectively ban such mendicants from the streets. The official soliciting Rabbi Zevin's views emphasized that no one had suggested restraining the poor from requesting charity from worshippers in synagogues; the proposed ban was to be limited to solicitation in public thoroughfares.
>
> Rabbi Zevin quotes chapter 17 of the Chafetz Chaim's *Ahavat Hesed*, a work devoted to the *mitzvah* of charity, in which the author reports the innovative move of establishing "federations" for the purpose of conferring stipends upon itinerant beggars in order to preclude them from soliciting alms from individual householders. The Chafetz Chaim frowns on this practice and among his sources cites the negative view expressed in the Gemara, *Baba Batra* 7b, with regard to the building of a walled enclosure around one's courtyard because the wall prevents the cry of alms-seekers from being heard.
>
> The well-known anecdote concerning the reaction of Rabbi Levi Yitzhak of Berditchev to a similar proposal is also noted by Rabbi Zevin in this context. The Berditchever sarcastically remarked that the idea is not at all novel; such a communal edict was long ago promulgated by the Council of Four Lands: Sodom, Gomorrah, Admah and Zeboiim. Clearly, Berditchev – and hopefully Tel Aviv also – would not want to be included in such an infamous grouping.
>
> In conclusion Rabbi Zevin suggests that many such paupers would cheerfully desist from these activities if their needs would be provided for by an adequate social-welfare allotment. Nevertheless, he agrees that steps may be taken to prevent beggars from accosting people on public thoroughfares, but argues that they should not be restrained from adopting a mendicant posture at a fixed location. In the final analysis, while undignified forms of public solicitation are to be deplored, it is unthinkable that a Jewish community bar any individual from seeking charity. "If there be among you a needy man, one of your brothers, within any of your gates, in your land which the Lord your God gives you, you shall not harden your heart, nor shut your hand from your needy brother" (Deuteronomy 15:7).

On analysis, we see that Rav Zevin's response contains three elements: (1) the social-communal one, that society must provide adequate social-welfare allotment; (2) halachic, basing himself on the Hafetz Hayyim's reference to *Baba Batra* 7b; (3) the moral and educational aspect, as indicated by the Berditchever's caustic comment, but even more so by the inner meaning of that passage in *Baba Batra*, which states clearly that one may not do that which "prevents the cry of the alms-seekers from being heard," and understood by the final biblical quote from Deuteronomy 15:17, that we must do nothing that might bring to the hardening of the heart. This, again, requires a *continuous* educational process, and, in a sense, justified the mendicants begging on the streets. "Continuous," because as Deuteronomy 15:11 states clearly:

> For the poor shall never leave out of the land: therefore I command thee, saying "Thou shalt open thine hand wide unto thy brother, to thy poor, and to thy needy, in thy land."

Or, in other words, open thy heart and not harden it against the importuning beggars.

This is, in fact, very clearly spelled out by the Hafetz Hayyim himself in a note to chapter 17 in *Ahavat Hesed*. For there he writes as follows:

> Recently there is a phenomenon of those who seek to prevent beggars from coming to the doorstops of householders [to beg for money] . . . and place a charity tax on all members of the city.
>
> And indeed, this is a great error (citing the passage in *Baba Batra*) . . .
>
> And now, let us make a reckoning of the various ills deriving therefrom: (1) . . . For over a period of time their wish will bring about a diminishing of the human characteristic of compassion. For this characteristic becomes firmly embedded in the soul through repeated acts [of charity]. But it will be diminished over further generations, if people will not see, with their own eyes, their neighbors' hardships. And, [when one does give charity to the impoverished], one also comes to a realization that one must thank God for one's own [satisfactory status] in contrast to the sight of the poor and groaning [beggar].[1]

I believe that our message must be clear and unambiguous, namely that not merely for humanistic reasons, but out of the true understanding of *halachah*, we must lay a far greater emphasis on our norms of social behav-

1. See also *Michtevei ha-Rav Hafetz Hayyim*, by his son Reb Aryeh Leib ha-Cohen, 2nd ed. (New York: 1953, part 2, p. 8, sect. 10).

ior. For our piety cannot be limited to our ritual behavior alone; rather our piety and "*frumkeit*" should also be directed towards our fellow beings.[1]

Finally, I should like to end with a quote from Eugene Korn's review essay, already mentioned above (in *Meorot* 8 [2010], 3):

> Orthodoxy's current pan-halakhism [which I see as primarily concerned with ritual, D.S.] seems to have lost interest in the human condition *per se*, and is rapidly losing the language to discuss universal human concerns like ethics, justice, spirituality and human purpose.

This is a trenchant criticism, on the one hand, and also admirably underscores the urgent challenge that we have been discussing throughout this study.[2]

---

1. Recently there has been developing in certain circles a greater sensitivity to social issues. Thus, the phenomenon of Bema'aglei Tzedek in Israel, and its parallel institutes in the USA, which gives a "hechsher" to enterprises, such as factories, restaurants, food shops, etc., which concern themselves with the needs (and legal requirements) of their employees, such as decent working hours, no less than minimum wage rates, social security, non-employment of juniors, etc., reflects this newly emerging awareness of human needs. For food to be declared kosher, one expects more than merely examining the slaughterer's knife and the lesions on the animals' lungs, but that the workers be afforded decent work conditions, a reasonable wage, normal working hours, safety and security, etc. Less than this would constitute an abuse of his basic rights, both legal and moral, and should be sufficient cause to refuse granting a "hechsher." And see above sect. 23 near n. 5.

The subject of ecology and conservation, which also may be related to this issue, is too broad to be discussed here, and I hope to deal with it in another framework. See, in the meantime what I wrote in the *Edah Journal* 2:1 (2002), 1–5, in an article entitled "Jewish Environmental Ethics," and most recently in an article entitled "Bal Tashchit: Waste Not Want Not," in *Beloved Words: Milin Havivin* 5 (2010–2011), 85–91.

2. It is fascinating to find a similar such criticism expressed by a contemporary Hindu thinker, Bharat Gupt, in his *India: A Cultural Decline or Revival?* (New Delhi: 2008, 14–15) speaking of the "Abrahamic traditions [being] . . . co-terminus with the commandments of the book," and that "Hinduism now needs to strongly resist this commandment-alization in order to save its original genius," because for Hinduism it is not the pursuit of commandments that is most central, but rather "a pursuit for realization." (I am grateful to Prof. Gupt of the College of Vocational Studies at the University of Delhi, for presenting me with his valuable study.)

APPENDIX

Charity before Prayer[1]

In Maria and Kazimierz Piechotka's classic *Wooden Synagogues* (Warsaw: 1959 [the English version]), in fig. 200, we have a view of the inside of the main doorway of the synagogue at Przedborz, slightly south of Warsaw (fig. 1). On the right-hand side as one entered (on the left in the photograph) there is a wooden charity-box, finely carved and locked with a small bolt. At its side may be seen a wooden plaque, also ornately carved, inscribed with the verses from Psalms 17:15 and 85:14:

> "As for me, I will behold Thy countenance in righteousness [*be-tzedek*]: I shall be satisfied, when I awake, with Thy likeness. Righteousness [*tzedek*] shall go before Him; and shall set us in the way of his steps."

There is here an overt play on the words *tzedek*, righteousness, and *tzedakah*, charity.

Generally, the words appearing on charity boxes are "[but] righteousness [*u-tzedakah*] delivereth from death" (Proverbs 11:4), and especially

---

1. This appendix is based on what I wrote in my *Minhagei Yisrael*, vol. 7 (Jerusalem: 2003, 25–33). Here, of course, it appears in the context of the principle of the ascendancy of charity as a social mitzvah, and one that may pave the way to real prayer.

on those of *hevrot kadisha* (burial societies).[2] However, the source of the first verse on the plaque at Przedborz may be found in a passage in BT *Baba Batra* 10a:[3]

---

2. This verse appears in the *sugya* (halachic discussion) in BT *Baba Batra* 10a. As to the use of charity boxes, see, for example, Victor Klagsbald, *Catalogue raisonné de la collection juive du musée de Cluny* (Paris: 1981, 118, no. 164 [Nuremberg, 18th cent.]), with the words "צדקה תציל ממות" "charity will save from death," and also "a gift in secret pacifieth anger" (Prov. 21:14). The use of this latter verse is also based on what we read in BT *Baba Batra* 9a, in the words of R. Eliezer: Greater is he who gives charity in secret than Moshe Rabbenu. For concerning Moshe Rabbenu it is written, "For I was afraid of the anger (אף) and hot displeasure (חימה)" (Deut. 9:19), whereas concerning one who gives charity it is written, "A gift in secret pacifieth anger (אף)," (Prov. 21:14). See further below. (And for more charity boxes, see Klagsbald, 119.)

This verse, "charity will save from death" appears most commonly also on wine beakers of *hevrot kadisha*. See David Altshuler, *The Precious Legacy* (Washington: 1983, fig. 153 on p. 159 [Mikolov, Moravia: 1836]), and cf. the charity box ibid., 85 from 1763. See also *The Jewish Museum of Budapest*, ed. Ilona Benoschovsky and Alexander Scheiber (Budapest: 1987, 93, no. 59), (and also additional burial-society boxes without this verse on p. 84, no. 60, from 1822, 96 no. 63, from 1855, and charity boxes on 95, 97–98, and cf. ibid., 116, 118, without the verse). So too in *Museum Narodowe w Warzawie: Judaica*, ed. Ewa Martyna, (Warsaw: 1933, 116, no. 115, from 1859 [without the verse]). These are but a few of the very numerous examples, that can be found in museum and private collections the world over.

Here it should further be noted that *Af* (anger) is "one of the angels of destruction, a prince of wrath and a ruler over the death of mortals. With *Hema*, *Af* once swallowed Moses up to his 'circumcised membrum,' but had to disgorge him when Zipporah (Moses's wife) circumcised her son Gershon, thus appeasing God's wrath against the Law giver who had, it appears, overlooked the covenantal rite [BT *Nedarim* 31a]. *Af* resides in the 7th Heaven and is 500 parasangs tall. He is 'forged out of chains of black and red fire,'" (*Zohar* [2.249b]; Ginzberg, *The Legends of the Jews II*, 308, 328; *Midrash Tehillim*). See Gustav Davidson, *A Dictionary of Angels, Including the Fallen Angels* (New York and London: 1967, 10). There is much to expand on this theme, but this is not the place therefor. In the meanwhile, see M. Moïse Schwab, *Vocabulaire de l'Angelologie* (Paris: 1897, 181); R. Reuven Margaliot, *Malachei Elyon* (Jerusalem: 1945, 208–213. It is, therefore, very understandable that this verse appear both on charity boxes and on those of the burial societies and their wine beakers.

3. This whole passage appears in R. Isaac Abohab's *Menorat ha-Maor*, third

> R. Dostai the son of R. Yannai preached as follows: Come and see, that the ways of the Holy One blessed be He are not as the ways of humans. Among humans, a man brings a great gift to the king, but it is not certain whether or not it will be accepted. [And even if it is accepted] it is not certain that he actually will get to see the king. But with the Holy One blessed be He, it is not so. A person gives a coin to a poor person, and he merits to receive the presence of the divine *Shechinah*, as it is said, "As for me, I will behold Thy face in righteousness: I shall be satisfied, when I awake, with Thy likeness."
>
> R. Eliezer gave a coin to a poor person and *then* prayed. He said, "As for me, I will behold Thy countenance in righteousness."

From this we may learn that after giving charity (*tzedakah – tzedek*)[4] to a poor man, a person may merit to behold the *Shechinah* and to make his requests in his prayers.[5]

R. Eliezer's statement is cited by the Rif (R. Yitzhak Alfasi) and forms the basis of the Rambam's formulation in *Hilchot Matnot Aniyim* 10:15 as follows:

> The greatest of [our] Sages would give a coin to a poor person before each prayer, and [only] afterwards[6] would pray, as it is said, "As for me, I will behold Thy countenance in righteousness."

---

candle, seventh principle, part 2, ed. Y. Fries-Horev and M.H. Katzenelenbogen (Jerusalem: 1961, 397 et seq. with interruptions and additions), and so too in Y. Al-Nakawa's *Menorat ha-Maor* (a book under the same name but by a different author), ed. H. Enelow (reprint Jerusalem: 1972), vol. 1, in the chapter on charity.

4. *Tzedek=tzedakah* throughout the whole *sugya*. See the enlightening observation of Naftali Wieder, in his (posthumous) volume *Hitgabshut Nusah ha-Tefillah be-Mizrah u-be-Maarav: Kovetz Maamarim* (Jerusalem: 1998), 539, n. 176. See further *Zohar* 3, 113b.

5. See Maharsha ad loc.

6. It would appear that the Rambam had a reading in the *sugya* in BT *Baba Batra*: והדר מצלי, "and afterwards he prays." See Raphael Natan Neta Rabbinovitz's, *Dikdukei Soferim* (reprint, NY: 1960) 22a. And it is interesting to note the formulation of *Semag* (*Sefer Mitzvot Gadol*), *Asin* 162 (134b): And R. Eliezer was wont to give a coin to a poor person every day, as it is said, "as for me, I will behold Thy countenance in righteousness."

The Meiri has a slightly different formulation (to BT *Baba Batra* ad loc.):[7]

> And the greatest of [our] Sages would give a coin to a poor person before praying, and then would pray, so that the mitzvah of charity could serve as an advocate between them and their father in heaven.[8] And an indication of this [may be found in the verse], "As for me, I will behold Thy countenance in righteousness."

So too we read in the *Shulhan Aruch Orah Hayyim* 92:10: "It is good to give charity before praying,"[9] and in *Yoreh Deah* 249:14: "It is good to give

---

7. Ed. A. Sofer (New York: 1957, 64).

8. This is based on the words of R. Eliezer be-R. Yossi in BT *Baba Batra*, ibid.: All charity and righteousness that Israel does in this world, [enables] great peace and great advocates [to serve] between Israel and their Father in Heaven [in the World to Come]. (On the word פרקליטין, see my *A Dictionary of Greek and Latin Legal Terms in Rabbinic Literature* [Jerusalem: 1984, 165–166].)

This motif is also to be found in Abohab's *Menorat ha-Maor*, 422: When a person leaves this world and he has in his hands charity and good deeds, they go before him to make for him a pathway of peace, and they serve as positive advocates for him before the Holy One blessed be He, and they do not allow the prosecutors to prosecute, as it is said, "If there is an angel with him [an interpreter, one among a thousand, to show unto man his uprightness]" (Job 33:23). And so too in Al-Nakawa, 34. And based on this, we find tombstones with the motif of a hand placing coins in a charity box. See for example fig. 3, from Mszczonow, in Poland, when we see a hand placing money in a charity box. Above is inscribed, "He hath dispensed, he hath given to the poor" (Psalms 112:9), and the verse continues "his righteousness endures for ever; his horn shall be exalted with honor," implying: after death. See below, n. 12 on the notion of "exaltedness."

On boxes inscribed with "A gift in secret pacifieth anger" (see above, n. 2, and below), see Monica Krajewskka, *Les Temps des Pierres* (Warsaw: 1981, 129), and cf. ibid., 109, 111, (in 111, there is also a cut-down tree, and for this motif see my *Minhagei Yisrael*, vol. 7 [Jerusalem: 2003, 365–368]); and see figs. 4–5, one from Venice and the other from Warsaw, found in A. Schwartzman, *Graven Images* (New York: 1993, 50–51).

9. See *Mishnah Berurah*, ibid., n. 36 for other customs, and the *Magen Avraham* 51:6, according to the Arizal. And see the comprehensive study of my colleague Prof. Moshe Hallamish, "*Ha-Tzedakah mi-Kabbalat Tzefat va-Elach*," *Sefer ha-Zikaron le-Avraham Spiegelman* (Tel Aviv: 1979, 169–185), (and again in his book *Ha-Kabbalah ba-Tefillah u-ba-Minhag* [Ramat Gan: 2000, chap.

a penny to a poor person before each prayer, as it is stated, 'As for me, I will behold Thy countenance in righteousness.'" On which the *Shach (Siftei Cohen)* wrote (ibid., note 10): "To a poor person, etc.: And how much more so if he gives to the [communal] charity box before prayer, and this is even preferable." And so wrote the *Tur* in *Orah Hayyim* 92 ad fin.: "It is good to give charity before prayer, etc."

Indeed, we find in the synagogue of the Rema in Cracow, that as you come into the lobby, there is a charity box fixed onto the wall (fig. 6).[10]

In view of the above, we may well understand why the charity box is

---

17, 383–400]), and in *Minhag Yisrael Torah*, 2nd ed., by Y. Lewy, vol. 1 (Israel: 1995, 132:2, 230–231). And see also in *Hanhagot Tzaddikim*, by H.S. Halevy Rotenberg, who states that R. Dov Baer of Mezridj (1704–1793) gave charity before every prayer service, vol. 3 (Jerusalem: 1991, 102, sect. 15). And so too (p. 91, sect. 18), R. Eliyahu ha-Ethmari from Izmir, the author of *Shevet Musar* (died 1729), wrote: "To give charity before praying, and one must say, 'As for me, I will behold Thy countenance in righteousness.'" (And cf. Hallamish, 172–174 who cited R. Yehiel Michel Epstein's *Kitzur ha-Shlah*, and especially n. 26.) Lewy, (ibid., vol. 2 [Jerusalem: 1988, 713, sect. 5]), cites R. Michel Rabinowitz of Slutzk as saying: "Before going to the synagogue one should set aside charity . . ." etc. As to giving charity at night, see R. Eliyahu Yohanan Guraryeh, *Hikrei Minhagim: Mekorot, Taamim ve-Iyyunim be-Minhagei Habad* (Kfar Habad: 1999, 240–248), and also R. Shlomo Tennenbaum's article in *Or Yisrael* 4/4 (16), (1999), 137–140, "*Minhag Netinat Tzedakah be-'Vayevarech David.'*"

10. On the upper section of the box is written, "Gold, silver and brass," and this is based on Exod. 25:3, "[And this is the offering which ye shall take of them]; Gold, and silver, and brass." The box was restored, the letters blackened, and there was fixed beneath it a metal plate with foreign (i.e., non-Hebrew) letters which cover the lower section of the box. See fig. 6b. One should note that in *Orah Hayyim* 92, which deals with the laws of prayer, we read "before praying" (קודם תפילה), meaning that the charity should be given *directly* before the prayer service; which in the laws of charity an additional word was added "before *all* prayer services" (קודם כל תפילה), according to the Rambam's formulation in *Matnot-Aniyim*, meaning that the obligation to give charity applies before *every* prayer service. At first sight, this would seem not to be in accordance with the view of the *Semag* (cited above, n. 6), who speaks of giving "every day" (בכל יום), but not necessarily before every prayer. Furthermore, the kabbalists ruled that one does not give charity at night (see above, n. 9), because this is the period of *din* – strict judgment – the implication being that one does not give before *maariv* (the evening prayer), and this view is not in accordance with the formulation of Rambam and the *Shulhan Aruch*.

fixed near the entry to the synagogue, so that on entering it one places one's coin into it before going to pray. And possibly, it is not by chance that often this box is fixed to the right of the door, as this would accord with the verse in Psalms 48:11. "Thy right hand is full of righteousness [*tzedek*]."[11] Indeed, we may find some support for this assertion in the notes to the *Sefer Minhagim* of R. Isaac Tyrnau (ed. S.Y. Spitzer [Jerusalem: 1979, 65–66, note 34]):

> On any day when one reads the portion in Deuteronomy 15:19, "All the firstling males . . ." one remembers the dead souls and gives charity,

---

11. We may also refer to Isa. 41:10 "yea, I will uphold thee with the right hand of My righteousness." See also Ps. 89:14, "high is Thy right hand." And compare BT *Baba Batra* 10b: Said R. Abbahu: Moses our Teacher said before the Holy One blessed be He: Master of the Universe, what will uplift the horn of Israel? He replied: "When thou takest" (Exod. 30:12, the verse beginning the passage that requests that each person give the half shekel, etc.). Said R. Abbahu: They asked Solomon the son of David: How far does the power of charity go? He replied: Go and see what my father David stated: "He hath dispersed, he hath given to the poor; his righteousness endureth for ever, his horn shall be exalted with honor" (Ps. 112:9). Rava said: From here "He shall dwell on high: his place of defense shall be the munitions of rocks: bread shall be given him; his waters shall be sure" (Isa. 33:16). Why "He shall dwell on high: his place of defense shall be the munitions of rocks"? Because "his bread he gave [reading נתן instead of ניתן] (and) his waters shall be sure."

It would appear that in order to fully understand the homily one should link up to the preceding verse: "He that walketh righteously (*tzedakot*), and speaketh uprightly; he that despiseth the gain of oppression . . . , he shall dwell on high" (vv. 15–16). Cf. Y. Abohab, *Menorat ha-Maor*, 422–423: The charity that Israel does is great and uplifts them. . . . So too in Al-Nakawa's *Menorat ha-Maor*, 34, basing itself on *Seder Eliyahu Zuta* chap. 1, ed. M. Ish Shalom, 2nd ed. (Jerusalem: 1960, 171): "He who gives charity to the poor, rises up and sits before the divine throne . . . , as is written 'he shall dwell on high.'"

See the editor's note to line 10, and ibid., p. 36. See furher in *Leviticus Rabbah* 34:9, ed. M. Margaliot, vol. 4 (Jerusalem: 1958, 791–792): Said R. Avin: This poor person stands at His right hand, as it is written, "For He shall stand at the right hand of the poor . . ." (Ps. 109:31). If you gave him [charity], know that My Name stands at his right hand, and will give you your reward. And if you do not give him [charity], know that My Name which stands at his right hand will punish you, as it is written " . . . to save him from those that condemn his soul" (ibid.). Cf. Abohab, 411, and also *Tikkunei ha-Zohar, Tikkuna* 19, 100b.

Figure 1. Main doorway of the synagogue at Przedborz, Poland
From *Wooden Synagogues*, by Maria and Kazimierz Piechotka,
Warsaw: 1959 (the English version)

Figure 2. Charity box fixed on the door of the Old Synagogue in Cracow, 1638
From *Wooden Synagogues*, by Maria and Kazimierz Piechotka,
Warsaw: 1959 (the English version)

Figure 3. "Giving Charity"; tombstone in Mszczonow, Poland
From *Graven Images*, by A. Schwartzman, New York: 1993

Figure 4. "Giving Charity"; tombstone in Venice, Italy
From *Graven Images*, by A. Schwartzman, New York: 1993

Figure 5. "Giving Charity"; tombstone in Warsaw, Poland
From *Graven Images*, by A. Schwartzman, New York: 1993

Figure 6. Charity box in the Rema Synagogue, Cracow
From *Wooden Synagogues*, by Maria and Kazimierz Piechotka, Warsaw: 1959 (the English version)

Figure 7. Charity box, Bohemia, early 19th century
From *The Precious Legacy*, by David Altshuler, Washington: 1983

Figure 8. Charity box in the synagogue at Litomirsky, Poland
From *Batei Kenesset be-Polin ve-Hurbanam*, by D. Davidovitz, Jerusalem: 1960

Figure 9. Doorway at the synagogue of Hodorov, Poland
From *Wooden Synagogues*, by Maria and Kazimierz Piechotka,
Warsaw: 1959 (the English version)

Figure 10. Charity box, Rothenburg, Germany
From *Wooden Synagogues*, by Maria and Kazimierz Piechotka, Warsaw: 1959 (the English version)

Figure 11. Charity boxes on the Matir Assurim Synagogue in Venice, Italy; 18th century
From *Aronot Ha-Kodesh ve-Tashmishei Kedushah me-Italiah be-Yisrael*, by S.A. Nahon, Tel Aviv: 1970

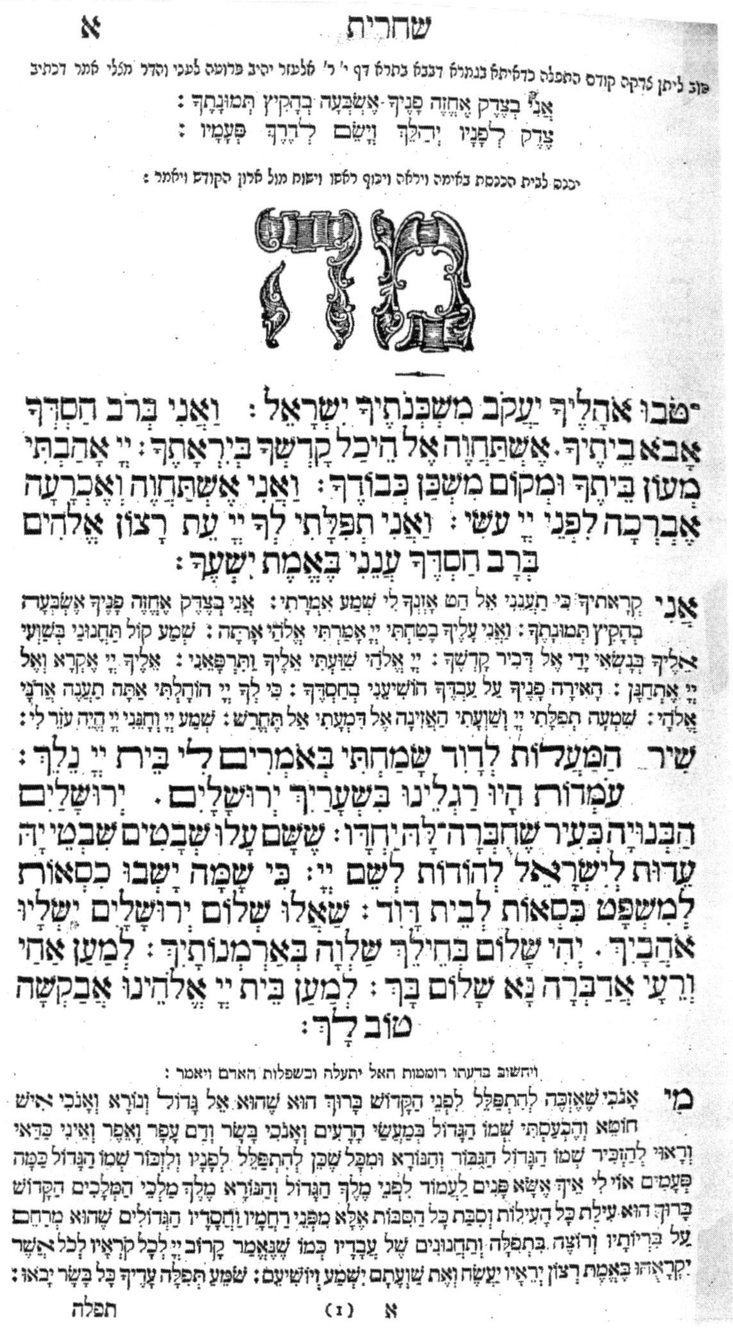

שחרית א

טוב ליתן צדקה קודם התפלה כדאיתא בגמרא דבבא בתרא דף י' ר' אלעזר יהיב פרוטה לעני והדר מצלי אמר דכתיב

אני בצדק אחזה פניך אשבעה בהקיץ תמונתך:
צדק לפניו יהלך וישם לדרך פעמיו:

יכנס לבית הכנסת באימה ויראה ויכוף ראשו וישוח מול ארון הקודש ויאמר:

מה טבו אהליך יעקב משכנתיך ישראל: ואני ברב חסדך אבא ביתך אשתחוה אל היכל קדשך ביראתך: יי אהבתי מעון ביתך ומקום משכן כבודך: ואני אשתחוה ואכרעה אברכה לפני יי עשי: ואני תפלתי לך יי עת רצון אלהים ברב חסדך ענני באמת ישעך:

אני קראתיך כי תענני אל הט אזנך לי שמע אמרתי: אני בצדק אחזה פניך אשבעה בהקיץ תמונתך: ואני עליך בטחתי יי אמרתי אלהי אתה: שמע קול תחנוני בשועי אליך בנשאי ידי אל דביר קדשך: יי אלהי שועתי אליך ותרפאני: אליך יי אקרא ואל יי אתחנן: האירה פניך על עבדך הושיעני בחסדך: כי לך יי הוחלתי אתה תענה אדני אלהי: שמעה תפלתי יי ושועתי האזינה אל דמעתי אל תחרש: שמע יי וחנני יי היה עזר לי:

שיר המעלות לדוד שמחתי באמרים לי בית יי נלך: עמדות היו רגלינו בשעריך ירושלים. ירושלים הבנויה כעיר שחברה לה יחדו: ששם עלו שבטים שבטי יה עדות לישראל להודות לשם יי: כי שמה ישבו כסאות למשפט כסאות לבית דוד: שאלו שלום ירושלים ישליו אהביך. יהי שלום בחילך שלוה בארמנותיך: למען אחי ורעי אדברה נא שלום בך: למען בית יי אלהינו אבקשה טוב לך:

ויחשוב בדעתו רוממות האל יתעלה ובשפלות האדם ויאמר:

מי אנכי שאזכה להתפלל לפני הקדוש ברוך הוא שהוא אל גדול ונורא ואנכי איש חוטא והכעסתי שמו הגדול במעשי הרעים ואנכי בשר ודם עפר ואפר ואיני כדאי וראוי להזכיר שמו הגדול הגבור והנורא ומכל שכן להתפלל לפניו ולזכור שמו הגדול כמה פעמים אוי לי איך אשא פנים לעמוד לפני מלך הגדול והנורא מלך מלכי המלכים הקדוש ברוך הוא עילת כל העילות וסבת כל הסבות אלא מפני רחמיו וחסדיו הגדולים שהוא מרחם על בריותיו ורוצה בתפלה ותחנונים של עבדיו כמו שנאמר קרוב יי לכל קראיו לכל אשר יקראהו באמת רצון יראיו יעשה ואת שועתם ישמע ויושיעם: שמע תפלה עדיך כל בשר יבאו:

תפלה א (1)

Figure 12. Mahzor, Altona 1826, the front page. At the top is written: "It is good to give charity before prayer."

> as it is written, 'Every man shall give as he is able' (16:17). And one makes a blessing (*Mi she-Berach*) at the Torah, for the charity is on his right, as it is said, "Thy right hand is full of righteousness." And so too the Torah is on his right, as it is said, "from this right hand went a fiery law for them" (33:2).

The practice of adfixing a charity box at the entrance to the synagogue is also mentioned in the *Minhag* book of Wermaiza, by R. Juspa Shamash, which was written around 1648. There, in section 284 (ed. Zimmer and Hamburger, vol. 2 [Jerusalem: 1992, 147]), we read:

> The synagogues of the men and the women, in each one there are two *hekdeshim* (boxes for "holy" charities), on the right and the left of the entrance[12] in both synagogues, and the charity to be found in them, one third thereof goes to the indigent in the land of Israel.[13]

Going back to the second verse we saw on the plaque at Przedborz, namely "Righteousness shall go before Him; and shall set us in the way of his steps,"[14] this verse also hints to the fact that charity should come before one continues steps that lead to prayer in the synagogue,[15] and

---

12. See editor's note 26 ibid., that R. Moshe Manheimer wrote, in his *Die Juden in Worms*, (Frankfurt am Main: 1844, 13): On the two sides of the entry [to the Vermaiza synagogue] there are charity boxes cut into the stone, as it is written "Righteousness shall go before Him" (Ps. 85:13). It is not clear to me whether he intended to tell us that this verse was inscribed on the boxes or that their placement is based on this verse. Be that as it may, the connection with the verse strengthens our understanding of the verse found on our plaque.

13. See ibid., sect. 285, 151–152, and especially the first annotation. See Y. Rifkind, *Yiddishe Geld* (New York: 1960, 33), and the article by A.N.Z. Roth, in *Yeda-Am* 15 (1971), 13. The editor, p. 147, n. 27, wrote: "Compare *Iggerot ha-Pekidim Me-Amsterdam*, vol. 3, Jerusalem: 1979, p. 90: It was the practice in several communities to fix in the synagogue a ballot box for the Land of Israel. What is particularly well-known is the metal charity box, in the form of an outstretched hand, with the inscription 'Eretz Yisrael' fixed into the wall of the cluize in Halberstat." See *Me-Halberstat ad Petah Tikvah: Zichronot ha-Rav Auerbach* (Jerusalem: 1987, 94). See further *Minhagei Vermaiza*, ibid., vol. 1 (Jerusalem: 1988, 10) in the annotation.

14. Cf. Al-Nakawa, 34.

15. See the charity box in the lobby at the entrance to the old synagogue in

as formulated by R. Moshe Yitzchak of Zlotva (died 1797): "Before the *Minhah* (afternoon service) and *Shaharit* (morning) service, each time one should give three coins for anonymous charity (מתן בסתר) to fulfill [the verse]: 'Righteousness shall go before Him.'"[16]

We are also well acquainted with the special charity box that was in the synagogue at Lotomirsk in Poland. It was carved out of oak, and affixed, as was the custom, next to the door of the synagogue. The anonymous woodcarver designed it in an original manner, namely in the form of a lion[17] placed on a high pedestal and holding in his clawed forefeet the

---

Cracow. See D. Davidovitz, *Batei Kenesset be-Polin ve-Hurbanam* (Jerusalem: 1960, plate 1, near p. 20). This is not the great synagogue that is in Kozmir in Poland, as indicated in *Beit-Yisrael be-Polin*, ed. Y. Heilprin, vol. 1 (Jerusalem: 1948, opposite p.17 [cf. fig. 2]). It has a baroque frame (17th cent.), and on the rim are the letters מתן בסתר יכפה אף = מ ב י א, "A gift in secret pacifieth anger" (Prov. 21:14). Cf. above n. 2. And below, in the escutcheon is written כי בצדקה יכון כסא לפ"ק – "for the throne is established by righteousness" (Prov. 16:12), the numerical value being 398=1638. There are also charity plates on which *matan be-seter* – "a gift in secret" is engraved. See, for example, *Danzig: Treasures of a Destroyed Community*, 1939, (New York: 1980, 117–118, no. 130).

16. *Hanhagot Tzaddikim*, vol. 3, 173, sect. 5. As to the motif of "three coins," this is by comparison with *Shulhan Aruch Orah Hayyim* 794:1, in the Rema: "And one should give [on the eve of Purim] three half *gedolim* (large coins) of these states, because there is no coin which is called "a half" . . . And in the State of Austria one should give half Wieners, which are also called "half." And earlier on there he explains why three: "Since the word *Terumah* (gift) appears three times in that passage" – he is referring to Exod. 30:13–15 – therefore one should give three. Its source is *Hagahot Mordechai, Megillah*, chap. 1, sect. 777, going back to JT *Shekalim* 1 ad fin.; ibid., 2:4. See also *Sefer ha-Minhagim le-Rabbenu Isaac Tyrnau*, ed. S.Y. Spitzer (Jerusalem: 1979, 154), and *Sefer Maharil: Minhagim*, ed. S.Y. Spitzer (Jerusalem: 1989, 422).

17. See above, n. 13, on the charity box in Halberstat with the outstretched hand. And see A.N.Z. Roth, "*Minhagim be-Yom 'Matnot Yad'*", *Yeda-Am* 15 (1971), 11–15. There are a number of such boxes from Moravia. See *The Precious Legacy*, 146–147, no. 132 (fig. 7), a box from Bohemia from the early 19th cent.; and ibid., 243, no. 83, and the bibliographic references cited by the editor (p. 278, n. 38). An additional example may be found in the guide to *The Jewish Museum of Prague*, ed. Volavkava (Prague: 1948, no. 2). See also H. Frauberger, *Uber Alte Kulturgegenstande in Synagogue und Haus*, 1903, (reproduction, Jerusalem: 1970, with the title *Objects of Ancient Ritual Jewish Art*), p. 63, from Weizehausen in Hessen. It has been remarked that there may have been an influence of Christian

actual box. The lion's open jaws served as the opening in which to place the charitable donations. On the sides of the pedestal are engraved the following inscriptions on the front façade: "The King who loves charity" (from the *Amidah* service), and "A gift in secret pacifieth anger" (Proverbs 21:14). On one of the side walls: " . . . and they shall not appear before the Lord empty. Every man shall give as he is able." (Deuteronomy 16:16–17)[18] (See fig. 8.)[19]

Perhaps the custom of giving charity at the entrance to the synagogue is also hinted at in the *double-entendre* of the inscription decorating the door of the wooden synagogue at Hodorov. (fig. 9.) The synagogue was built between the years 1642 and 1652. There we read, on the right side, "Open to me the gates of righteousness: I will go into them, and I will praise the Lord" (Psalms 118:19). And on the other side the inscription reads, "[Open ye the gates,] that the righteous nation which keepeth the truth may enter in" (Isaiah 26:2) "to prostrate before the Lord."[20] And underneath is written, "and walketh unto the house of God with excitement (ברגש)" (Psalms 55:15).[21] Obviously, the simple meaning of these inscriptions refers to the opening of the doors of the synagogue, which are the "gates of righteousness," in that they enable one to pray and thank the Lord. However, we would suggest that they also are intended to indicate to those entering that

---

art in the form of "arm reliquaries." See, for example, P. Lasko, *Ars Sacra 800–1200* (England: 1972, figs. 226–227), from the 12th cent. Another variation of these charity boxes may be found in those coming from the region of Alsace. See the Israel Museum Catalogue, *Yahadut Alsace: Kehillah Kafrit, bein Masoret le-Emancipatziah*, ed. A. Motzvaski-Schnapper (Jerusalem: 1991, 15, 55).

18. See what I wrote in *Minhagei Yisrael*, vol. 6 (Jerusalem), 6 on the Polish "Schulklopfer" that has on it carved lions, stressing the "heroism" (*gevurah*) of those who rise up early to go to the synagogue, based on *Shulhan Aruch Orah Hayyim* 1:1: "He shall gird himself with strength (*yitgaber*) like a lion to rise up in the morning for the service of his Creator" – the words of Yehudah ben Tema, in *Avot* 5:20, (*Minhagei Yisrael*, vol. 6, 1).

19. The picture is to be found in Davidovitz's book.

20. Or perhaps "with enthusiasm." This is not an actual verse, but a combination of a verse and something in the style of a verse. The words "Open ye the gates" are not written there, but this is the obvious connection with its placement next to the entrance.

21. See what I wrote in *Minhagei Yisrael*, vol. 6, p. 6, on the Polish "Schulklopfer" with this verse carved on it.

they should make their charitable donations,[22] and thereafter pray and praise the Lord with the confidence that their prayers will be accepted.[23]

R. Avraham ha-Levi Sheftelish, a disciple of the Rema, R. Moshe Isserles, and the father of the *Shlah*, R. Isaiah Horowitz, wrote in his *Yesh Nohlin*, chapter 2, section 5 (ed. princ. [Prague: 1615], ed. H.Y. Waldman [Jerusalem: 1993, 144–145]), as follows:

> It is well that one give charity every day anonymously when entering the synagogue to pray. For R. Eliezer would give a penny to a poor person and then pray (BT *Baba Batra* 10a), as it is written, "As for me, I will behold Thy countenance in righteousness." And this is the meaning of what the Sages said (in BT *Berachot* 8a): A person should always enter the measure of two entrances and [then] pray . . . , for concerning charity it is written, "But thou shalt surely open thy hand wide," (Deuteronomy 15:8) (פתח תפתח) – twice. And at least he should enter the synagogue twice every day, once for *Shaharit* (morning prayer) and once for *Aravit* (evening prayer).[24] And this constitutes "two entrances," namely: twice opening one's hand in charity on entering the synagogue . . .

Furthermore, we have found that many of the righteous scholars insisted that, at the time of giving charity, one should say the verse, "As for me, I will behold Thy countenance in righteousness."

22. Another example of a charity box next to the entrance to a synagogue is the *opferslock* in the synagogue in Rothenburg. See *Notizblatt der Gesellschaft zur Erforschung Judischer Kunstdenkmaeler, E.V.* 6 (1906), 15, in the article by Fritz Epstein, "Kultusbauten und Kulturgegenstande in der Provinz Hessen" (in reprint, Jerusalem: n.d., published *Atika*, 19). (Fig. 10). See further ibid., 15 (=19) from the Munich synagogue, late 18th cent. (?). One may assume that the letters 1795=תקנה=תקנה לפ"ק. But perhaps it is also hinting at the fact that giving charity will lead to one's amelioration.

23. In accordance with this formulation of R. Aharon Shmuel Kaidenover, (Minsk 1624–Cracow 1676), in his *Kav ha-Yashar*, chap. 88: Being that charity is the spice for all prayer, just as the spices are good for all foods, sweetening the dishes, so too charity is good before prayer.

24. However, cf. above n. 9, that according to the kabbalists one does not give charity at night, because it is the period of *din* – strict judgment. As to "the measure of two entrances," see *Tur Orah Hayyim* 90:10, and Bah ad hoc., based, inter alia, on BT *Berachot* 8a.

Finally, we should note that the practice of adfixing a charity box near the entrance of the synagogue, was not limited to Eastern Europe. For we have found just such a one at the entry to the Florentine synagogue, *Matir Assurim*, (fig. 11). There, there are actually seven separate, but connected boxes for the upkeep of the synagogue (בדק הבית), for the old-age home, for charity, for [synagogal] lighting, for the hospital, for Jerusalem, and for R. Meir Baal ha-Nes. This "installation" is from the seventeenth century, though the inscriptions "old-age home and hospital" are later additions from the nineteenth century, and come to replace the earlier ones.[25] In this case, the officers of the community went far beyond what was the usual practice in order to cover all the needs of the community.

The giving of charity prior to beginning one's morning prayer again underscores the moral priority of relationship towards one's fellow human even before one turns to one's Creator. This is clearly mirrored in the tradition attributed to the great Kabbalist R. Hayyim Vital,[26] that, when one rises in the morning, even before one goes to prayer, one should remind himself of the mitzvah "to love one's neighbor as oneself" (Leviticus 19:18).[27] Surely, this would be a clear expression of one's hierarchic scale of ethical values.

25. See S.A. Nahon, *Aronot ha-Kodesh ve-Tashmishei Kedushah me-Italiah be-Yisrael* (Tel Aviv: 1970, 130).

26. *Shaar ha-Kavanot* 1b. See in detail Moshe Hallamish, *Kabbalah in Liturgy, Halakhah and Customs* (*Ha-Kabbalah be-tefillah be-Kabbalah u-baMinhag*, [Ramat Gan: 2000, 357–382], [Hebrew]).

27. See Rashi (Lev. 19:18), (basing himself on *Torat Kohanim* and JT *Nedarim* 9:4) that R. Akiva said "This is a great Torah principle (כלל גדול בתורה)." See further Rambam, *Hilchot Deot* 6:3. See R. Yitzhak Yaakov Fuks, *Halichot Bein Adam le-Havero* (Jerusalem: 2008, 1–8, 27 et seq.); R. Asi ha-Levi Even Yuli, *Shulhan Aruch ha-Middot*, vol. 2 (Jerusalem: 2009, pp. pass, etc).

Indices

INDEX OF BIBLICAL SOURCES AND COMMENTARIES

INDEX OF MAIN HALACHIC SOURCES

MISHNAH

TOSEFTA

YERUSHALMI

BAVLI AND COMMENTARIES

MIDRESHEI HALACHAH VE-AGGADAH ETC.

RAMBAM AND COMMENTATORS

TUR AND SHULHAN ARUCH AND COMMENTARIES

INDEX OF NON-JEWISH SOURCES

INDEX OF NAMES*

* I have not referred to any of my own writings.

GENERAL INDEX